A Comprehensive Look at

FRAUD IDENTIFICATION AND PREVENTION

A Comprehensive Look at

FRAUD IDENTIFICATION AND PREVENTION

James "Rick" Youngblood, CPP, CFE

CRC Press
Taylor & Francis Group
Boca Raton London New York

CRC Press is an imprint of the
Taylor & Francis Group, an **informa** business

CRC Press
Taylor & Francis Group
6000 Broken Sound Parkway NW, Suite 300
Boca Raton, FL 33487-2742

First issued in paperback 2019

ISBN-13: 978-1-4987-0032-0 (hbk)
ISBN-13: 978-0-367-87133-8 (pbk)

Library of Congress Cataloging-in-Publication Data

Youngblood, James R., 1960-
    A comprehensive look at fraud identification and prevention / James R. Youngblood.
      pages cm
    Includes bibliographical references and index.
    ISBN 978-1-4987-0032-0
    1. Fraud. 2. Fraud--Prevention. 3. Employee crimes--Prevention. 4. Corporations--Corrupt practices. 5. Identity theft. 6. Computer crimes. I. Title.

HV6691.Y68 2015
364.16'3--dc23
                                          2014046047

Visit the Taylor & Francis Web site at
http://www.taylorandfrancis.com

and the CRC Press Web site at
http://www.crcpress.com

This book is dedicated to my lovely wife, Rosanne,
and our wonderful twins, Nick and Casey.

Contents

Foreword

Rick Youngblood is extremely knowledgeable about fraud and scams and often sends out warnings to other security professionals to help get the word out about the latest scheme to prey on unsuspecting victims. In this text, he delivers an up-to-date assessment of various fraudulent schemes that we hear about on an almost-daily basis.

We all have received the e-mails and letters touting that we were *chosen for a great opportunity* and all we have to do to be a part of this FREE money is "confirm" our Social Security number (SSN) (Translation: *Give* us your SSN.) or send a check to someone to pay expenses so they can send us a check for $1 million. Unfortunately, we have not met anyone who has been sent money by a Nigerian prince or encountered victims who said that someone *gave* them something for nothing. There is always a catch, and many times, the fraudster costs unsuspecting victims their lifetime savings. The old adage is right: "If something sounds too good to be true, it probably is." Rick Youngblood is helping inform others. We all know someone who has either been a victim or who is a potential victim. As more individuals are educated about scams, the fraudsters change their modus operandi so victims think they are making good decisions—not realizing they have fallen victim. The modus operandi of security must change as well.

Lately, we are hearing about businesses or credit card companies that have been hacked, and many of us were victims simply because we used a debit or credit card in the wrong place at the wrong time. Unfortunately, we fear this trend will become more commonplace, and the only way to prevent it from happening is by educating individuals and enhancing information technology (IT) security protocols. Much of our personal and confidential information is stored "in the cloud" and is susceptible to attack. Security professionals such as Rick Youngblood help to keep our personal information personal.

No one is safe. Bank employees and postal service clerks many times cannot tell when they see a fraudulent check or money order. The schemes and scams have become sophisticated and appear to be legitimate. As new software is developed to either detect or prevent cyberattacks, the scheme becomes more advanced and evolves to circumvent the controls that are in place. Preventing fraud and scams is an ever-changing process, and we must quickly adapt to meet the new challenges. Keep in mind this golden rule: "If it sounds too good, it's probably a scam."

Lawrence J. Fennelly, CHL III, CPO, CSS
Marianna A. Perry, MS, CPP

Fraud and Prevention

The Path of Least Resistance

The focus of this book, as given in the title, *A Comprehensive Look at Fraud Identification and Prevention*, is a detailed discussion on the many faces of fraud. In addition to providing a detailed discussion on the wide range of fraud issues, the focus also is on prevention measures. The methods of prevention are based on what is referred to as the *path of least resistance*. The focus or direction of the path is to take the would-be criminal away from a person or organization who utilizes the various outlined prevention tools to search for a much easier target.

With fraud or many other types of criminal activity, these crimes are going to occur against a number of victims. These victims can be suspecting or unsuspecting, and the criminal elements will take the path with the fewest barriers in the way that leads them to a target. When road crews construct a new highway and there is an option of using explosives and cutting a path through a large rock-based hill or diverting the roadway around the obstacle, the path of least resistance will take the crew on the easier and least-expensive path. The question is which option offers the least resistance.

The same road construction analogy can be applied to protecting an individual or organization against becoming a target and eventual victim of fraud. It might sound like a cynical option or means of protection, but as stated, criminal activity is going to take place, and with many faces of fraud, the options for the criminal are unlimited. These individuals have the benefit of time and can be selective of who to target and the method(s) they will use to commit the fraudulent activity. Do they go through the rock mountain or around?

It is imperative for the security professional or any individual to develop an understanding of the prevention tools available for diverting fraudulent attacks. They can put forth an effort to create a rock mountain or do nothing and leave an open path to their front door. Every business or individual is an attractive target for fraud, but they also control the amount of barriers on the path of least resistance. If prevention activities can be implemented by the business or individual, the path of fraudulent activity can be controlled.

Opportunity

The opportunity for a burglar looking to enter an office building could be an unsecured back door. If this same door is locked at closing, the burglar has to look for another entry opportunity or create one. The internal questions the burglar has to ask, "Does the entry opportunity available or created provide undetectable access to commit the desired crime?" "If not, what location provides an opportunity to commit a burglary that offers the easiest path to avoid detection?"

The fraud-related theory of the path of least resistance has a partner in opportunity. Criminals looking for individuals or businesses to target for fraud-related activities have to search for an opportunity.

Business owners and security/loss prevention personnel have to evaluate their organization to identify fraud opportunities. The question to answer is, "Within our daily operating functions, are we creating an opportunity for fraudulent activity, or can fraud opportunities be easily created by employees or outside personnel?"

Individuals going through their daily activities also have to address the aspect of fraud-related opportunities. A major issue for the individual could be a lack of knowledge regarding the fraud-related threats they face. Their goal has to be to develop detailed knowledge of fraud-related threats. Once they have developed this level of understanding, the individual can work to stop creating opportunities to become a fraud victim:

- Criminals or employees looking to commit fraud against a business look for a window of opportunity in operating policies and procedures.
- Criminals looking to commit fraud against an individual hope to create a window of opportunity.
- Individual fraud opportunities are created by building a level of trust with the targeted person.
- Criminals also provide targeted individuals with an enticing personal opportunity that leads to successful fraud.

To move off the path of least resistance as it relates to fraud victimization, the overall goal is to identify and eliminate the opportunity.

Temptation

From a business perspective there is a need to understand and eliminate areas of opportunity. From a temptation perspective, these are areas of opportunity that are created within the daily operating procedures of the business. Understanding the areas of opportunity created by the employee in an effort to commit fraud is also important, but these are areas that lack temptation. An employee with the purpose of committing fraud is not driven by temptation but by opportunities within the business operation.

The goal of any business is to work toward eliminating business practices that can create the temptation to commit fraud. If the organization has strong dual control and two-person rule operating policies, employees face low levels of temptation. If one employee has the sole responsibility of overseeing the accounts payable area, this could create a high level of temptation. The employee who knows there are no checks and balances in the daily operation of their specific department could be tempted to commit fraud.

This is not to say all employees left alone to perform their job in an organization with weak fraud prevention policies are going to steal. The business has to develop an understanding that there is a certain section or percentage of the workforce that could be swayed to commit fraud based on the opportunity created in their operating procedures. A business-created opportunity or weakness in its operating system can provide a level of temptation for some associates.

About the Author

James "Rick" Youngblood, CPP, CFE, has extensive experience in the fields of loss prevention, security, investigations, law enforcement, and fraud. A retired chief warrant officer from the US Army with more than 21 years on active duty and in the National Guard as a CID (Criminal Investigation Command) special agent, Rick has authored numerous articles on the topics of fraud, security, and loss prevention for many national publications and has provided presentations on fraud, security, and loss prevention for many national and international organizations, including ASIS (Advancing Security Worldwide®), Association of Certified Fraud Examiners, Institute for International Research, and more. He is also a current and longtime member of the ASIS Crime and Loss Prevention Council and is a member of the ASIS Investigations Council.

Rick holds a master's degree in financial management and a bachelor's degree in criminal justice/business management.

Rick currently resides in Phoenix, Arizona, with his wife, Rosanne.

Chapter 1

Fraud

1.1 Fraud Overview

Fraud or the various types of fraud can be discussed, categorized, identified, or listed in different groups, subsets, or individual classifications. A business or organization can be the target of internal fraud through poor hiring practices or as a revenge tactic of a longtime employee. This same business can also be the target of external fraud and attacked through weaknesses in its computer operating systems, a covert attempt to extract money via opportunities available in their financial operating practices, or poor record keeping of products coming into and out of the loading dock. The business can also be the target of fraud by individuals working together from inside and outside the organization.

An individual can also become the target from many different angles, with a criminal or criminals attempting to assume the target individual's identity and to open fraudulent bank accounts in their name. A person committing fraud against an individual can also work on a confidence-type fraud and gain the trust of the intended target. Once the targeted person realizes trust was placed in the wrong person, most or all of their personal assets can be stolen.

The Internet has also become a popular avenue for committing varying types of fraud against a business or individual. A small business can be targeted in the same manner as an individual for the purpose of business identity theft and account takeover. Individuals are popular targets for fraud through the use of unsolicited e-mails and a growing number of advance fee schemes.

The tactics used to steal money or property from a business or individual are many, as are the prevention measures that can be used to stop the attempted fraud or force the fraudsters to pursue an easier target. The key to fraud prevention is based on awareness, detection, and ultimately prevention. It is vital for the individual or business operation to develop an understanding of the various aspects of fraud and their particular threat level. For the purpose of understanding threat levels and sometimes the simplicity of erecting the necessary barriers to prevent the fraud, the crime of identity theft (discussed in detail in Chapter 10) is used in the discussion that follows.

All individuals and small businesses are susceptible to becoming victims of identity theft. To place the barriers necessary to prevent identity theft, the individual has to have knowledge of the fraud. Understanding how the fraud of identity theft takes place, it is easier to make an effort to erect barriers for prevention:

- A person who has not been a victim of identity theft cannot develop an understanding of the threat.
- A person who has been a victim of identity theft understands the amount of time and money involved to clear their good name.
- Once victimized, a person can understand the potential financial loss associated with being a victim of identity theft.

If the victim of identity theft could have gained knowledge of the overall fraud and the long-term ramifications, they would have most likely erected the necessary barriers, basically taking them off the path of least resistance and making others a more attractive target.[1] The same theory can be stated about individuals who were arrested and charged with the crime of driving while intoxicated (DWI).

1.2 Study Analysis

Police officers across the country work a shift knowing individuals operating a vehicle on the roadways are intoxicated. These police officers also know their duties will bring them across the path of intoxicated drivers. The intoxicated driver operates a vehicle with the hope of not attracting the attention of a police officer or rolling through a DWI checkpoint.

A person identified and arrested for DWI can expect to go through a long process of paying higher insurance rates, having an interlock device[2] placed in their vehicle, and having limited driving privileges. In addition, there are large fines and court costs associated with the crime of DWI. If those arrested hire an attorney, their out of pocket costs will increase as a result of driving while intoxicated. On average,[3] it costs a person arrested for DWI $10,000. After all of the associated fees related to a DWI conviction are paid and the driver can operate a vehicle on an unrestricted license, the person has most likely wondered countless times why they did not spend $20 on a taxi ride.

The problem for many individuals who have been charged with the crime of DWI is that they developed an understanding of the associated costs after they were arrested. A prudent individual might investigate the long-term ramifications of a DWI arrest and make the right choice of using a designated driver or taking a taxi.

This DWI analogy can be related to understanding the ramifications of becoming a fraud victim. Both businesses and individuals can suffer the long-term consequences associated with fraud losses, as well as the time requirement necessary to repair a personal credit history or the integrity of a company's name.

As the $20 taxi ride removes the impaired driver off the path of least resistance, it is vital for individuals and any type of business operation to develop an understanding of fraud awareness, detection, and prevention.

1.3 Internal Fraud

Internal fraud, also called occupational fraud, takes place when a person or group of people employed by a business use their position in an effort to conduct illegal activity. This illegal activity can take many forms, and no department within an organization is immune. In addition, there are no boundaries on who within the company walls will take the opportunity to defraud an employer using internal fraud. Internal fraud has a history of being committed by a person working in the mail room, the Accounting Department, the loading dock, management, department directors, as an owner, and more.

To establish a strong foundation of internal fraud awareness, prevention, and detection, organizations need to ensure they develop strong policies for employee hiring (Chapter 2). Also, all organizations, large and small, need to develop an understanding of how fraud-related opportunities are developed and compromised (Chapter 3). Initially, an internal fraud awareness, prevention, and detection program has to begin with understanding internal controls.

1.3.1 Policies and Procedures

Beginning with new employee orientation and reviewed on a periodic basis, all employees need to be aware of and adhere to internal policies and procedures. An organization has to develop these policies and procedures to establish a strong internal fraud prevention program.

1.3.1.1 Code of Conduct

The code of conduct will differ based on the organizational goals and business direction. No matter the organization, a code of conduct has to be developed that is company specific, basically the standards and values the organization wishes to establish as guidelines for successful operation.

An effective code of conduct has to have senior level buy-in and support. For the code of conduct to be respected by all employees, the enforcement of violations has to be consistent across the board. Rules and compliance should not be based on position, job title, and tenure.

Organizations that have established a code of conduct should develop an annual training policy. In addition to establishing code of conduct training classes, all members of the organization have to fall under a mandatory attendance policy. Associates noticing certain high-level employees are exempt from code of conduct training can be led to believe management's actions can also be exempt.

For the organization's code of conduct policy to have longevity, it has to be revised as the business operation evolves. Employees required to sit through a code of conduct training class that was created 10 years previously will most likely have the information fall on deaf ears.

1.3.1.2 Conflicts of Interest

Conflicts of interest can have varying definitions within an organization and are based on the daily operating activities. Employees working within any business operation need to be able to recognize a situation for which a conflict of interest can arise. The main question that needs to be answered by any employee making a business decision for their employer is; "Will this decision affect my ability to be impartial?" If a department manager is dating a subordinate, will all disciplinary decisions toward that individual be impartial?

Along with establishing code of conduct training classes for all associates, discussion has to take place on what constitutes conflicts of interest within the organization.

1.3.1.3 Mandatory Vacation Policy

Individuals committing internal fraud are normally reluctant to take any time off from their job. The rationale is that if another person has to assume their duties for a period of time, the fraudulent activity could be discovered. This is especially true for employees working in any department that deals with organizational assets. Many of these frauds require day-to-day monitoring to prevent discovery by a third party, therefore requiring the associate to be at his or her desk each and every day. By establishing a mandatory vacation policy, organizations have a better opportunity to discover improper activity.

1.3.1.4 Proper Use of Corporate Credit Card

No matter the size and scope of the organization, certain associates need to be issued a corporate credit card. On issue of the corporate credit card, associates need to be instructed on what expenses can and cannot be processed on the card. Based on the organization, the expense policies can vary, with some more liberal than others. To prevent a violation of corporate credit card policies, new hires should be briefed on the card policies during orientation. What might have been acceptable with a prior employer might not be allowed in the new organization.

Corporate credit cards should also have set credit limits. These credit limits should be based on the job level of the associate and the estimated amount of the associate's legitimate expenses. An associate issued a corporate credit card who makes one annual training trip a year does not need a card with a high credit limit.

As discussed previously and throughout this book, the goal of any fraud prevention program is to eliminate temptation.

1.3.1.5 Expense Report Policies

As with the corporate or business policies related to the use of a corporate credit card, associates need to be made aware of the unique requirements pertaining to the completion and submission of expense reports. This is especially true for associates new to the organization. All new hires need to be briefed on expense report policies during new hire orientation.

In addition, organizations and businesses need to establish expense report review policies. Prior to employees being reimbursed for company-related expenses, managerial sign-off has to take place. Company policy should also dictate mandatory expense levels for all categories of associates. These expense-level policies should also detail who is authorized to approve high-dollar expenses.

1.3.1.6 Use of Company Assets

During the course of any business, some associates are issued company property to be used as part of their daily operation. Based on the business, the type of company property issued will vary. A good example of associates using business assets is the issuance of a company vehicle. All associates utilizing a company vehicle need to understand the policies regarding when the car can be used.

Some organizations allow company vehicles to be used in almost the same manner as a private car. Vehicles issued by state and federal governments have stricter use policies. To avoid misuse, all associates need to be briefed on the proper use of company vehicles. The same requirement holds true for associates using any type of company assets and equipment.

1.3.1.7 Purchasing Guidelines

Some associates working within an organization will be given the task of purchasing material. Based on the scope of the business, the type, amount, and costs of material will vary. The same holds true for associates working within the business. Employee job titles and position levels should also dictate purchasing amount guidelines. A lower-level associate should not be authorized to make high-dollar or high-quantity purchases.

Based on company purchasing guidelines, all associates need to be made aware of the policies and their exact purchasing power. In addition, corporate policies should dictate who is authorized to approve high-dollar purchases. A manager of three low-level purchasing associates should not have approval authority for high-dollar-item expenses.

1.3.1.8 Disbursement Guidelines

A typical business operation has associates that purchase material for the company and those who disburse money to pay for material and other expenses. As discussed for the organizational purchasing guidelines, all businesses need to establish payment guidelines. These should also be based on job position and associate level within the organization. The disbursement guidelines should also dictate amount approval levels and verification prior to the money leaving the organization.

Strong purchasing and disbursement guidelines need to be discussed with all new hire associates. Plus, company policies should dictate that associates review their individual purchasing and disbursement levels on at least an annual basis. The greater the level of fraud awareness activity within the organization, the lower the level of individual temptation.

1.4 Understanding Rationalization

There are several contributing factors to why certain employees will engage in committing fraud against an employer. Many of these factors are discussed in further detail in the following chapters and in the opening discussion of opportunity and temptation. A major factor in the understanding of why employees commit fraud against their employer relates to rationalization.

Basically, if employees can rationalize their pending fraudulent activity or necessity they can convince themselves of its legitimacy. A popular phrase used by associates who committed fraud against their employer is, "I was entitled due to being underpaid for the job I perform." Their rationalization revolves around the thought process that they should be paid more for the job functions they conduct. Following that same thought process is the statement that, "If my boss will not give me a raise, I take an equivalent amount in company assets."

On the surface of this discussion, a normal-thinking individual will look at the activity as stealing and ask the following questions:

- Why not ask for a raise?
- If I am unhappy with my salary, why not look for another job?

From an employer's perspective, the hope is to have a workforce staffed with normal-thinking individuals. These people cannot, in their right minds, understand the thought process of the self-perceived underpaid associate's rationalization.

On the other hand, self-perceived underpaid associates can convince themselves of the justification of their activities.

Other common excuses used for fraudulent activity conducted as a result of rationalization are the following:

■ The perception the organization is corrupt. If the organization is perceived not to be acting aboveboard, then why should the associate?
■ "I am not stealing the money, just borrowing." "I was going to pay it back."
■ "Working here has created a high level of stress that led to my drug habit. Since my employer caused my drug habit, the employer can pay for my drugs."
■ "The money will never be missed. They created these loose account reconciliation procedures, so they deserve to be ripped off."
■ "It's the economy, stupid. I am not stealing from my employer; I am doing what I can to feed my family."
■ Testing the procedures: "I was not stealing; I was looking for opportunities where others could steal from the company."

To lower the potential levels of rationalization within an organization, it is necessary to create a working environment free of fraud temptation and opportunity.

1.5 External Fraud

External fraud from a business perspective pertains to outside threats created with the purpose of falsely obtaining organizational assets. These assets can be in the form of financial gain, illegally obtained company property, or payment for nondelivery or underdelivery of product. A majority of external frauds begin with a person who is in a nonemployee status targeting the business. This same individual can target the business for the purpose of fraud and attempts to be hired by the organization. Finally, the individual working in an external capacity can solicit the assistance of a current employee and the two work together to defraud the organization. No matter the direction of the fraud attempt, it is vital for all businesses (large and small) to develop an understanding and awareness of the threats faced.

The goal of any business as it develops a fraud prevention policy is to understand the path of least resistance. This understanding has to be based on knowing that individuals who want to commit external fraud will look for weaknesses in the business operation and procedures. A business operating under the assumption that "it can never happen to us" is placing company assets directly on the path of least resistance. A business that develops detailed understanding of external threats and establishes a strong fraud prevention and employee education posture will place its competition closer to the path of least resistance.

From a perspective of policies and procedures discussed concerning internal fraud, the same focus has to occur when working to combat external fraud. A strong education policy on the code of conduct also has to bring into the discussion how associates interact with business relationships outside the organization. In addition to applying the code of conduct to prevent external fraud, associates all need to be educated on outside conflicts of interest.

Employee relationships with vendors, suppliers, delivery drivers, and customers have to be a part of the overall discussion and training on what constitutes a conflict of interest. Because many of the external fraud threats will come from these relationships, associates need to understand their boundaries and how external fraud can take place in relation to these outside contacts.

> **CASE STUDY 1.1**
>
> The crime of adultery is on the legal books in many states across the country. Even though adultery is listed as a crime, it is not prosecuted as a stand-alone offense. The only entity that prosecutes the crime of adultery is the US military. The rationale for prosecuting service members who committed adultery is not to ensure the integrity of the family unit. The rationale for prosecuting adultery in the US military is based on service members being targeted for bribery and extortion.
>
> Any service member involved in an affair can be approached by their adulterous partner or an outside third party. In an effort to keep the indiscretion from a spouse, service members could possibly be asked go through extraordinary measures at the request of the individual who has knowledge of their extracurricular activity. Service members can become a target to supply money, property, or even military secrets.
>
> To prevent service members from falling victim to bribery and extortion as the result of being caught in an adulterous relationship, military policy has to be strict enough to deter such activity.

When organizations develop and deliver training on code of conduct and conflict of interest to their associates, the direction has to be based on the worst-case scenario. Associates need to understand their outside activities can result in a similar type of situation in which they are forced to commit fraudulent related activities to keep an individual with inside information silent. An associate involved in minor kickback activities or vendor favoritism can perceive these activities as a minor violation of a code-of-conduct policy.

What the associate might fail to understand is the initial intent of the outside party. What might appear to the associate as a friendly agreement could be the beginning of a fraud-based setup on the part of the outside party. Associates need to understand the lengths some individuals looking to commit fraud will go, and even their slightest indiscretion could result in them being blackmailed to keep information on their activities silent.

A major part of any organization's training on its code of conduct and conflict of interest has to be based on individual integrity and ethics. Basically, this is an understanding that all associate activity has to be based on the premise of "doing the right thing even if no one is looking."

1.6 Gift Policies

Standard operating procedures in many organizations require associates to interact with outside suppliers and vendors. These interactions involve the employee being the recipient of something paid for by an outside party that conducts business with the associate's employer. Many of these interactions involve the following:

- Employees being taken to dinner by a vendor while attending an out-of-state trade show.
- A golf outing paid for by a vendor or supplier.
- A trip to a local sporting event that is paid for by a vendor or supplier.
- A working business luncheon paid for by a vendor or supplier.
- A business discussion that takes place during happy hour at a local establishment and the tab is picked up by the vendor or supplier.
- Gifts received by employees from vendors or suppliers. The occasion for the gift can be associated with a birthday, holiday, or anniversary.

There are numerous reasons for individuals who provide services to an organization to pay for meals or other activities as a result of normal business operations. The issue for employers is to maintain some type of control over the value of gifts received by their associates and the frequency of entertainment activities.

A large majority of outside vendors and suppliers choose to pick up the tab for a meal or after-dinner drinks. Meal purchases, paying for a round of golf, or taking the purchasing team to a ball game is a way of saying thanks. The gray area for business owners and managers resides in the intent of the gratuities and the level of the activities. Whenever associates receive a free meal or tickets to a ball game, owners and managers need to consider the ramifications of the gray area acts:

- Is the outside vendor/supplier providing gratuities to their associate to receive preferential treatment?
- Is their associate requiring a certain level of gratuities for the vendor/supplier to continue conducting business with their organization?
- Could this relationship result in a kickback-type operation?

To avoid a fraudulent relationship developing from employee/vendor relationships as they pertain to free meals and game tickets, internal policies need to provide associates a detailed understanding of acceptable levels of gifts and other gratuities. Based on the operational activities of the individual business, the gratuity amounts and frequency will vary. It is up to the organization to establish standards on the cost level of outside gifts or gratuities their associates can accept.

Notes

1. It could appear cynical when discussing the need to place others on the path of least resistance when it comes to identity theft or other frauds. It is necessary to develop an understanding that fraud is going to take place on all levels. The goal of any business or individual is to lower their level of attractiveness for people searching for fraud targets.
2. Interlock devices are required in many states after a person has been convicted of DWI. A person with an interlock device in his or her vehicle cannot start the car without blowing into a tube in the same manner as would be done for a Breathalyzer test. If the driver has not been drinking, the vehicle can be started. If the driver has alcohol on his or her breath, the vehicle will not start.
3. Solomon, C., DUI: The $10,000 ride home. http://money.msn.com/auto-insurance/dui-the-10000-dollar-ride-home.aspx (accessed July 20, 2104).

Chapter 2

Employee Theft and Fraud

2.1 Introduction

Employee theft and fraud are present in almost every business, and the individuals involved can range from the fast food counterperson to the chief executive officer (CEO) of a major corporation. Many times, the theft is generated by opportunity because of a weakness in operating procedures. Other times, the individual obtains the position for the purpose of committing fraud. Either way, the organization needs to ensure there are sound operating policies for daily business activities and work to make sure only quality applicants are hired and retained.

With a majority of employee fraud, the activity takes place based on an opportunity presented in the daily operation of a business. Based on the nature of the business and the internal operating and staffing policies, the defined opportunity can vary. What needs to be understood on the part of owners and managers of a business is that the fraud opportunity created can be based on what is internally perceived as a cost-saving measure.

To cut corners, a business might reduce the number of employees to lower the annual payroll expense. If the additional duties created by lowering employee levels can be added to the duties of the remaining staff and daily operations remain at the current pace, this decision might sound like a quality cost-saving move, taking on the term of "doing more with less."

Many times, doing more with less can lead to a lower employee head count and lower operating profit. On the surface, a business can look at lowering employee payroll expenses as a cost-saving measure, one that can add to the bottom line. If the cost-saving analysis stops with cutting staffing levels, the business operation could be creating fraud-related opportunities.

With any changes made to the daily operating activities of any business as part of a cost-saving measure, it is necessary to conduct some type of a cost/benefit analysis. The cost/benefit analysis has to answer the question: "Will the cost savings from lowering staffing levels have a negative or positive effect on annual losses caused by internal fraud?"

A major issue for any business that adopts the theory of doing more with less is the increased workloads on the remaining associates. These increased workloads also include the assumption of duties generated by the departing staff members. By adding additional areas of responsibility to the remaining staff, management can be creating fraud opportunities through their internal violation of the two-person rule. Simply stated, do these staffing cost-saving measures allow the same employee to write all business checks and reconcile the business bank accounts? (The two-person rule and other business-related staffing fraud prevention measures are detailed in Chapter 3.)

A simple perceived cost-saving measure that could lead to increased fraud losses is discussed next.

A small retail business operation might look at installing an internal video surveillance and point-of-sale (POS) system as an unnecessary business expense and overlook the cost factor associated with employee theft and "sweethearting."[1] The initial expense of the video surveillance/POS system could be $5,000 as an up-front capital expense, with minimal monthly operating cost. With a less-than-desirable inventory control system and inability to monitor the store activity in a real-time or recorded video, the owner could be losing more than the amount of the security system from internal fraud and employee theft.

Many times, business owners or company officers look at the bottom line through fixed costs and keeping variable costs in line with sales or production. By not having a firm handle on the associated costs of internal fraud and employee theft, these losses can be written off as a cost of doing business.

If the business owner previously discussed would have bitten the bullet and laid out the capital expense for a video surveillance and POS system, it could have quickly been discovered that the business was losing hundreds of dollars a week through fraud and employee theft. What the owner failed to do was overcome the initial shock of a $5,000 capital expense. When compared to the loss of $200 to $300 a week through employee fraud, the system would have paid for itself in about six months and eventually ensured an increase in the overall bottom line.

Business owners and managers can take several steps to decrease the fraud-related opportunities within their organization. Many of these steps are discussed throughout this chapter.

No matter the eventual fraud prevention measures implemented by an organization, the foundation necessary to protect the company assets has to begin with hiring quality associates.

When analyzing any business operation and working to ensure quality associates are hired, it is necessary to conduct background checks. The type of and intensity of looking into an applicant's background for preemployment screening varies on a legal basis state to state. Human resources personnel have better understanding of what can be researched or checked as part of an applicant's background verification.

2.2 Preemployment Background Verification

Prior to making new hire decisions in a business or organization, some type of preemployment background verification needs to take place. Based on the size of the operation and assets available in the hiring and personnel budget, the company needs to decide how intensely applicants will be screened prior to being hired. At the least, an applicant's work history needs to be verified through discussions with previous employers. The length of each prior position is vital to an extensive work history verification to ensure time gaps in the work history are not longer than reported by the applicant on the job application or résumé.

Beginning with the application for employment, the need to establish the integrity level of the prospective employee is important. Unreported time gaps in their employment history can be uncovered early in the application process and save the business or organization money on conducting additional background verification steps. In addition to verifying previous employment timelines, actual positions held and reported on the application and résumé also need to be confirmed. Just because the applicant can provide job-related discussion concerning the position desired does not mean the person held or worked in the positions listed on the job application.

Another great tool that can be used as part of a preemployment background verification is a review of the applicant's credit report. Prior to obtaining an applicant's credit report, the following information needs to be understood: According to the Small Business Administration, employers are required to obtain written permission from prospective employees prior to obtaining and looking at their individual credit report. During the application process, if a decision is made not to hire an applicant based on information in the applicant's credit report, the employer has to provide a copy of the credit report to the prospective employee. The employer also has to inform the rejected applicant of the applicant's right, under the Fair Credit Reporting Act (FCRA), to challenge the information listed in the credit report.[2]

Prior to making an offer of employment, having the ability to review the information in the applicant's credit report will allow the employer access to vital information about the potential future associate. Information in the credit report will show the approximate year of issue of the Social Security number (SSN), as well as the state of issue. (In 1986 it became mandatory for parents to apply for an SSN for newly born children. Prior to 1986, most people applied for and obtained an SSN around the age of sixteen, when they decided to enter the workforce.[3])

The credit report can also provide information on the credit history of the applicant. The report can answer questions on the applicant and determine if there is a history of paying bills in a timely manner, if there was delinquency, or if they failed to pay debt obligations. Failure to pay owed debts can result in the amount being charged off by the issuing financial institution, business, credit agency, and so on. Any employer who conducts credit checks on prospective employees can work to ensure they are not placing a person with a poor credit history in charge of company assets.

The credit report can also provide information on names associated with the SSN, as well as current and previous addresses. Multiple names reported on an SSN can reveal multiple names used by the job applicant. The multiple names used can also reveal a history of identity fraud for that particular SSN. (SSN information and the potential for identity theft and identity fraud are discussed in detail in Chapter 10.) The address information available on the credit report can be cross-checked against the work history reported on the application and résumé.

Companies can also choose to verify the applicant's name, SSN year of issue, and related SSN address information through various companies that provide simple checks of the SSN. The fees associated with the SSN name verification are minimal and vary per the companies offering the service. The ability to access this type of SSN verification information is vital to the new applicant verification process, and it can be obtained at a minimal cost.

A popular tool used by numerous companies, large and small, is to contact previous employers to verify a job applicant's prior employment information. Because of legal issues, many companies have varying policy requirements on the type and level of information they can provide for employment verification. A popular block of information many organizations choose to provide to the hiring company is position held and dates of employment.

A simple search of the Internet on negative prior employment reference checks can lead to discussion of legal cases in which the company reporting negative information on a former employee was taken to court. Whether right or wrong on the reported employee information, many companies choose to provide simple employment information to avoid the potential for lawsuits brought by the former employee.

Any information the hiring company can obtain from a prior employer reference check is vital to the background verification of the applicant. Organizations need to know the individuals they are hiring and the work-related experience of that particular applicant. One tool available for companies looking to obtain detailed information on an applicant from a former employer or employers is an employee reference release. This is a form (it is hoped prepared with legal counsel) that protects the former employer from potential legal action on any negative information provided during the employment verification process. This release, signed by the individual seeking employment, states the individual signing the form agrees and holds harmless the reporting person or organization (former employer) against adverse information released pertaining to the applicant.

When developing a new hire release form, the company can choose to develop the document in-house through its legal department or obtain a blanket form through a third-party vendor. With a world of information available on the Internet, it is easy to locate more than one business offering to sell or develop a custom-fit release form.

Companies choosing to have job applicants sign a reference release form can obtain a wealth of positive or negative information pertaining to the job seeker.

Organizations also have to be aware of what is referred to as a negligent referral, which, basically, is the potential ramification of not providing a true and accurate account of why a former employee was terminated:

CASE STUDY 2.1

Companies hiring new employees have a risk of processing a job applicant who was recently fired by a former employer. During the employment verification process, the former employer provides the position held and the dates of employment. (Many human resources policies require only providing the basic information on previous employees to prospective employers.) The basic information is provided to the prospective employer without consideration of whether the former employee was fired for misconduct. Based on the position held and the daily operating activities of the business, the reasons for misconduct can vary. From the position of a financial institution, the misconduct could be as in the following example:

In the financial institution community, a teller at bank A is fired for stealing cash from the teller drawer. Weeks later, bank A is contacted by bank B for a former employee reference verification. All bank A provides is the position held and dates of employment. What happens if the teller commits the same crime while working at bank B? Can bank A be sued by bank B for providing a "negligent referral"?

If bank A provided the actual cause of termination, bank B could have avoided a loss by not hiring the terminated teller.

Former employers walk a slippery slope when contacted by prospective employers about a former associate who was terminated for fraud, theft, or other criminal activity. With the increase in negligent referral cases across the country, should former employers consider revealing information on serious misconduct? If the former employer chooses to reveal the information to a prospective employer, the information needs to be delivered in a straightforward manner without offering a hint of bias.[4] The question remains whether there is an obligation to provide a negligent referral. From a moral perspective, the information could be reported in a clear and concise manner. From a legal perspective, there is no duty to report.[5]

Prospective employers should conduct preemployment background verifications and take into consideration the potential for negligent referral. Employers who terminate an employee for fraudulent activity also need to consider providing an accurate account of why the individual was terminated. While conducting a new hire background verification, the hiring organization should ascertain exactly why the candidate left a former employer. In an effort to ensure that the reference information provided by the former employer is accurate, the use of a new hire release form is vital.

From the perspective of a path of least resistance, potential employers can choose how far off the path their new hire verification policies will take their organization. The more detailed and extensive the verification policies, the greater the level of deviation off the path will be. Employers advertising on their company website that they require all candidates to sign a new hire release form can save time and money. By not having candidates with questionable backgrounds apply because they have to sign a release form, less time is wasted processing paperwork and conducting negative verifications.

All employers need to look at the level of effort placed in conducting reference checks on prospective employees. Smaller business operations might have between five and ten employees and operate on tighter margins for inventory, theft, and profit for the business owner. One bad employee hire can easily wipe out the end-of-year profit of the business through sweethearting, embezzlement, or outright theft. Larger business operations operate on much larger margins and can invest more money in new hire screening. (Their employee theft and fraud issues are discussed further in this chapter and in Chapter 3.)

2.3 Small Business Theft/Fraud

Small business operations, especially those specializing in the food and retail industry, have to maintain strict procedures for new hiring. In cities across the nation, main streets are lined with single-unit mom-and-pop operations that conduct daily business with fewer than twenty employees. No matter if the small business has a name connected to a well-known global enterprise, such as McDonald's, the daily operation of these franchise locations is conducted by individual owners. Even though there is the name of a multimillion-dollar corporation on the building, the individual owner is responsible for operating the business and hiring new employees.

Small businesses and franchise companies, where the owner has between one and ten stores, all operate within tight margins, with a limited amount of capital available for purchasing inventory, advertising, hiring costs, and so on. On average, the typical small business/franchise owner spends between 30% and 40% of gross sales on payroll. With so much invested in the operating expense of employees, it is vital to a successful business that the organization hire, train, and maintain loyal associates.

When it comes to the profit margin or the annual percentage of profit based on gross sales, there is no set industry figure. Based on the type of business, location, and local economic conditions, the percentage of end-of-year profit based on gross sales will vary. For a typical small business operation, the percentage of profit to gross sales is between 25% and 35%.[6]

For a small business to be successful, much attention has to be given to the employees. With retail operations, the location has to be stocked with associates who have the personality and ability to sell. For operations with a fast turnaround of patrons, the associates need to be able to react quickly, think on their feet, have quality interaction with the customers, and prepare or stock depleted items. Especially when the owner is not in the location during the hours of operation, the employees need to be trusted and have a success of their employer's business mentality. Ideal employees need to be trusted to operate on a success of the business mentality weather the owner is present or not.

Annual payroll expense and tight operating margins coupled with the hourly pay rate as well as the daily operating costs of the business are major concerns for the small business owner. Employers are mandated by federal law to pay all associates the minimum wage. Many cities and states have set their minimum wage higher than the federal requirement, and employers have to pay the required hourly amount. In many regional areas around the country, there is a set minimum wage, and at times, there is an unmandated minimum wage that an employee expects. This wage is paid to employees in the region by some employers and even though it is higher than the required standards, it is expected by those seeking employment in the region. Any employer operating in these regions is faced with a greater burden on the annual payroll percentage of the business.

For any small business owner to be successful and profitable, the owner needs to provide the following:

- A quality product
- Easy accessibility to the public
- Products that are competitively priced in the region
- Operating hours consistent with customer needs
- Energetic and trustworthy employees

An ideal small business operation should be successful if it is operating under these five points. Success can also be achieved if one of the five points is taken away, excluding the energetic and trustworthy employees. The small business owner not only has to trust the employees for successful operation, but also the associates have to operate under the umbrella of trust.

The small business owner needs to develop an understanding of why it is important to identify and eliminate job candidates who will most likely defraud their operation. The owners also need to identify the candidates who display a strong level of integrity and place these individuals in their business operation. In addition, the business owner needs to eliminate opportunities for fraud in daily operation to ensure the associates working for the company perform their duties in a professional manner.

Within the security, loss prevention, and law enforcement communities there are many theories regarding why some people commit fraud and most others do not. It basically comes down to evil, integrity, and temptation. The evil is the 20% of the population who are inherently dishonest. The middle 60% of the population are honest and go throughout their daily lives operating under this umbrella. However, the middle 60% can be tempted and under the right circumstances will commit fraud. The remaining 20% of the population are honest to the core and will not submit to temptation.[7]

Within any business, every attempt should be made to identify the top 20% of job applicants and place as many as possible into the operation of the business. It is also vital to identify the bottom 20% and allow these individuals nowhere near the business operation. The middle 60% of the public can be hired and operate successfully within any business operation. This 60% of the population is why it is necessary to understand the many avenues of small business fraud/theft. This understanding of fraud awareness will allow the business owner to remove all avenues of temptation.

Small business owners need to develop an understanding of the tactics used by the bottom 20% in an effort to defraud their organization. The discussion next details some tactics used to extract money and merchandise from a small business, along with possible prevention measures.

2.3.1 Getting Hired to Steal

Some people apply and aim to be hired by a small business for the sole purpose of slowly stealing merchandise, taking small amounts of cash from the register, or sweethearting sales to friends or associates.

2.3.1.1 Remedy

Small business owners need to adhere to the strictest new hire verification standards, including speaking with character references and prior employers. It is vital for the business owner who is conducting background verification of former employers to make sure to speak with the actual business owner or someone to whom the applicant directly reported. Do not ask for a former employee reference verification from whoever answers the phone. It is also necessary to obtain the phone number for the business to be called from directory assistance and not directly from the applicant. An applicant can provide a phone number to a drop house where there is an associate who answers all incoming calls and provides any positive information the person calling wants to hear.

2.3.2 Protecting the Company Bank Account

The job applicant who seeks a position for the purpose of fraud will also obtain a job from a small business that does not use direct deposit on payday. Many small business operations do not want to pay the extra expense of using a payroll-processing company and issue the employees an actual check on payday. A newly hired employee who obtained the job for the purpose of fraud will work at the company to receive the actual paycheck. The information on the face of the check (bank name, routing number, account number) can now be used to create counterfeit checks in the name of the issuing company or person. With each counterfeit check processed or cashed outright, the dollar amount comes out of the small business owner's bank account.

2.3.2.1 Remedy

Many small business operations need to issue an actual check to employees on payday. It is possible for the information on one of the issued checks to be used for counterfeit purposes. To protect the assets of the company, the business owner has to establish two separate bank accounts: one account for the purpose of issuing payroll checks and maintaining a balance in that account to cover the total cash amount of the checks issued to employees. All money received through the daily operation of the business (cash, checks, and credit card deposits) needs to be deposited into an account separate from the check-issuing bank account. If checks are counterfeited on the bank account used for issuing checks, the total assets of the business are not at risk.

It is necessary to point out that counterfeit or forged checks processed through a business account can be identified as fraudulent by the business owner. Even though the monetary amounts of these bogus checks was extracted from the business account, the money will be credited back to the account holder on identifying the checks as fraudulent and the completion of the necessary paperwork. Although the business account holder is not ultimately responsible for the monetary amount of the bogus checks, having unexpected dollar amounts removed from a business account can cause legitimately issued checks to bounce. This activity can cause harm to the overall integrity of the business.

2.3.4 Protecting the Credit Card Swipe Machine Master Code

Almost any business, large or small, has one or more devices used to swipe and process credit/debit card transactions (Figure 2.1). The money from each transaction, minus a small percentage, is deposited into the merchant account of the business. The credit card transactions occur with a swipe of the card's magnetic strip, the machine reading the data on the strip, and the customer approving the dollar amount of the transaction and providing a signature. A debit card transaction begins with the same process but concludes with the customer entering a four-digit personal identification number (PIN) into the machine. A charge can also be placed against the customer's credit card by manually inputting the sixteen-digit card number and card expiration month and year. The business needs to obtain approval of the card holder to process a manual credit transaction.

Figure 2.1   Credit/debit card swiping machine.

The business owner can use the card-swiping machine to void credit/debit card transactions and to credit a monetary amount back to a credit card. To process either a credit card void or return transaction, the four-digit master code has to be entered into the swiping machine for verification. Without entering the master code, neither procedure can occur.

With the possibility of use of the credit card machine master code by a dishonest employee to process a return transaction to any legitimate credit card and not one of a previous customer, unauthorized withdrawals of money can occur from the business owner's merchant bank account.

2.3.4.1 Remedy

The small business owner needs to set the operation of the credit card swipe machine so that employees can only process card transactions with the presence of the actual card. All other transactions involving the manual entry of the credit card number, sale voids, and returns should only be completed by the owner/manager with the entry of the manager's code.

To prevent large amounts of money from being withdrawn from the business merchant account through unauthorized credit card returns, an additional bank account should be created by the owner. The small business owner should open a separate company bank account for the purpose of transferring a set percentage of the daily assets received through credit/debit card transactions. This process will leave a smaller dollar amount of available assets in the merchant account that can be withdrawn in the event of fraudulent activity.

For a small business to operate successfully and with an end-of-year profit, the owner needs to make sure as much temptation as possible is eliminated in the day-to-day operation of the business. As discussed, poor operating practices or fraud-related opportunities could lead an employee from the 60% category to engage in fraud or theft. This is especially true for any small business that hires teenagers or has one or more quick service restaurant franchise operations.

Small business owners need to develop an understanding of not creating opportunities of temptation that could cause the middle 60% of employees to commit fraud or steal from their organization. Next, some tactics used to extract money and merchandise from a small business are detailed, along with possible prevention measures.

2.3.5 Not Conducting Store Inventory

A good business owner should conduct an inventory of merchandise at least once a year, but an ideal plan would be to do so on a quarterly basis. Store associates need to be involved in the inventory process to show everyone working in the business there is an accountability process.

2.3.5.1 Remedy

Begin an inventory process at the business location and involve store employees. A location inventory should be conducted at least annually. To ensure the integrity of the operation, inventories should be conducted on a quarterly basis. In addition, the exact dates and times of the upcoming inventories should not be made known to store associates.

2.3.6 Scheduled Visits to the Location by the Owner

Owners of a small business set up an operation by which a manager completes the scheduling, hiring, and training and oversees the daily store activities. The business owner might visit the location on Friday to issue paychecks or on a set time each week to meet with the manager. Knowing the set dates and time the owner will be at the location can raise the temptation level within the organization. In addition to raising the temptation level of the employees for fraud/theft, poor operating practices can also develop. The old expression "while the cat's away, the mice will play" is evident in almost any business operation.

2.3.6.1 Remedy

The store owner needs to develop a pattern of dropping by the location at various days and times throughout each week. Once in the location, the owner needs to make his or her presence known to the associates working. The business owner should also make the effort to engage in conversations with the associates. These conversations can vary in content, with the purpose of showing the associates that they are part of a team and the business owner is concerned about their progress and well-being.

In addition, if the business owner is going out of town on vacation for a week or two, this information should only be shared with the trusted store manager.

2.3.7 Set Dollar Amount Promotions

Some stores, especially franchise operations, have promotional nights when a certain product is sold at a discounted price to generate additional sales and location traffic.

> **CASE STUDY 2.2**
> **Dollar Scoop Night**
>
> I used to work for a large franchise organization that specialized in selling ice cream products. Several times throughout the year, the home office would schedule a promotional sales event. These events were referred to as "Dollar Scoop Night." For $1, a customer would receive a single scoop of the ice cream of their choice. Promotional advertising indicated that all the customer needed to make the purchase was a single dollar bill, with the sales tax amount included in the purchase price.
>
> Having the ability, as a customer, to hand over a single bill to make a quick purchase is a time-saving benefit. As a store operating benefit, more customers can be moved through the line at a faster pace while collecting a single dollar without having to make change for every transaction.
>
> Unfortunately, this practice worked to create both an opportunity for fraud and an increase in the levels of temptation. After many of these dollar scoop night sales promotions, at various locations across the country, it was evident that each and every ice cream cone prepared and handed to the customer was not processed through the cash register. Postaudits and visual video confirmation proved the sales staff at many locations did not properly account for each cone sold.
>
> Private investigators hired to covertly record the register activity on the promotional nights revealed cones being prepared and handed over the counter to customers. With some of the transactions observed the product and payment transaction took place as normal. However, other transactions involved the store personnel receiving the payment and the money being placed in a specific location on the counter. It was hoped that at the end of the evening the stack of cash would have been recorded as a bulk sale. A subsequent register audit revealed there were no bulk sale amounts recorded at the end of the evening prior to totaling the daily register sales.
>
> Additional usage audits of raw material compared to sales recorded revealed more ice cream product was used in the production of the cones provided to the

customers than money recorded in the register, basically indicating that more cones were prepared and delivered to the customers than the number of items recorded in the register.

Although these promotions are a good marketing tool, they can also raise the temptation level for fraud and theft. If customers are walking through the serving line purchasing a product for which they can hand over a single dollar bill or two and not expect change or a register receipt, the potential for fraud on the part of the store employees increases. If an employee is able to accept a rounded monetary amount for payment of a product purchased, the need to provide change back to the customer from the cash register drawer is eliminated. If the register drawer is not opened from a recorded transaction and a receipt is not generated, the temptation to pocket the cash increases.

2.3.7.1 Remedy

Small business owners should continue to increase customer sales and traffic through product promotions, but each item sold has to be at a dollar amount that requires change to be returned. Small business owners also need to initiate a guaranteed receipt policy. Develop signage placed in customer view by the register that states: "If you are not provided a sales receipt, the purchase is free." Additional information that needs to be placed on the receipt guarantee sign is a contact number. The number provided for the customer to call can be an individual associated with the business or one of many third-party vendors that provide receipt guarantee services.

The business owner can set up a guaranteed receipt service through one of the many mystery shopping organizations that track and report on nonreceipt transactions.

2.3.8 Teenage Employees Working in a Fast Food Restaurant on Game Night

In any small business retail company where most employees are paid minimum wage, it is almost impossible not to hire teenagers. This is not to say all teenage employees are going to steal or commit fraud. What is at issue is the temptation for employees working at the small business/fast food restaurant who attend high school in the same geographical location as the store to provide free or discounted product to school friends. This situation is especially true during the time frame after the end of the Friday night home football game. Students will visit the local fast food restaurants where their friends are employed and receive free or discounted items. The reason for the free giveaways range from loyalty to school classmates and resentment on the part of the student employee for having to work on a home game night.

Local school student employees have been known to commit the free giveaways to friends not only after home sporting events but also on any night of the week. The main temptation is the absence of the owner or manager overseeing the operation.

The absence of the owner or manager can also lead to sweethearting among younger associates and their school friends.

2.3.8.1 Remedy

The number one prevention tool to control fraud and theft in a small business operation is the installation of a video monitoring system. Video cameras mounted on the wall in open display can work to serve multiple purposes:

- The cameras let the employees know their activities are under constant surveillance.
- Friends visiting the establishment might be reluctant to accept or request free or discounted items if they know their activity is being monitored.
- Having open video surveillance monitoring and recording can also work to prevent robberies.

In addition to having video monitors around the store, it is a good idea to have a camera pointed directly over the cash register(s). This lets the employees know their register activities are under surveillance. With a surveillance system installed in the retail location, it is imperative to set up the system with remote monitoring. The remote monitoring allows the owner to look in on the location's activities from a laptop computer or tablet. It should also be common knowledge for all employees that the store owner has the ability to remotely monitor the activities inside the retail location.

An additional fraud/theft procedure any retail store owner should employ is the eyes and ears of their friends. An owner of a restaurant can offer to pay for the meal purchased by a friend who agrees to consume the product inside the location. This allows the friend to monitor the activities of the store employees to ensure operating procedures are adhered to by the employees and all sales are recorded through the cash register. Friends can also be solicited to visit retail locations to make a purchase or shop, with the purpose of monitoring employee activities.

Another prevention tool, as discussed previously, is the unscheduled store visits by the owner.

2.3.9 Trading Pizzas for Tacos

In many strip malls across the country, customers have the ability to easily walk to several fast food restaurants from a central location in the parking lot. Most of these restaurants close around the same time while some offer twenty-four-hour service through the drive-up window.

A popular method to defraud store owners out of inventory is for employees on the closing shift to cook excess product at several different restaurants. Instead of throwing the food in the trash, the associates at the pizza restaurant will trade the product for tacos at the neighboring location.

2.3.9.1 Remedy

The restaurant owner has to establish food preparation policies during the slow hours after the dinner rush. Prepared items should be a smaller percentage of the amount of product on hand during peak customer traffic hours. It is also vital for the store owner to make surprise visits to the location prior to and at closing time.

With all the potential for fraud and theft in a small business, it is vital for the owner to develop and practice strict new hire standards. This is to include the verification of prior work history and the interviewing of references. Job applicants should be required to provide references who can validate prior work performance. The interviewing of the references provided has to be completed in a detailed process to ensure the potential candidate can be trusted. For recent high school graduates, having the ability to speak with former teachers and school administrators can assist in the selection of trustworthy candidates.

For the small business owner to be able to ask the questions necessary to validate the integrity of the applicant, job candidates should be required to sign an employee release form.

CASE STUDY 2.3
Getting Hired to Steal

I worked for a large national financial institution in the Security/Fraud Department. Over a short time period, one bank branch had numerous $500 to $2,000 charge-offs.[8] The returned items were counterfeit checks that were deposited into customer accounts, and once the deposit item funds were available, withdrawals were made against the accounts. The bank accounts where the counterfeit checks were being deposited belonged to random customers who frequented that particular branch location. The bank accounts of the random customers were assigned/housed to the bank branch in question,[9] and all had higher-than-average balances and transaction activity.

Video surveillance of the individuals making the counterfeit check deposits and the subsequent withdrawals indicated the individuals were all different people, with no pattern of the same individual pictured conducting numerous fraudulent transactions or withdrawals. Video surveillance actually showed one person making the deposit, with a different person making the withdrawal; both individuals presented identification in the name of the account holder.

With no set pattern of suspects conducting the deposit and withdrawal activity on the accounts of one individual branch, the focus of the investigation shifted to looking into the computer activity of the branch associates. Each person working within the entire financial institution has a unique and individually assigned log-in name and password. With the ability to limit the focus and search of a small list of log-in names, it was easier to identify the bank teller who accessed the branch accounts where the fraudulent activity took place.

The suspected branch teller was researching high-dollar and high-activity accounts and providing the account numbers to individuals he was associated with in a sophisticated fraud ring. The suspected teller in question was also providing the names and addresses of the legitimate account holders to his associates. The account holder data was used to produce counterfeit pieces of identification in the account holders' names with the various fraud ring members pictured on the pieces of identification.

With the investigation identifying a suspect teller who worked at the branch in question, the teller was called in to the branch manager's office and was met by a bank security officer and a member of the law enforcement community. Once the police detective identified himself to the suspect, the suspect handed over a business card of his lawyer and refused to provide any information. He was later charged with various counts of bank fraud and was released on bail pending trial. To the best of my knowledge, he never showed up for trial.

The sole purpose of the suspect seeking a job and working for the bank was to commit fraud.

2.4 Hiring Quality Teenagers

As discussed previously, many small business operations and fast food restaurants rely on younger employees to conduct their daily operations. Many of these younger employees are still of high school age and offer little in the way of a prior work history.

One area where employers can look when hiring school-aged associates is the local high school and college DECA (Distributive Education Clubs of America) programs. School-related DECA programs have a mission of preparing students for careers in business, marketing, management, finance, hospitality, and so on.[10]

Business owners and managers should contact their local high schools and colleges to determine if they have a DECA program. If these local schools participate in DECA programs, efforts should be made to hire quality associates who participate in DECA activities.

2.5 Nonprofit Organization Fraud

A nonprofit organization is one that is established to serve the public, and all revenues are disbursed back into the business. There are currently twenty-six categories of nonprofits that are recognized by the Internal Revenue Service (IRS). Nonprofit organizations can range from a charity, to a religious organization, to the local community group that organizes youth soccer programs. A more official account of a nonprofit organization is that it is one that has the purpose of being scientific, religious, literary, or charitable.[11]

Basically, a nonprofit organization is a business operation that generates revenue and accepts charitable donations but does not declare an end-of-year profit like a normal business. Many nonprofit operations have obtained a tax exempt status through the IRS and are categorized as having a 501(c)(3) status.[12]

Organizations operating in a nonprofit status are well known for their charitable activities and work within communities supporting activities such as youth sports. These organizations are also known through news stories in cities throughout the country when it has been discovered that a member of the company was embezzling money.

The reasons for individuals working in these nonprofit organizations to commit fraud vary, and the positions held in the organizations of those who do so range from a bookkeeper to the chief executive. Individuals working in high positions in the organizations who commit fraud tend to steal around four times the amount as a person in a lower position. However, embezzlement cases involving charitable organizations typically involve female employees. These employees traditionally work for the organization for at least four years, have no criminal record, and make less than $50,000 per year. Traditionally, most people within a nonprofit organization who commit fraud work in the financial area of the business. These positions include the accountant, bookkeeper, or an associate who signs and issues checks.[13]

Not all, but many, nonprofit organizations that fall victim to internal fraud tend to operate on the path of least resistance. These same organizations that fall victim to internal fraud have operating procedures that open up the avenue of temptation to the 60%. Newspapers are full of stories outlining the bookkeeper who stole thousands of dollars from a local charity and had worked at this same company for over twenty years. The reasons vary regarding why the individual chose to commit fraud against a longtime employer, but the facts of most cases point to poor internal controls. These controls revolve around allowing individual control of bookkeeping duties. This could be because of budgetary constraints in the hiring of new employees or a development of trust with a long-term and loyal associate.

No organization, large or small, should allow one employee to operate in both areas of accounts receivable and accounts payable. One employee operating with this much freedom in the Bookkeeping Department can:

■ Create fictitious invoices to cover money embezzled from the organization.
■ Keep bank statement information secret from board members and management.
■ Create bogus financial documents to hide fraudulent activity.
■ Outright steal donations paid with a check by opening a business bank account in the name of the organization and then transfer those funds to a personal account. Typically, this individual will have access to the organizational paperwork necessary for opening financial accounts.
■ Operate for years under the radar while presenting a stronger-than-accurate company financial situation.

The only business or organization that should allow one employee to be in charge of both accounts receivable and accounts payable is a sole proprietorship with only one employee. All other businesses and organizations need to separate accounting duties and move off the path of least resistance. In order to prevent fraud and embezzlement in a nonprofit organization, the following procedures need to be followed:

- Conduct a complete internal audit at least annually; ideally, have the audit conducted by a disinterested third party.
- Never allow one employee to manage accounts receivable and accounts payable.
- Establish dual-control procedures for activities related to the organization's financial activities.
- Make sure the organization's bank statements are made available to the founder or board members on a quarterly basis.
- Develop a policy of dual-signature requirements for checks written over what the company believes to be a large amount.
- Keep the financial activity of the nonprofit separate from the accounts of the organization founder, owner, or board members.

2.6 Embezzlement

Embezzlement in the simplest terms is theft or larceny. It is the taking of property or assets by a person who was placed in a position of trust. This same individual has to have had a responsibility over the property or assets.[14]

A large majority of embezzlement incidents take place at the hands of employees from small businesses, nonprofit organizations, and large corporations. Unlike embezzlement cases discussed previously with nonprofit organizations, the likely suspects can be any employee in the organization and the embezzlement can take place outside of employees with accounting responsibilities.

A popular form of embezzlement, sometimes referred to as siphoning or shrink, takes place in the retail industry. This includes any retail operation that involves customers making a purchase and the store employee receiving the payment for the product. The most popular areas where siphoning/shrink takes place are retail stores or restaurant operations. Unlike small business fraud discussed previously in the chapter, the retail operation or restaurant can be a single-unit operation or a store that is part of a national chain. Retail organizations such as Target that operate thousands of locations across the country can suffer a financial loss through embezzlement. The embezzlement can be at the hands of a single employee stealing money from a cash register at one Target location. The same holds true for any restaurant or small retail operation, no matter the size and financial assets of the parent company.

The goal of the suspect employee is to take money from the cash register while working to ensure the money in the register at the end of their shift is equal to the amount of the transactions recorded through customer sales. The sales associate will process a majority of the customer-based transactions according to procedure. Other transactions that involve the intent of the sales associate to steal money from the register will take place based on the employee's knowledge of the register's operating system.

The activities used by employees stealing cash from the business vary, and the focus needs to be placed on identifying their specific accounting system. An individual accounting system has to be used by the embezzling employee for the employee to be able to account for how much money was not recorded through the register. At the end of their shift, the money in the register drawer has to balance with the internal register totals.

Most cash register change drawers have five slots for coins. Typically, four coin slots will be used in a typical retail operation (quarters, dimes, nickels, and pennies) cash register. Employees who typically embezzle money through the retail cash register will use the fifth slot to place random coins. The random coins of varying value act as their individual accounting system to track the amount of money to remove from the cash drawer. The basic method is pennies count for a dollar, nickels for five dollars, and so on. The history of interviewing associates who have embezzled money through a retail store cash drawer has shown the fifth slot accounting system varies per individual.

In a typical restaurant setting, the employee or employees working behind the bar will use a popular method of having a glass containing straws by the cash register. Next to the full glass of straws is an empty glass, and throughout the shift, straws will be taken from the full glass and placed into the empty glass. Based on the accounting system of the stealing employee, each straw placed in the empty glass has a certain monetary amount assigned. At the end of the shift, the employee or employees have a count of how much money to remove from the register.

There are no catchall methods a retail location owner or manager can use to stop all employee embezzlement from the cash register. Outside of initiating a Las Vegas–style camera monitoring system of placing video surveillance on each register and employee, a better prevention system would be to develop an awareness of associate activities operating around the cash register.

Some of the awareness activities that store owners or managers need to develop are as follows:

■ Look for odd coins placed in the open slot in the cash register drawer.
■ Look for counting systems in the bar area of a restaurant, such as the straw method.
■ Have a friend or hire a mystery shopping company to watch the restaurant bar activity. One key area to look for is associates making change from the tip jar or tip bucket.

■ During busy times in retail locations, especially fast food restaurants, two or more employees will work together to embezzle money. Employees will go through the process of switching out cash register drawers, leaving the swapped out drawer on the retail counter while customers are making purchases. One or more employees will process transactions involving a few dollars using the register drawer on the counter.

■ Develop a guaranteed receipt policy and make the benefit of a customer not receiving a receipt worth alerting a store manager. This policy will work to alleviate employees opening the cash register drawer to make change by using the No Sale key or recording a penny sale.

■ The receipt policy will also eliminate percentage sales. Employees will ring a sale into the register at a low percentage of the total item price. If the employee knows a popular item costs $5.50 with tax, the employee might record the transaction in the register as a sale of $0.55. Using a 10% accounting method, the employee knows he or she can remove $4.95 from the register.

■ Watch for certain employees who seem to have a lot of sale voids throughout their shift. The sale can be voided after the customer makes the actual purchase. Excessive voids can also be used to throw off the actual totals of the recorded register sales.

Leaving the retail side of a business, another popular method of employee embezzlement is through what is called kickbacks. Based on the operational aspect of the business, most operations need to purchase wholesale items for retail sales or purchase raw materials. No matter the types of materials required for successful operation of the business, the vendors selling the items to the company have been known to recruit employees to engage in kickback schemes. To ensure the vendor has a continuing business operation with the company, the vendor gives a percentage of the items sold to the business back to the person in charge of purchasing, basically kicking a profit back to the employee for continuing to do business with the vendor.

Outside of the employee and vendor participating in unethical activity, the continued relationship could cause the business owner to pay a higher price for material. Once the vendor has the employee operating in a kickback scheme, the crime of blackmail enters the picture. To increase the profit level of material sold to the business, the vendor can raise prices. Knowing his or her job could be in jeopardy for participating in a kickback scheme, the employee approves the price increase.

To identify and stop kickback activities in a business operation, the following steps should be followed:

■ Make sure all material price increases are approved. Business operations should develop an approval committee to analyze vendor activity and material purchases.

■ Establish a competitive bid policy for material purchases.

■ Make similar material purchases through more than a single vendor.

- Switch purchasing employees so they oversee different vendor groups every six months.
- Watch for odd relationships between purchasing employees and vendors.
- Watch for the delivery of substandard material from a long-term vendor. If the vendor has an employee on the hook for receiving kickbacks, the vendor knows the associate will accept the product as delivered.
- The same theory holds true for long-term vendors that begin to make deliveries past the promised delivery date.

Embezzlement in an organization can take many forms and be committed by all levels of employees within the business; the monetary amounts taken can range from $500 to millions of dollars. The suspects can range from the volunteer managing the weekly donations at the community church to the widely televised case of Bernie Madoff. The rationale or motivation to commit embezzlement can range from out-and-out greed, as with the Madoff case, to other areas of rationalization. For the typical business organization, the rationale for the employee can vary:

- Feelings of being unappreciated for the level of work performed.
- Belief of being underpaid for the perceived quality of work performed.
- Individual belief the money is only being borrowed and will be repaid before anyone notices.
- The common response, "It was only a small amount of money."
- "Everyone else is doing it."
- Knowledge of fraud being committed by a boss or upper management.
- Individual financial necessity because of a recent unexpected large expense, foreclosure, family health issues, and so on.
- Belief there are no audit procedures in place and they will not get caught.
- An individual belief the employee is smarter than management and associates working in the Audit Department.

2.7 Two-Person Rule/Separating Accounting Duties

As discussed with frauds pertaining to nonprofit organizations, the loss took place because one employee was allowed to perform accounting duties by monitoring both accounts receivable and accounts payable. In the business world, a large majority of employees performing duties in some type of financial capacity are honest and go to work with no intent to steal or commit fraud. As long as the business can weed out those applying for a job who fall in the 20% category of evil and understand only another 20% fall in the category of outright honest people, operating policies have to be developed to prevent the middle 60% of people from falling to the temptation of fraud. The temptation is driven by opportunities that arise from lack of policies, procedures, and staffing that protect against the temptation:

- All organizations need to develop and adhere to policies that require departmental audits at least annually.
- The procedures of the organization should not allow employees to perform cross-functional financial duties.
- Employee staffing policies should not allow one employee to oversee both accounts receivable and accounts payable.

CASE STUDY 2.4
Two-Person Rule

Entry into a secure vault containing top secret information or entry into a secure area in a nuclear power plant require adherence to the two-person rule. The rule restricts entry to secure areas by a single individual. The purpose of the two-person rule is to prevent one person from removing secret information, taking unauthorized photographs, or intentionally causing damage. With a two-person rule, unauthorized incidents are less likely to take place.

Although conducting accounting duties in many business operations do not rise to the level of the two-person rule requirement at a nuclear power plant, in an effort to prevent fraud, the development of a like policy is necessary. It is not necessary for companies to hire two employees to work the same financial department job, but initiating a policy requiring two employees to approve a business expense can eliminate the temptation to commit fraud. The two-person rule can also be used by requiring two employees to approve payments to vendors or an increase in material pricing.

Companies can also have a policy of separation of duties. Any position within the company where one employee can commit fraud and cover up the activity needs to be eliminated. To continue with the vendor example discussed, it is not wise for an organization to allow an employee working in the Purchasing Department to approve a vendor request for an increase in material pricing. The same is true for allowing an employee who issues checks that pay the company bills to also approve the bills to be paid.

The examples discussed might seem simple or common knowledge to many, but they have been allowed in businesses and nonprofit organizations across the country. The owner of a company or department head or ideally a security or loss prevention professional working outside the direction of the finance area should conduct a vulnerability audit of the procedures and employee functions. The vulnerability audit is an overall analysis of reviewing the department policies and procedures and the day-to-day functions of each employee performing finance-related duties.

The person conducting what I refer to as a vulnerability audit reviews the procedures and employee functions through the eyes of a criminal. The auditing individual has to conduct the review and look for vulnerabilities that would appeal to a thief and answer the following questions:

- Do our financial department operating policies place the company on the path of least resistance?
- Are there any daily functions performed by employee A that place the company on the path of least resistance?
- Do our policies conform to the theory of the two-person rule?
- Have all of the avenues of temptation in our financial business operations been eliminated?
- Are all of our company employees treated fairly and with respect?
- Are our company payroll structures competitive within the marketplace?
- When analyzing company financial operating procedures and thinking like a thief, could successful fraud be committed?

When discussing employee theft/fraud, numerous books can be written detailing a vast amount of frauds committed by employees during the history of business. Many internal frauds have been assigned a name that falls into the category of embezzlement, nonprofit fraud, and so on. Also, there are countless variations of successful fraudulent acts committed by employees that were spun off the named criminal activity.

The purpose of this chapter and book is not to provide a detailed account and name for each type of fraud committed by employees. The purpose is to raise the awareness of employee fraud and discuss procedures that allow a business to hire applicants with the least amount of potential to commit fraud. Once hired and working for the business, the organizations need to operate on a foundation of eliminating areas of temptation within each employee's job duties and functions. Policies and procedures also need to focus on eliminating temptation on the part of the employees while making sure not to create a big brother–type working environment.

Fraud prevention in any business is based on working to hire the 20% of the population who are inherently honest, eliminating the avenues of temptation for the middle 60%, and developing policies and procedures that are based on preventing successful fraud if a person from the bottom 20% was accidently hired—taking the entire business operation off the path of least resistance.

Notes

1. *Sweethearting* is defined as a person working in a sales capacity allowing friends and family members to purchase items at a discounted price. This activity is popular in bar settings, with bar staff providing a friend with drinks all evening, not ringing up the purchases, and charging the patron for a single beverage at the end of the night. The arrangement between the patron and employee is for the person who drank virtually free all evening to leave a large tip for the drink provider.
2. Small Business Administration, Pre-employment background checks. http://www.sba.gov/content/pre-employment-background-checks (accessed May 16, 2014).

3. Appendix A provides a breakdown of the SSN prefix information. The first three digits of the SSN reference the zip code in the mailing address used on the application to apply for the Social Security card. The mailing address does not have to be the same as the mailing address used to apply for the Social Security card.
4. Meason, C., How to handle reference calls for employees who were fired, http://work.chron.com/handle-reference-calls-employees-were-fired-11844.html (accessed May 30, 2014).
5. Edwards, L. B., and Culley, S. R., The employer reference problem: how much, if anything to disclose. http://www.rumberger.com/?t=11&la=721&format=xml (accessed May 30, 2014).
6. Morgan, R., What is the average gross profit margin for a small retail business? http://smallbusiness.chron.com/average-gross-profit-margin-small-retail-business-22607.html (accessed May 30, 2014).
7. It is unclear who actually developed this theory of 20-60-20. It has also been discussed in smaller terms as 10-80-10 and wider ranges of 15-70-15 to 20-60-20. I have always discussed the fraud theory in the 20-60-20 range.
8. A *charge-off* is a dollar amount charged back against the cost center number of a bank branch for any items processed at that location that were later determined to be a forgery or fraudulent item.
9. All accounts within this financial institution are assigned to the location where they were opened and branch associates can easily access reports containing customer information for local accounts.
10. For information about DECA, go to http://www.deca.org/about/ (accessed October 19, 2014).
11. What is a non-profit organization? http://www.nonprofit.pro/nonprofit_organization.htm (accessed June 2, 2014).
12. Ibid.
13. Bush, C., Life planning—beware of fraud in non-profit organizations. http://www.cbwealthadvisory.com/nonprofits.php (assessed June 2, 2014).
14. FindLaw, Embezzlement. http://criminal.findlaw.com/criminal-charges/embezzlement.html (accessed June 2, 2014).

Chapter 3

Organizational Fraud

3.1 Introduction

Organizations, large and small, conduct business operations on a daily basis with each entity operating in a manner suitable to their company mission statement and goals. Organizations susceptible to fraud include the following:

- Multimillion dollar, national and international, organizations
- Large businesses operating across many states
- Regional business operations offering a wide variety of services
- State or city operations with a more limited scope of operation
- Nonprofit operations, including churches and charities
- Single-unit mom-and-pop operations

As indicated, any organization conducting business operations where assets are available can become a victim of or a target for fraud. The focus of the fraud can range from extracting money, inventory, or intellectual assets through avenues created in the day-to-day business activities from operations, control procedures, and employee hiring.

When addressing the issue of fraud in the workplace, large corporations employ professional security and loss prevention departments. These departments work within the corporation to ensure there are strict hiring standards, accounting practices, inventory control, access control, and all other related operations so the assets of the company are secure. This is not to say the large corporations are not immune from fraud, but they place their operation in a better position to deter and prevent fraud.

From a position of the path of least resistance, the path is diverted to make the midsize, nonprofit, and mom-and-pop operations a more appealing target. In many midsize-to-smaller operations, they operate with smaller budgets, and many times employees wear multiple hats. This practice can lead to overlooking certain security and loss prevention procedures, with a lower level of resistance presented. With the smaller mom-and-pop operations, budgets are even tighter, and the idea of "it won't happen to me" is commonplace.

The importance of operating any size business or corporation is not in the amount of time and money spent working to prevent and deter fraud; it resides in the knowledge available on where the business is vulnerable to fraud, both internal and external fraud.

The knowledge required to place the business off the path of least resistance resides in the education level of the owners or employees given the task of protecting the company assets. The education level is not based on years of college experience or degrees held, but how well the business owners and loss prevention employees are educated on fraud identification and prevention.

3.2 Analyzing Fraud Potential

Chapter 2 on employee theft and fraud discussed the theory of 20-60-20 as it pertains to categories of individuals in society. Twenty percent of the population is inherently honest and will not be swayed into dishonesty, no matter the temptation level. Another 20% of the population is inherently dishonest, and it is hoped these individuals are weeded out during the applicant screening process as part of a detailed preemployment background verification. The remaining 60% of the population does not enter the workforce to commit fraud or steal. The opportunity level created by company operating procedures could cause an otherwise-honest individual to commit fraud or steal (temptation).

A proper understanding of organizational fraud potential resides in the category of opportunity.[1] To develop a complete understanding of opportunity, company policies and procedures have to be addressed to cover the two-sided aspect of fraud potential:

1. Do the daily company operating procedures and actual day-to-day business activities create an opportunity for fraud/theft?
2. Do the daily company operating procedures and actual day-to-day activities allow gaps where an employee can create the opportunity for fraud/theft?

When looking to conduct a fraud/theft prevention analysis of a business operation, it is necessary to identify areas of opportunity:

- Organizationally generated opportunities identified through weaknesses in daily operations
- Employee-generated opportunities identified through weaknesses in daily operations

3.2.1 Quit Being Reactive

Business organizations across the country suffer losses through fraudulent activities conducted by internal employees or external consumers. Based on the industry and the size of the financial loss to the organization, follow-up procedures will vary. Loss prevention/security policies in one organization might dictate procedures related to suspect identification and case referral to law enforcement. Other organizations could have internal policies that dictate the necessity of collecting restitution from the individual responsible for the loss. In an effort to show good faith to the suspect, promises are made not to pursue prosecution if restitution is paid. No matter the loss prevention/security policies relating to follow-up procedures caused by fraud losses, the goal of any organization has to revolve around the idea of "quit being reactive."

Successful businesses operate off the policy of a proactive approach to attract customers and increase sales:

■ A retail location that does not invest in advertising, offer competitive pricing, and work in a proactive posture to increase customer volume will fail while the competition grows.
■ A technology business hires the best and brightest associates in an effort to develop the latest gadget that sets them apart from the competition.
■ Successful restaurants offer a quality product at a competitive price. Menu items are continuously changed to offer new options to their customers.

No matter the type of business operation, to be successful, a proactive approach has to be adopted to ensure sales growth and future success.

Internally, in these same organizations, the method to reduce losses from fraudulent activity has to be addressed in a proactive manner. A rancher can ensure the integrity of his herd remains intact by erecting fencing around the property. If this same rancher takes a walk around the perimeter of his property and notices a hole in the fence line, the proactive measure would be to fix the breach prior to livestock walking away. A reactive rancher would not check the fence line for a breach until the livestock head count decreased. Now, the reactive rancher has to spend time rounding up the herd and repair the hole in the fence line.

Loss prevention/security managers have to apply the same principle of proactive versus reactive methods in an effort to prevent fraud-related financial losses. These proactive measures are going to vary based on the operating practices of the individual businesses, but the principle remains the same.

3.2.2 Talk across Departments

Organizational operation types vary from retail, manufacturing, wholesale sales, delivery, food service, and so on. No matter the operational focus of the organization, each is unique as it pertains to its individual business environment. The same is true for departments working within the overall business operation. Each department is unique concerning how it conducts business and contributes to the organization's bottom line.

When fraud and financial losses take place in an organization, all eyes turn toward those responsible for loss prevention and security. Questions are raised about how the fraud loss took place, where the internal weaknesses were, whether the offender can be prosecuted, and whether restitution is possible. To avoid department heads and other high-level associates from looking toward the Loss Prevention/Security Department for the answers after a fraud loss, the organization can develop a stronger proactive prevention posture by involving the entire company in a continuing risk analysis process.

Areas of opportunities can be identified by developing fraud focus groups or fraud working groups. These groups should consist of representatives from the various departments across the organization. The purpose of the working groups is to discuss areas of potential weakness within the departments as well as gaps that can develop between cross-departmental interaction.

Many associates working for an organization have developed years of experience and can be considered experts in their field. Employers use this employee expertise as part of their daily operational mission. From a fraud prevention perspective, why not use these same job-specific experts to identify areas of weakness in the organizational operating system?

Fraud groups can meet on a regular basis and brainstorm potential areas of weakness within the company's operating system. These sessions not only will open up information sharing but also will work to increase overall communication. Without effective communication, groups, associations, corporations, partnerships, and so on cannot be effective.

3.2.3 Think Like a Thief

Law enforcement detectives and investigators look at the overall crime in an effort to determine motivation and identify the perpetrator. Successful investigators use the evidence at the crime scene, witness interviews, and other investigative tools to identify the person or persons who committed the crime. A major factor of connecting the suspect to the crime is motivation. Investigators have to ask the question: "What motivated this individual to commit the crime?" Motives can range from revenge, a need for money, jealousy, or opportunity.

Investigators analyzing a fraud loss within an organization can also look at varying motivating factors. The rationale for a person to steal from his or her employer could be motivated by an increasing personal debt level or revenge for being passed over for a promotion. No matter the individual motivation to commit fraud against an organization, the main factor all fraud investigators need to consider is opportunity. Fraud investigators working in an organizational setting have to ask the question: "Where are the opportunities for fraud?"

The follow-up question would revolve around the topic of, "Where are the fraud-related opportunities within the organization?" To answer this question, the security/loss prevention professionals have to use their years of experience and case-related facts to think like a thief and identify the areas of opportunity.

Loss prevention/security professionals have to develop a proactive mindset when looking to lower the potential for fraud losses. The goal is not to wait until the crime takes place. The goal is to identify the areas of weakness and prevent the loss from taking place.

A successful method of fraud loss prevention in an organization is to think like a thief.

3.3 Individual Analysis

I was asked recently to provide information for an article titled, "Why is one house broken into over another?" Instead of researching past crimes of neighborhood burglaries, I placed myself into what I called the mindset of a criminal. The first question to be considered was: "If I wanted to break into one or more houses on my street, how would I know if the residents were not home?" The answers came down to knowing a resident's set pattern of activity.

The activity levels did not revolve around constant surveillance, but things noticed during my daily travels in and around the neighborhood. After about a week of analyzing the residential activity in the neighborhood, I was able to develop several points that a burglar would look for in selecting a potential victim. Basically thinking like a potential thief.

When analyzing a neighborhood in an effort to select potential homes to burglarize, who better knows the daily activities of the residents than a person living on their street? The same holds true for a person working in an organization. Who better knows the daily activities of the business operation than loss prevention/security professionals who interact with the various departments as part of their duties? When conducting a fraud analysis or as part of an overall fraud prevention program, loss prevention/security professionals need to look for fraud opportunities using the mindset of a thief, asking the question: "If I was going to commit fraud in this department, how would I go about it?"

The same thief posture analysis can also be a successful part of the fraud focus group discussions. Who better knows the weaknesses in an organizational department than those working there on a daily basis?

3.3.1 Talk to the Person Who Committed the Fraud

Organizations handle employee theft differently. One company might choose to collect all of the evidence to submit to local law enforcement, it is hoped for prosecution. Another might use the threat of turning the case over to law enforcement to persuade the suspect into paying restitution. The size of the fraud loss could also be a factor, with the organization satisfied with simple termination. No matter the path an organization chooses to pursue after identifying an internal suspect after a fraud loss, it is vital to gain as much intelligence from the person as possible. Investigators need to determine the motivating factor behind why the person committed the fraud. The main information the suspect can provide pertains to the opportunity. Was the opportunity for the fraud based on one of the following questions?

1. Did the daily company operating procedures and actual day-to-day business activities create an opportunity for fraud/theft?
2. Did the daily company operating procedures and actual day-to-day activities allow gaps where an employee could create the opportunity for fraud/theft?

Investigators working within the organization can gain quality fraud prevention-based information as a result of a person providing answers to these questions. All fraud awareness and prevention programs have to be developed around the thought process of eliminating opportunity.

Speaking with those individuals who have committed fraud against an organization can provide vital information on fraud-related opportunities. They can answer the question: "Do our operating policies leave open windows where fraud can take place, or do these same policies allow an individual to create an opportunity to commit fraud?"

In addition, the following questions can further assist the organization in closing the windows of fraud-related opportunity:

■ Did the employee notice a weakness in the operating procedures and see an avenue for fraud? If so, did this otherwise-honest employee (60%) simply take advantage of the opportunity?
■ If the employee was buried under an increasing mountain of debt, did the employee probe the operating procedures in an effort to create an opportunity to commit fraud?
■ Does the employee have knowledge of others committing the same type of fraud within the organization who were not caught? Many times, employees will notice fraudulent activity taking place (opportunity) and not see any negative ramifications as a result of the fraud. This leaves the thought process: "They got away with it."
■ Was their fraudulent activity the result of negative issues with the organization or management? Basically, does the employee feel underpaid or not appreciated for his or her performance, or did the employee receive some type

of negative feedback from management? With this thought process, some associates will look to get back at the organization and seek avenues to commit fraud.

No matter the rationale used by an employee to commit fraud, the information the employee can provide on weaknesses and opportunity within the organization can work to create a strict fraud prevention program.

3.3.2 Restitution versus Prevention

Organizations develop policies pertaining to addressing the potential for fraud and the resulting losses. Many organizations face fraud loss potential from an external threat, particularly in the financial services community. Financial institutions face a daily threat from those looking to commit bank fraud through check forgery, new account fraud,[2] and counterfeit checks. A successful new account fraud scheme can cost the financial institution thousands of dollars in lost revenue. The individual who commits the new account fraud typically assumes the identity of another (see Chapter 10 for a detailed discussion on assuming the identity of another), making the proper identification of the suspect difficult.

Many frauds committed against financial institutions are part of gang activity. These are not the typically perceived drug-based street gangs, but individuals in the country from eastern European and West African countries. These are sophisticated groups who utilize technology and identity theft to commit fraud.

This is not to say financial institutions are the only organizations susceptible to fraud losses. Any business operation can be a victim of external fraud and suffer a financial loss.

Based on the organization, each has a different primary focus on how to direct their loss prevention/security assets. A range of directions exists:

- Investigating the fraud loss to identify the offender and seek criminal prosecution
- Identifying the suspect to seek restitution and recover lost assets
- Understanding the fraud loss opportunity identified and capitalized on by the perpetrator

Once an organization suffers a financial loss because of either internal or external fraud, it is necessary to pursue prosecution. The goal of prosecuting the suspect is to ensure punishment based on the laws broken and to send a message to potential future offenders. If the suspects can be identified as the result of a fraud loss investigation, efforts also need to take place to try to recover the lost assets.

Ideally, the primary focus of any loss prevention/security operation is to identify the fraud opportunities present and build in prevention measures. Prosecution and asset recovery should be pursued after the loss, but the primary goal has to be to prevent the loss from taking place.

From a job performance perspective, the problem with having the primary focus of the Loss Prevention/Security Department directed toward fraud prevention is the measurability factor:

- If the loss did not take place, was this lack of loss based on the efforts of the loss prevention/security professionals?
- How can the success of preventing fraud losses be counted as part of job performance if no losses took place?

If the focus is based on the amount of lost revenue recovered, management has a measurable benchmark. Unfortunately, the recovery rate of revenues lost because of fraud is a small percentage of the overall loss amount.[3] Another attractive incentive to use restitution of fraud losses as the primary focus of the Loss Prevention/Security Department resides in revenue generation. Loss prevention/security departments are non-revenue-generating cost centers, prompting department managers to focus on bringing assets back into the organization. Basically, restitution amounts provide a measurable benchmark, but a loss never taking place does not. Is it better financially for an organization to have its loss prevention/security assets chase money that is already out the front door or to never let the money go out the door—restitution versus recovery?

Organizations that are susceptible to external fraud threats need to develop a prevention posture as it pertains to their internal loss prevention/security policies. The goal, as stated previously, is not to round up the herd after discovering a hole in the fence line. The goal should be based on ensuring the integrity of the herd by making sure the fence line is secure.

A good posture for any organization to develop pertaining to fraud prevention is to identify the opportunities. Once these fraud opportunities are identified regarding both internal and external threats, they need to be eliminated.

3.3.3 Employee Education

Based on the size and scope of an organization, each will face different threats related to fraud. In an effort to create a team environment and it is hoped lower fraud-related opportunities, it is important to establish an employee education program. The goal of the program should be to educate employees within the organization on the many aspects of fraud and the threats faced within their business operation.

Employees are the lifeline of any business, and efforts need to be made to create a total team concept. As with law enforcement, the only interaction of many individuals with the police is negative, typically being pulled over and cited for a traffic violation. Having only a negative experience with law enforcement, the benefits of the total services they provide are overlooked. Gone are the days of the walking beat cop who talked with the business owners and communicated with the citizens. The beat cop worked to build relationships between the community and the police department and was there at the first sign of trouble.

The same negative experience with law enforcement can be carried over to the organization. Typically, an employee's first and only interaction with members of the Loss Prevention/Security and Audit Departments is negative. This initial interaction could be based on a minor policy infraction, the termination of a coworker, or the need to seek information about knowledge of a recent fraud incident.

To provide a more pleasant interaction experience with internal investigators, it is time to go back to the police beat officer method. Beginning with new employee orientation, loss prevention/security/audit (internal investigators) representatives need to be present. The purpose of having internal investigators present at new hire orientation is to provide an overview on organizational fraud and its effects on the entire business operation, providing discussions on how fraud losses to an organization provide a negative effect on the bottom line. These negative effects could possibly become a factor for all employees of the organization.

Research has shown organizations that develop and deliver fraud awareness training programs to their entire workforce have lower losses related to internal and external theft. In addition, the length of the fraudulent activity is shorter. Employees imbued with knowledge of how to recognize fraud can identify potential areas of loss and report the information to internal investigators on a much faster timeline.[4]

The following should be contained within the employee fraud identification and awareness program:

■ A discussion should take place regarding the many aspects of fraud that are industry specific.
■ Once the types of fraud are identified, employees need to gain knowledge regarding how the threats can affect the entire organization.
■ Information should be provided on the proper manner to report suspicious activity.
■ Information should be conveyed on how the financial losses caused by successful fraud attacks affect the bottom line of the organization. The more money lost to fraud, the fewer assets are available for business growth, expansion, research and development, travel, employee development, and raises.
■ Also, employees within any organization need to be educated on the types of fraud targeted toward the individual, including information in employee fraud awareness programs on identity theft (Chapter 10), phishing (Chapter 11), and advance fee fraud (Chapter 9). Organizations that provide information to their associates on individual fraud show management is also interested in the associate's financial well-being and not just the business bottom line.

3.3.4 Developing Incentives to Stay

The reasons or rationale used by employees of an organization who were terminated for committing fraud vary. No matter the type of fraudulent activity committed, people have different excuses for their activity. The reasons can range from

- Revenge based on prior disciplinary issues
- Revenge based on a belief they were passed over for a promotion
- Revenge based on the belief they have no future growth opportunities
- Revenge based on a belief of not belonging

A major portion of any fraud prevention program has to revolve around employee education, employee awareness, and development of a team atmosphere. Organizations spend a lot of money hiring and training their associates. Efforts need to take place to show employees their value to the organization and that management is interested in their retention and growth, basically developing a team atmosphere.

Associates working for a more welcoming organization will be less likely to act in a revengeful mode versus an operation for which the employee does not believe he or she is part of a team.

In addition, during the new employee hiring process, it is necessary to identify highly motivated applicants. These motivated individuals have been known to integrate faster into the working aspect of day-to-day operations. Also, highly motivated applicants become motivated associates who have the best interests of the organization at heart.[5]

3.3.5 Avoiding Complacency

Individuals looking for opportunities to commit fraud operate on the theory of the path of least resistance, selecting target organizations that erect the fewest barriers in their fraud prevention policies or practices. Organizations that work to eliminate opportunities for fraud divert from the path of least resistance. A major factor concerning the path of least resistance is complacency, which generally means being happy with the current organizational environment and working to maintain the status quo. Prior to suffering a large fraud-related loss, an organization could have operated for years in a passive fraud detection and prevention capacity. As long as there is no major activity that disrupts daily operations, is it necessary to continuously overhaul the loss prevention/security posture?

When addressing complacency as it pertains to fraud prevention within an organization, it is important to look at the total picture of all aspects of the business operation:

- Are the efforts of the fraud detection and prevention program based on a reactive approach?
- Are efforts made to eliminate fraud opportunities based on lessons learned from a recent loss?
- Are the years of individual employee knowledge utilized to develop a detailed fraud prevention policy?

- Has the manager of the Accounts Payable Department (or any department) been asked about any weaknesses in the department's daily operation where fraud losses can occur?
- Has the same question been asked of an employee in any department within the organization? It is important to obtain fraud-related information from employees other than those at management levels.
- Has the loss prevention/security manager with years of experience within the organization conducted a threat assessment of daily operations? Ask if the manager can identify opportunities to commit fraud within the organization.
- Has the same question been asked of the associates working in the Loss Prevention/Security Department?
- Has the same question been asked of employees working in the various departments across the organization? Who can better identify fraud-related opportunities within sections of the organization than associates with direct working knowledge of the departments?
- Has every effort been made to glean as much information as possible on fraud-related losses from the person who committed the crime? These losses include those from both internal and external fraud incidents. Organizations might want to consider forgoing a case referral to law enforcement based on fraud intelligence obtained.
- Are the loss prevention/security policies based on the recovery of fraud losses as a measurement baseline versus having a prevention-first policy?
- Do management and internal investigators include employees on fraud discussion and working with the organization to prevent losses?
- Are the employee growth policies of the organization based on creating a team environment?

3.4 Segregation of Duties

The goal of any fraud prevention policy has to be based on the elimination of opportunities in an effort to avoid employee-related theft. Many organizations create areas of opportunity for fraudulent activity based on assigned job functions. As discussed in Chapter 2, it is necessary to establish a two-person rule and a policy of separation of duties. Key areas within an organization for which it is imperative to ensure separation of duties are

- Inventory control
- Verification of product delivery
- Verification of products loaded for delivery
- Account reconciliation
- Authorization of accounts payable
- Authorization of accounts receivable

3.4.1 Inventory Control

It is vital that an organization conduct a routine inventory of merchandise available for sale and items in stock. Organizations that operate in a production capacity need to have an understanding of their raw material. Once the various items are manufactured, there has to be an accurate count of product available for delivery. No matter the nature of the business operation, it is imperative to have a process in place to determine the available inventory. To ensure accuracy of the inventory process, at least two people must be involved in the process. A business should never allow the individual conducting the physical count of items to be the same person recording the number of items available on the inventory control sheet.

A business operation has to have procedures in place to manage its inventory, along with the number of times a year to conduct the process. To ensure the integrity of the inventory control process, employees should be made aware of the potential for random counts. To add credibility to the potential for random audits, it is necessary to conduct random audits.

> **CASE STUDY 3.1**
>
> While working as a US Army criminal investigator, there were certain job functions that required issuing undercover purchase funds. Working on the Drug Suppression Team was one of those specific job functions.
>
> Undercover agents had to sign for and were issued cash that was to be used to make drug purchases. If any undercover funds were spent, the agents were required to record the amount on a specific form. Once this form was submitted, management had an understanding of the amount of undercover funds each agent had on hand.
>
> To ensure the integrity of the available funds on hand, being called in for a random count of undercover funds was always a possibility. Never knowing when a random count was going to occur eliminated the temptation of borrowing from the available undercover funds.

3.4.2 Verification of Product Delivery

For large business operations, most items purchased are delivered at a loading dock. A smaller business operation could accept deliveries through the back door. No matter the location where product is received, strict controls have to be in place to ensure the integrity of these items.

At no time should a business allow the same individual who conducts the physical count of the items delivered to be the same person who records the number received on the invoice. In addition, no business operation should allow delivery drivers to individually conduct the delivery count process. The driver should be allowed to conduct his or her own count of the number and types of items delivered.

To add further credibility to the delivery count process, it is necessary to include the driver in the process. Prior to the business accepting the delivery, it is vital to ensure the driver's count agrees with the number of items received by the business.

3.4.3 Verification of Products Loaded for Delivery

A business needs to maintain tight controls of items delivered to the business. The same holds true for all products loaded onto a vehicle for shipping purposes. Whether these items are loaded onto pallets or packed in boxes, at least two employees need to be involved in the counting process. At no time should the same employee be given the task of counting items loaded to be shipped and verifying the quantities on the shipping documents.

> **CASE STUDY 3.2**
> **Floors and Tile**
>
> Floors and Tile[6] is a large national wholesale operation that sells various types of tile. The sizes, shapes, and types of tile available for sale vary, as does customer demand for the product. One customer might choose to enter a location and purchase a few boxes of tile. Other customers will enter a location and purchase sixty boxes of tile and the related products needed for installation. Typically, customers making large-quantity purchases will pay for the material and schedule a pickup time and date.
>
> On the scheduled pickup date, the Floors and Tile procedures are as follows:
>
> ■ Customer service is notified by the individual making the material pickup with the name of the client who placed and paid for the order.
> ■ To ensure the individual making the scheduled material pickup is authorized to take delivery of the tile, proper identification is required.
> ■ After proper identification is made, the warehouse is provided with the order sheet, and the items are placed on a pallet or pallets.
> ■ Once all of the purchased tile-related items are packaged for delivery, they are transported to the loading dock.
> ■ Prior to loading the prepurchased material, a supervisor is required to compare the items loaded against the quantities listed on the order sheet.
> ■ An additional item and quantity verification is made against the in-store computer order form.
> ■ If all three checks agree (computer order form, paper order sheet provided by customer service, and the actual material loaded onto pallets), the material is loaded and signed for.

The detailed product verification process for Floors and Tile works to ensure the customer only receives the amount of product purchased. The verification process also works to ensure employees working in the warehouse do not load extra product for certain customers as part of a sweetheart fraud process.

3.4.4 Account Reconciliation

Based on the size and scope of a business operation, there can be a single bank account to handle the daily transactions of the business. Larger organizations can have several accounts that receive money for deposit and money disbursed to cover expenses. No matter the number of bank accounts used by a business operation, it is necessary these accounts be reconciled for the operation to have an understanding of available funds.

When an individual or audit department looks to reconcile a business bank account, the process involves three steps:

- An understanding of the available balance as noted on the bank statement
- An understanding of items and amounts deposited into the specific bank account that have yet to clear or have shown up on the statement
- An understanding of checks/automatic debits and amounts that have not shown up on the bank statement

Once all of the amounts related to these three areas are known, the business can have an understanding of the available funds in a specific account.[7]

To prevent fraudulent attacks to continue for an extended period of time, it is vital each business bank account be reconciled as soon as the monthly statements are received. If a business chooses to reconcile its monthly bank accounts on a quarterly basis, this leaves a sixty-day window when fraudulent activity can continue. If fraudulent activity is taking place on a business bank account, the sooner the activity is identified the quicker the process can be shut down.

To ensure the integrity of the activity taking place on a business bank account, the following procedures need to be implemented (including internal practices to prevent employee bank account fraud):

- Establish a policy to reconcile all business bank accounts immediately on receipt of the bank statement.
- Establish a separation-of-duties policy; mainly, any individual who has a responsibility for writing business checks should not be involved in the statement reconciliation process.
- Establish a separation-of-duties policy for employees involved in business account depository procedures not being involved in the reconciliation process.
- To stop potential fraudulent activity on a business account, the company should keep a detailed ledger of all checks written and their amounts. With the ability to access bank account statements online, the business should delegate a trusted employee to ensure checks showing up as debited against the account are for actual approved items as written and listed on the ledger. The business also has to establish a policy of not allowing the person who conducts online verification of checks debited against the business account be any individual involved in creating the check ledger.

Businesses can also adopt a policy of conducting account reconciliation on an almost-daily basis. With the availability of online banking and the ability to access daily account activity, fraudulent attempts can be identified in a shorter time frame.

3.4.5 Authorization of Accounts Payable

No single employee should have the business responsibility of maintaining the entire accounts payable responsibilities. Accounts payable activity gives those associates working in this department the authority to write and disburse checks. Checks disbursed through the Accounts Payable Department are written to suppliers or vendors. With little or no oversight of an individual or individuals, money can flow out of the business and into the bank accounts of dishonest associate(s).

Without a system of checks and balances operating in the Accounts Payable Department, a dishonest employee can simply write checks to cover fictitious invoices. Checks written to cover these bogus invoices can be mailed to a post office box or mail drop[8] location and retrieved by the dishonest employee or an accomplice.

Company checks written to pay suppliers and vendors need to be crossmatched against the actual invoices provided for services rendered. At no time should the employee in charge of issuing checks to cover invoices be the same person who created the list of payable invoices.

With proper checks and balances for the accounts payable system,

- A list of payable invoices should be created and listed in detail on a ledger-type system.
- The Accounts Payable Department should create a listing or ledger of checks written to provide payment for invoices listed on the payable invoices ledger.
- A disinterested third party should crossmatch the information on the payable invoices ledger with the checks written on the check ledger.
- At no time should the same employee be involved in creating both the payable invoices ledger and the check ledger.

3.4.6 Authorization of Accounts Receivable

Businesses across the country operate in a manner that is consistent for their success. Some operate on a cash or credit card–based sales system; others provide a product to their customers on a credit basis. Based on the terms of the credit provided to the customer, payments are made to the business to pay off the debt created from the sale. The Accounts Receivable Department or section is responsible for processing the payments made to the business.

To ensure all assets due to the business wind up on the company books, it is vital to establish a strong antifraud accounts receivable policy. The purpose of the antifraud policy is to ensure a separation of duties for associates working in the accounts receivable area and to eliminate temptation.

A popular fraud scheme used by associates working in accounts receivable departments across the country is referred to as *lapping*. Lapping occurs when money is skimmed from a payment made to a business. To show the initial payment as processed in full, a portion of a subsequent payment made to the business is used to cover the amount originally stolen.

- Customer A makes a $1,000 payment to a business.
- Employee B takes or steals $250 of customer A's payment.
- To show customer A as having a payment account in good standing, $250 is needed by employee B.
- Customer C makes a payment to the same business totaling $1,250.
- Employee B takes $250 from the payment of customer C and uses this money to show customer A as having made a required $1,000 payment.
- Now, customer C's payment is short $250.
- Employee B has to take $250 from the payment of customer D. Eventually, money must be taken from customer E to cover the shortage of the payment made by customer D.
- To keep the fraud afloat and show all subsequent customer payments as paid in full, employee B has to continuously keep a separate set of books. If employee B does not make the necessary account adjustments on a daily basis to show all subsequent accounts as paid in full, the fraud will fall apart and be discovered.[9]

Employees stealing from the Accounts Receivable Department of any business can also engage in the alteration of internal accounting statements, use credit memos to cover missing assets, or create fraudulent write-offs. No matter the technique used by an associate to commit accounts receivable fraud, there are several prevention measures a business can employ:

- Never allow one employee to have sole responsibility for all accounts receivable activity.
- Establish mandatory vacation policies.
- Have employees trained to perform job functions in many areas of the Accounts Receivable Department and initiate a job rotation policy.
- Ensure all checks received are immediately stamped "For Deposit Only."
- Have customer payments sent directly to a lock box.[10]

3.5 Removing the Temptation for Fraud

No matter the internal fraud prevention control procedures implemented by a business, it is also necessary to identify areas of opportunity. As discussed in Chapter 2, there is a certain percentage of the population that could fall to temptation. Areas of fraud-related opportunity present in a business operation also provide a level of temptation.

Temptation is based on areas of opportunity that might lead an honest employee to think about committing fraud or theft. The goal of any business operation is to eliminate the areas of temptation for all employees, including those intent on committing fraud or theft.

3.5.1 Cameras on the Loading Dock

To ensure the integrity of the company loading dock, a twenty-four-hour video surveillance system should be installed. Signage should be posted in any company location where video surveillance is operating. Also, video monitors need to be placed where they can be easily accessed and observed by management.

3.5.2 Installing Motion-Sensitive Lighting

To conserve assets allocated for business-related utilities, many business operations turn off the lights in areas that are not occupied. From a cost-saving perspective, this is a good business procedure. Unfortunately, employees develop an understanding of the locations within the business where this practice takes place. To eliminate the temptation for fraud/theft, motion sensors should be installed in these areas that automatically turn on the lights to illuminate the entire area. These same light-controlled areas should also be equipped with motion sensor video monitoring.

3.5.3 Trash Control Procedures

It is hoped the only items going into the dumpster are actual trash. Without strict trash control procedures, businesses can have items placed in the dumpster and later retrieved by off-duty associates. To control what is actually placed into the trash or dumpsters, the following prevention procedures need to be established:

■ Establish a flat-box policy inside the business operating area. Having empty boxes around the loading dock area, warehouse, and so on provides an inviting temptation for fraud. Items can be placed into empty boxes prior to an employee taking the boxes to the dumpster. To avoid retrievable items from being placed in the outside dumpster and decrease the temptation, all empty boxes need to be flattened. The requirement to flatten and stack empty boxes prior to disposal can eliminate the overall shrink numbers.

■ Employees placing business-related items into the trash or dumpster will later have to return to retrieve their stolen goods. If possible, the area where trash is dumped during the course of daily business operations needs to be in a secure location. This location should be located within the secure area of the business and not be accessible by outside individuals. If off-duty employees and outside individuals cannot gain access to the trash area of the business, the temptation of placing items in the dumpster is eliminated.

- If possible, all business-specific dumpsters should be designed so the lids can be secured with a padlock. These dumpsters need to remain locked during nonbusiness hours and only unlocked when being loaded with trash or emptied by the trash management company.[11]
- To ensure the integrity of the trash taken out of the business operating area and placed in a community dumpster, a two-person rule should be established. When large amounts of trash that accumulates throughout the business day is taken for disposal, policy should dictate two employees are involved in the transfer and dumping process. For safety purposes, the business owner has to ensure the areas where the community dumpsters are located are well illuminated. Community dumpsters are those located in the back of a strip mall-type location, and many business operations use them for trash disposal. Employees should not feel like a trip to the dumpster is from a scene in a horror movie. These areas need to be brightly illuminated for security and safety purposes.
- If staffing does not permit establishing a two-person rule for garbage disposal, the job of taking refuse to the dumpster should be rotated.
- To remove the temptation of placing company items inside trash cans, clear trash bags should be used.

3.6 Merchant Fraud

A large majority of retail organizations provide the customer the opportunity to use a credit/debit card to complete the transaction. To complete a retail transaction, the customer has to swipe his or her credit/debit card through what is referred to as a swiping machine (Figure 3.1). With credit/debit cards processed through these machines, the customer has the choice of how the transaction is treated. The sale can be processed as a credit card sale or as a debit card sale that requires the input of a personal identification number (PIN).

To obtain a swiping machine, the business owner or representative has to establish a merchant account through their financial institution. Once the merchant account is opened and the swiping machine issued, all credit/debit card transaction amounts are deposited into the business account. Based on the financial institution setting up the merchant account, the sale amounts are deposited into the business bank account within one to three days.

In an effort to commit fraud and obtain customer credit/debit card account numbers, individuals will target small business operations.

CASE STUDY 3.3

Almost every business, large or small, that offers a product for retail sale has one or more machines used to swipe and process credit cards. These machines are good tools for the merchant, allowing the merchant to sell a product with the almost-instant satisfaction of knowing the money presented by the customer is available and will be credited to the business.

Figure 3.1 Swiping machine for credit/debit cards.

A popular scam used by individuals looking to commit fraud is to target smaller business operations.

■ The smaller business is an ideal target because it most likely keeps its merchant account statements in house or in a location where they can be easily obtained. Many larger business operations will likely have their credit transaction documents held by an outside firm, which might question why the business needs to obtain a few months of transaction information. Once explained to the accountant or holding firm why the documents are needed, the intended fraud might be discovered and prevented. The individuals attempting to target the smaller merchants for fraudulent purposes want the fewest number of individuals in the financial document search process.

The scam or fraud is simple in nature: One person or several people will walk into various stores in a strip mall-type setting and claim to be from XYZ Merchant Services or some other made-up company name. These individuals will present business cards and convince the store owner or manager they can save them money on the percentage charged to process their credit card transactions. The first question asked of the business owner is regarding the percentage charged for each credit card transaction. Most business operators do not have this information immediately at hand, and this is the point that a representative from XYZ Merchant Services asks for the past few months of their credit card-processing statements and related bank information so they can be reviewed and a lower per transaction percentage rate can be offered. They will tell the store owner they need to look at a few months of financial statement data so they can get a handle on the number of transactions per month, average dollar amount, and dollars processed. This is conveyed to convince the business owner the representative is looking out for the owner's best interest and will help save money processing credit card transactions.

One target area of this type of merchant fraud is to have the small business owner turn over all credit card–related financial information, mainly the bank account information where the daily credit/debit card transactions are deposited. This information in the hands of an individual hoping to commit fraud against the small business can be used to drain the available funds from the depository account.

This type of fraud starts out with the business as the target, but the main focus is to obtain the individual credit card account information of the customers who purchased an item or items through the retail store. These past customers can have their credit card accounts hacked by the fraudsters, leaving a weak path regarding how the information was obtained from fraudulent purposes.

The simple prevention procedure is not to provide account documents to any organization that was not solicited by the business. It is also important for any business seeking to set up a credit card–processing account to do their due diligence and research the business prior to establishing an account or providing any business or personal information.

3.7 Know Your Vendors/Suppliers

As discussed in Chapter 2, organizations need to develop strong and detailed new hire screening procedures. Each and every business operation has to be able to ensure all associates have been thoroughly screened during the new hire process, ensuring only quality associates become part of the operational family.

The same desire should hold true for individuals providing services to the organization. Prior to selecting a company to provide services to a business, the individual or individuals making the decision need to ensure the same hiring and screening processes are maintained. To ensure the integrity of vendors and suppliers conducting business in any organization, the following questions need to be asked by the decision makers:

- How detailed is your new hire screening process?
- Does your organization conduct random drug testing?
- Do your employees receive any type of training on code of conduct/conflict of interest?

If an organization is going to take the time to establish a fraud awareness and prevention policy to stay off of the path of least resistance, it should only conduct business with like-minded companies.

Notes

1. For the purpose of the opportunity discussion, the focus is directed toward the 20% (inherently dishonest) of the population based on the 20-60-20 theory. If a business places its focus on eliminating the opportunity for fraud based on the motivations of the inherently dishonest, it will also take away any prospects of temptation for the middle 60%.
2. New account fraud is discussed in detail in Chapter 10 on identity theft.
3. The low recovery percentage rate discussed is based on personal observations made as a loss prevention professional across many industries. Conversations with other industry professionals and information gleaned from annual fraud loss reports cannot produce a solid loss recovery percentage number. All are in agreement the percentage of fraud losses recovered are minimal.
4. Association of Certified Fraud Examiners, Report to the nations on occupational fraud and abuse, http://www.acfe.com/uploadedFiles/ACFE_Website/Content/rttn/2012-report-to-nations.pdf (accessed July 21, 2014).
5. Prevention a Sound Investment, Theft and fraud in the workplace, http://www.prevention-commerce.com/pcevf.asp (accessed July 14, 2014).
6. Floors and Tile is a fictitious entity, but the analysis provided is indicative of proper inventory control operations for large wholesale organizations.
7. Epstein, L., Reconciling bank accounts for your business, http://www.dummies.com/how-to/content/reconciling-bank-accounts-for-your-business.html (accessed August 16, 2104).
8. *Mail drop* is a term used to describe business operations that offer services to their customers to send and receive mail. These are legitimate business operations and provide a convenience factor to their customers.
9. Accounting Tools, What is lapping fraud? http://www.accountingtools.com/questions-and-answers/what-is-lapping-fraud.html (accessed August 21, 2014).
10. *Lock box* is a service provided by a bank for the receipt of customer payments. Instead of the customer mailing a payment directly to the business, it is sent to a special post office box for processing. Once the payments have been processed, the money is deposited into the business bank account.
11. Preventing internal theft in businesses, http://www.sandiego.gov/police/services/prevention/tips/internaltheft.shtml#trash (accessed August 14, 2014).

Chapter 4

Small Business Fraud

4.1 Introduction

Based on the individual or organization asked, many definitions will be provided on what constitutes a small business. A small business can be operated as a corporation, partnership, or sole proprietorship. The specialty of a small business can vary from an agricultural operation, fast food restaurant, retail store, a partnership operating several franchise locations, and so on. The number of employees working in a small business will also vary from a single person to a few hundred. Based on the business operation, production needs, daily sales, and other items will dictate the number of employees required to conduct operations.

The annual revenue of a small business is also based on the specialty of its day-to-day operation. A small business operating a single fast food restaurant can bring in $200,000 to $300,000 a year; a 100-employee computer-programming company can have annual revenues in the millions of dollars.

What makes a small business more susceptible to fraud than a large, 1,000-employee corporation is the amount of annual revenue the business can allocate to loss prevention. Many large corporations have security and loss prevention departments that operate with the sole purpose of protecting company assets. A small business is more likely to divert a majority of company assets to daily operations, growth, and sales. The large corporation is most likely to have one employee designated as the director of loss prevention/risk management. A small business can have one employee whose responsibility covers numerous day-to-day operational activities.

As discussed in Chapter 2, there are many areas in which any business/organization can become a victim to employee fraud. The individual vulnerabilities are based on internal operating procedures and hiring practices.

As discussed in Chapter 3, there are many areas within a small business where the business can become a victim of fraud from sources located outside the business operation.

Because of the operational activities of many small businesses, the focus of this chapter is a discussion of both the internal and external threats to small business operations. Because many small businesses operate on tight budgets and with limited personnel devoted to fraud/loss prevention, a broad discussion of vulnerabilities of the businesses has to take place.

4.2 Small Business Identity Theft

During local newscasts, it is almost impossible not to hear of a person who lost an entire life savings as a victim of identity theft. In addition to the many stories pertaining to the constant flow of identity theft victims, the television, radio, and Internet have advertisements pertaining to identity theft prevention tools.

Although a popular type of fraud against the individual, a small business can also become a victim of identity theft. With identity theft, the goal is to assume the identity of another. The same end game is desired for small business identity theft: a person or persons working together to use the good name of a legitimate business operation. The goals of those looking to commit small business identity theft vary, but if successful, a legitimate company will suffer some type of financial loss.

To take over the good name of a legitimate business, there are several steps that can be taken.

4.2.1 Employer Identification Number

Like a Social Security number (SSN), a business has an Employer Identification Number (EIN), sometimes called a Federal Tax Identification Number (TIN). Like an SSN (XXX-XX-XXXX), the EIN contains nine digits (XX-XXXXXXX). Prior to 2001, the first two digits of the EIN were based on the geographic region of the business location. Ten different regions across the country had specific two-digit numbers they would assign to new applicants (see Table 4.1). After 2001, the assignment of EINs was centralized, and a two-digit number could be assigned to a business for any of the ten regions. The remaining seven digits of the EIN make up a specific number assigned to the individual business.[1]

An individual can protect their SSN and only provide the number to others if they choose to do so. Unfortunately the protection of a business EIN is not as simple. There are several Internet-based companies that can legally provide the EIN of a business. For anyone looking to begin the process of small business identity theft, locating the EIN of a target company is an easy first step.

Table 4.1 Employer Identification Numbers (EINs) According to Regional Assignments

Campus/Other Location	Valid EIN Prefixes
Andover, Massachusetts	10, 12
Atlanta, Georgia	60, 67
Austin, Texas	50, 53
Brookhaven, New York	01, 02, 03, 04, 05, 06, 11, 13, 14, 16, 21, 22, 23, 25, 34, 51, 52, 54, 55, 56, 57, 58, 59, 65
Cincinnati, Ohio	30, 32, 35, 36, 37, 38, 61
Fresno, California	15, 24
Kansas City, Kansas	40, 44
Memphis, Tennessee	94, 95
Ogden, Utah	80, 90
Philadelphia, Pennsylvania	33, 39, 41, 42, 43, 46, 48, 62, 63, 64, 66, 68, 71, 72, 73, 74, 75, 76, 77, 81, 82, 83, 84, 85, 86, 87, 88, 91, 92, 93, 98, 99
Internet	20, 26, 27,45, 46 (47 is reserved for future use) **Note:** Prefixes 26, 27, 45, 46, and 47 were previously assigned by the Philadelphia campus.
Small Business Administration (SBA)	31

Source: "How EINs are assigned and valid EIN prefixes." http://www.irs.gov/Businesses/Small-Businesses-&-Self-Employed/How-EINs-are-Assigned-and-Valid-EIN-Prefixes (accessed June 9, 2014).

4.2.2 Company Letterhead

Almost all business operations have their official company letterhead stationery. Most company letterhead contains the business name, contact information, and some type of individual company logo.

Once a small business is targeted for identity theft, it is necessary to develop a company letterhead in the name of the entity. It is fairly easy to obtain correspondence from a small business or any business to obtain the company's letterhead information. In addition, company information can be obtained from the data on its business website. This company website information can be used to create fraudulent company letterhead.

As discussed concerning company/website hijacking in Chapter 11 on cybercrime/fraud, company logos can be copied from the legitimate website and placed on the bogus letterhead.

4.2.3 Business Owner Information

Based on the nature of the business, it is fairly easy for individuals looking to commit small business fraud to obtain the name or names of business owners:

- If the business deals with contracting, a simple check of the state's websites will provide the name of the individual who is the registered license holder. The basic information required to locate the principals of the business is the state-issued license number.
- Any business registered as some type of corporate entity has to list the principal officers with the corporation commission of the state. A visit to the state's corporation website will provide this information.
- There are several websites available that will provide the names of company owners. All the individual seeking the business-related information needs is the state that issued the business license.
- With the various tools and websites available, a determined individual can locate most business-related information. Unlike the privacy associated with a person's SSN, business information is more accessible.

After obtaining the necessary business-related information (TIN, company letterhead, owner information), it becomes possible to commit small business identity theft. To add further credibility to the small business information already obtained, fraudsters can also establish business legitimacy.

4.2.4 Establishing Business Legitimacy

Based on the desire of those committing small business identity theft, additional steps can be taken to add legitimacy to their operation:

- Leasing commercial space in the name of the legitimate business. Outside of restaurant or retail operations, many small businesses operate from a commercial business location. During the takeover process of a targeted small business, those perpetrating the fraud will obtain the company information required to lease commercial office space.
- To process credit card transactions, a business has to open a merchant account for the purpose of processing credit/debit card transactions. In an effort to add legitimacy to a fraudulent business operation, a merchant account will most

likely be opened in the name of the unsuspecting legitimate business operation. (See Chapter 3 and the section in this chapter on establishing fraudulent merchant accounts for additional information on merchant accounts.)

■ For many businesses to operate, various types of paperwork have to be filed with the secretary of state's office. This can include address information, business trade names, company officers, and so on. States will also issue some type of business tax identification number for the purpose of paying state and local sales taxes.

For the purpose of committing small business identity theft, bogus paperwork (on the fraudulent company letterhead) can be filed with the secretary of state's office to change the company address and officer information.[2]

Once all of the information is collected on a small business operation and business legitimacy is established, various types of fraudulent activity can take place. These are discussed next.

4.2.5 Opening Lines of Credit

It is common practice for those committing the fraud of small business identity theft to open lines of credit in the name of the target company. Once these criminal elements have obtained the necessary company information, line-of-credit accounts can be opened with various retailers. Based on the company where the line of credit is established, items will be purchased that can be quickly sold or exchanged for cash. These bogus purchases are conducted quickly after the line of credit has been established. The goal is to max out the credit amount before the legitimate company realizes an unauthorized credit line was opened in its good name.

Individuals looking to commit small business fraud, as it pertains to bogus lines of credit, are typically not satisfied with the opening of a single fraudulent account. After obtaining the necessary small business information, their goal is to open as many lines of credit as possible. Having access to multiple fraudulent lines of credit allows for the purchase of a large number of items in the name of the legitimate and unsuspecting small business.

4.2.5.1 Obtaining a Fraudulent Small Business Loan

In addition to applying for and opening lines of credit, another popular method is to obtain a small business loan. After the identity thieves have obtained the company information necessary for the loan documents, these forms are completed and submitted for approval. The individuals committing small business loan fraud hope they have selected an operation with a a solid financial reputation and unblemished credit records.

After the required small business loan documents are submitted, the loan officer looks over the paperwork and loan request. The loan officers review the documentation and business owner information as if they are approving a legitimate loan request. If the individuals looking to commit small business loan fraud have collected the correct personal and business information, the loan request typically is approved.

Once approved, the requested loan amount is delivered to the individuals representing themselves as the legitimate small business owners. With this type of scam, the people committing the fraud have access to money loaned in the name of the legitimate small business operation. Unfortunately, the actual small business owners become aware of the fraud once the collection notices arrive at their door.[3]

4.2.5.2 Establishing Fraudulent Merchant Accounts

To protect against the fraud of identity theft, a person has to keep tight control over who has access to their SSN. As discussed with business operations, it is fairly easy to locate a TIN. It is also a simple process to obtain or create the company letterhead of a targeted business. With this information, coupled with fraudulent documentation of the legitimate business owners, it is an easy process to open a merchant account.

Merchant accounts are used to process credit/debit card transactions for purchases made by customers. Credit cards are swiped through a credit card swiping machine (see Chapter 3 for an image of a swiping machine). If the physical credit/debit card is not present, the business owner or any associate can manually enter the number into the swiping machine. Either way, a monetary amount can be processed against the credit/debit card.

In an effort to use a legitimate business as part of fraudulent activity, merchant accounts are opened in the name of the unsuspecting business. Once the merchant account is established, unauthorized transactions are processed. The credit/debit cards processed through these unauthorized merchant accounts are either stolen or counterfeited.[4] The credit/debit cards can belong to an individual consumer or a legitimate business.

No matter the type of credit/debit card or the actual account holder, money from each transaction processed is deposited into the bank account of the individuals committing the merchant account fraud.[5] Once the individuals committing the merchant account fraud are satisfied with the amount of money obtained, it is withdrawn from the bank, and they move on to the next target.[6]

From a liability factor, the business that had its good name used as part of the merchant account fraud is not responsible for the financial losses to the various credit/debit card account holders. They could, however, have their business reputation tarnished with numerous complaints from consumers and other business operations that had unauthorized charges made against their credit/debit cards.

As discussed in Chapter 10 on identity theft, it is necessary to obtain the services of an identity theft protection company. Once the services of an identity theft protection company are obtained, the business owner will be notified if attempts are made to open unauthorized bank or merchant accounts.

4.2.5.3 Opening Unauthorized Credit Card Accounts

Another popular method of small business fraud is using the company information collected to establish business legitimacy and open credit card accounts in the name of the unsuspecting business. The information used to open these credit card accounts is the good name of the business and its owner(s).

In an effort to gain the greatest bang for their buck, the individuals committing this type of fraud will open as many credit cards as possible and max out the cards as quickly as possible.

4.3 Small Business Account Takeover

Most small business operations have company credit cards and lines of credit that were opened by the owners or their authorized representatives. When a person or group of individuals begins looking into a small business for the purpose of committing fraud, they can come across vital company information. Information discovered during the search process can contain company financial information, such as credit card account numbers and line of credit data. Once this information is in the hands of unauthorized individuals, the organization will become a victim of small business account takeover.

The intent of those involved in a small business account takeover is to use the credit reputation of the organization to make unauthorized purchases. These purchases are made using counterfeit credit/debit cards in the name of the business and accessing legitimate lines of credit.

In an effort to conceal the unauthorized account activity, individuals committing this type of fraud will learn the purchasing habits of the small business. By purchasing business-related items, the illegal activity might be overlooked during the account reconciliation process.

Individuals committing small business account takeover will also uncover the personal account information of the actual owners. This information is uncovered during the data search process and will be used in the same manner to conduct unauthorized purchases. In an effort to prevent small business and individual account takeover fraud, it is vital the owners follow the prevention measures outlined here and in Chapter 10.

4.4 Small Business Fraud Prevention Measures

To protect a small business from identity theft and account takeover, the following prevention measures need to be understood and implemented:

■ Protect all company documents. This includes bank account statements, credit card statements, loan documents, and so on. People will look through company trash and recycling bins in an effort to locate sensitive information. Prior to discarding any sensitive information relating to a business or individual owner, it has to be shredded. This includes all company invoicing documents, purchase information, and so on.

Individuals looking to commit small business account takeover will attempt to locate purchasing information that is specific to the target business. A person committing account takeover fraud will attempt to gain knowledge of ordinary items purchased by the business as part of normal daily activity. Once ordinary buying activity is learned, like items will be purchased using company credit card information. As previously discussed, a wise business will have some type of suspicious transaction prevention tool active on its accounts.

■ Protecting business information is not limited to financial and purchasing documents already in the hands of the business owner. It is necessary to make sure all sensitive information intended to be delivered to the business actually arrives. Many small businesses operating in a strip mall-type setting will have their mail delivered to a community cluster mailbox (Figure 4.1). The postal service worker opens the back of the box and inserts the mail into the designated slots. The business owner will retrieve the mail from this cluster mailbox.

Many people committing individual and small business fraud will gain unauthorized access to the back of the cluster mailboxes and steal sensitive mailed items. To prevent the potential theft of mail from these cluster boxes, the use of an official US Post Office box provides a more secure environment. (Cluster mailbox theft is discussed in detail in Chapter 10.)

■ Make sure all employees understand phishing (see Chapter 11 for additional discussion of phishing and other computer-related e-mail frauds) vulnerabilities. In many business operations, employees are constantly accessing company computers as part of normal business activities. Employees send and receive e-mails throughout each business day. An employee acting in what the employee believes to be the best interest of the business could become an unwitting accomplice to fraud.

Individuals looking to target a small business for fraudulent purposes will use many phishing techniques. These techniques involve contacting employees via the telephone and through e-mail and social media websites. The intent of the criminals is to convince an employee to open a link sent through an e-mail or to provide sensitive company information over the telephone or through a social media website. By opening a link sent through an e-mail on

Figure 4.1   A community cluster mailbox in a strip mall-type location.

a company computer, the employee could be allowing malicious software to be installed on the company's computer. Employees can also download and install malicious software sent through a social media website. The employee is convinced the software is beneficial for continued business operations. No matter how the software was installed on the company computer, the intent is to gain access to private business information, ideally obtaining business credit card and financial account information.[7]

Employees need to develop an understanding of the various phishing techniques, which are further detailed in Chapter 11.

■ Sending company account information through e-mails or other web-based services can make the business more susceptible to small business fraud. For many business owners and employees, using the Internet is a convenient method of conducting daily business activities. Company policy should forbid the sending of personal information, financial account information, and account numbers via e-mail or other web-based services. Policy needs to dictate this sensitive information can only be sent over a secure website. A secure website is one that has *https* in the website's Uniform Resource Locator (URL).[8] (See Chapter 12 for further discussion of secure websites.)

■ It is important for any business owner to treat sensitive company information as they would their personal financial data. To prevent individual identity theft, it has always been advised that an individual check his or her credit report at least once a year. The same holds true for the credit accuracy of any small business. It is important to monitor the credit profile of a small business through any of the credit reporting and monitoring agencies.

- In addition to monitoring the credit standing of a small business, the owners need to reconcile bank statements on a monthly basis. Keep a detailed ledger of all checks written in the daily course of business operations and make sure these are the only checks appearing in the month-ending bank account statement. (See Chapter 3 for further discussion of bank account reconciliation.)

- A small business owner has to treat the sensitive information associated with the company as he does with his own personal data. As discussed in Chapter 10 on Identity Theft, it is vital that all small business owners hire the services of a credit monitoring organization. These monitoring organizations will alert the business owners of any attempts to open unauthorized financial related accounts.

- Credit card abuse is a major area of fraud for small businesses. Gaining access to the credit card accounts of a small business is a goal for those committing account takeover fraud. It is vital for all small business owners to check the account activity of all credit and debit card accounts associated with the small business. Financial institutions allow account holders to set up a user name and password to access their credit/debit card accounts online. To detect early attempts at account takeover fraud against the small business, account reconciliation is a major prevention measure.

- Financial institutions provide a service to their account holders to monitor transaction activity. Based on transaction historical activity, account holders are notified by their financial institution of suspicious debit or charge attempts. To protect a small business against account takeover fraud, the owners need to allow their financial institution to provide fraud alerts.

- Conducting detailed background verifications on all applicants is vital to steer a small business off the path of least resistance (refer to Chapter 2).

- To protect sensitive information, many government agencies operate on a "need-to-know" policy. The same holds true for the success of a small business. Sensitive company and financial documents need to remain locked in secure devices. Access to sensitive files should only be granted to those employees with a business need.

- Every small business operation needs to make sure all computers contain antivirus, spyware, and malware software. Company computers also need to be backed up on a daily basis to ensure continuous business activity in case of a cyberattack.[9]

- All small business financial activity should be conducted on a dedicated computer. To ensure protection of company financial account information, employees should not be allowed to access social media websites from the dedicated computer. In addition, the dedicated computer should not be used for sending e-mail or any type of web-surfing activity.[10]

- To further protect small business computer systems, it is necessary to establish a password policy for all employees. Passwords need to be changed at least every ninety days and be somewhat complex. A solid password should be at least eight characters in length and have at least one uppercase letter, one lowercase letter, a number, and a symbol. Passwords should not be a name or a password that was previously used or contain repetitive letters or numbers. (See Chapter 12 for additional discussion of secure passwords.)

- No matter the protection measures put in place by the company owners to prevent small business fraud, it is only as secure as the employees allow. Employees can become the first line of defense in identifying and preventing fraud. Establishing regular fraud and computer security training sessions is necessary for business security. If an organization is going to take the steps necessary to conduct detailed new hire background verifications, it should also invest in making its employees part of the business. Trusted employees who know they are actually part of the small business family will work to protect the business and ensure future growth. A small business owner willing to take the time to include employees in the protection of the operation goes a long way in showing concern for future job security.

    If the company is devastated by small business identity theft or account takeover fraud, the guarantee of future operations is in question.

- A small business owner needs to implement all the prevention measures available to guarantee future operations. The goal is to move the small business as far off the path of least resistance as possible. However, there is no 100% guarantee of total fraud prevention. It is vital for a small business owner to purchase insurance to protect the company assets against fraud.

Notes

1. Internal Revenue Service, How EINs are assigned and valid EIN prefixes. October 2014. http://www.irs.gov/Businesses/Small-Businesses-&-Self-Employed/How-EINs-are-Assigned-and-Valid-EIN-Prefixes (accessed June 16, 2014).
2. Colorado Secretary of State, Business identity theft resource guide. http://www.sos.state.co.us/pubs/business/ProtectYourBusiness/BITresourceguide.html (accessed June 14, 2014).
3. Ibid.
4. Individual or business credit/debit card information (account number, user name, expiration date, and the card security code) is obtained through one of the numerous schemes discussed throughout this book. Once this information is gathered, a counterfeit card is produced, and the vital information is transferred to the magnetic strip on the back of the card.

5. When a merchant account is opened, there has to be a corresponding bank account where money from the daily transactions is deposited. Depending on the merchant account, the money is transferred to the bank account within one to two days.
6. BusinessIDTheft.org, Business ID theft provides criminals with more options and potential targets. http://businessidtheft.org/Education/BusinessIDTheftScams/OtherSchemestoDefraud/tabid/177/Default.aspx (accessed August 12, 2014).
7. Microsoft Safety and Security Center, How to recognize phishing e-mail messages, links, or phone calls. http://www.microsoft.com/security/online-privacy/phishing-symptoms.aspx (accessed June 15, 2014).
8. Colorado Secretary of State, Business identity theft.
9. Beesley, C., Seven ways to protect your small business from fraud and cybercrime. May 8, 2013. http://www.sba.gov/community/blogs/7-ways-protect-your-small-business-fraud-and-cybercrime (accessed June 19, 2014).
10. Ibid.

Chapter 5

Investment Fraud

5.1 Introduction

Many people lose money to fraud because they respond to unbelievable opportunities presented in unsolicited e-mails; these e-mails offer a large payment for simple participation. Others respond to letters or fake lottery award notices that offer a cash payment for a simple up-front fee. People have also fallen victim to fraud by participating in work-at-home schemes, telemarketing fraud, or advance fee fraud.

Many of these fraudulent crimes require an active participant and an opportunity created by a person or group looking to commit fraud. Based on the type of fraud targeted toward the consumer, the individuals committing the activity can cast a wide net with the hope of catching as many fish as possible. The payout from the individuals acting as willing participants in what initially comes down to an opportunity to "get something for nothing" is drawn in by the money-making potential. Basically, minimum development is required of the criminal to attract the targets; the criminal then waits for a positive response from the intended target audience. The attraction for the targeted audience involves an impressive monetary reward for little participation.

With investment frauds, the individuals putting the schemes together must be somewhat more detailed in the hope of a larger monetary return. In basic consumer fraud, the victim will provide money as part of the scheme, and contact is broken off by the person who initiated the fraud. Investment schemes require more up-front involvement of the criminal during the development process. This includes coming up with a convincing money-making attraction that actually provides a rate of return for the initial participants.

The "too-good-to-be-true" money-making endeavor, which actually provides a return for initial investors, provides an increased attraction level to those offered the opportunity to participate. A more savvy or alert individual could possibly see through the loss potential of many consumer-directed schemes that simply require a one-time up-front fee, with no proof of participant success. With many investment schemes, the targets are drawn in based on the success of the ground-floor participants. According to the thought process: "If it worked for them, how can it fail?" This thinking leads to the target being grateful for having the opportunity to participate in a proven money-making endeavor.

Based on the knowledge of how the many victims of consumer- and individual-related frauds were drawn into the various scams, the assumption can be made that the initial investors in investment schemes are ground-floor targets for all frauds.[1] With investment schemes, a willing target audience is necessary to build the base or ground level of the fraud. Many of these initial investors or participants reach a level of success and might not be harmed financially as the scheme proceeds. Following the assumption mentioned, the question can be whether ground-floor participants of investment schemes are setting themselves up as future victims of consumer or individual frauds.

No matter what happens with the ground-floor participants of an investment scheme, they are required to bring success to the overall operation. Once the operation has been established with a certain level of success, the initiators of the schemes can now bring in additional participants. By adding participants to the investment scheme, the individuals initiating the fraud can see the invested money levels increase. Unfortunately, those entering the scheme during the later stages fall victim to the fraud and suffer financial hardship.

5.2 "Ponzi" Schemes

The term *Ponzi scheme* gets its name from an Italian immigrant who arrived in the United States in 1903 aboard the *SS Vancouver*. Charles Ponzi initially landed in Boston and worked many odd jobs in the United States and Canada. In addition to working in several different career fields and not achieving success, Charles Ponzi dabbled in some criminal activity, which landed him in jail on a few occasions. Eventually returning to Boston in 1918, Charles Ponzi continued working in odd jobs before launching an investment scheme that made him a lot of money and cost his investors millions of dollars.[2]

Ponzi eventually launched an investment business that was driven by the purchase of international reply coupons (IRCs). The IRC scheme revolved around purchasing the IRC stamps in a foreign country and later selling them in the United States at a higher price. Ponzi promised investors he could provide a return on investment of around 50% in a short period of time. The time frame on return of investment was around ninety days, which offered an attractive financial opportunity for many. In a short period of time, the investment money flowed in, and Ponzi was making a large monetary return.[3]

As the investment endeavor by Ponzi grew, the number of investors increased. The problem with this particular business opportunity was that the earlier investors were paid with the money provided by newer investors. As long as the new money flowed in to the business, current investors received the return percentage promised. In addition to the investors making an unheard of amount of return on their investment, Ponzi was also reaping profits in the millions of dollars.

In August 1920, the *Boston Globe* began an investigation into the extreme profits made by Ponzi and the investment business. This investigation caused panic for the investors in the company, and it also began a run on the business. Investors began pulling their money out of Ponzi's business, causing its eventual collapse.[4] Although the investment opportunity created by Ponzi was not referred to as a Ponzi scheme, later crimes of a similar nature were branded with the name.

A simple explanation of a Ponzi scheme is that it is an investment opportunity offered with an acceptable return. The percentage returned to the investor and the time frame of the return is based on the level of desired attractiveness to recruit participants. Initial investors put up a set amount of money with the promise to receive a substantial return. To provide the promised return amount to the initial investors, the managers of the scheme have to recruit additional participants. These additional participants are attracted by the proven rate of return to the initial investors. Unfortunately, the initial investors are paid their return from the money provided to the company by the subsequent participants. As long as new investors can be attracted to the business and invest their money, the house of cards will not crumble.

The issue with Ponzi schemes of this nature is the growth rate. For example:

- Ten initial investors place $100 each into the business.
- The initial investors are promised a rate of return of 40% per quarter.
- After the first quarter, the initial investors can be paid their promised return, totaling $400, from the initial investment capital generated. This will only leave $600 in the business.
- By using initial capital money to pay back investors, the scheme can only stay afloat for two and one-half quarters or seven and one half months, leaving no profit for those starting the business.
- To make the required return-on-investment payments and a substantial profit for those who began the operation, additional investors are required. Assuming those generating the scheme plan to keep all of the initial $100 payments made to join the scheme, all of the money required to make the quarterly interest payments has to come from new investors.
- To keep the same amount of quarterly capital generated at the beginning of the business ($1,000 = ten $100 investors), fourteen new investors need to be recruited at $100 each.
- This provides the business with an additional $1,000 of investment capital and $400 to pay the quarterly return payment.

- Now, the business has twenty-four investors and a return payment due of $960 ($40 for each of the twenty-four investors).
- To stay afloat, the business needs to add an additional twenty investors at $100 each. The investors now total forty-four with a return payment of $1,760.
- This is a simple scenario, but it shows the number of new investors needed to keep the current investors satisfied with their promised return amounts and allow those initiating the scam to keep the initial payments for all investors. The ever-increasing number of new investors required to make the rate-of-return payments will eventually become unsustainable.

The generation of Ponzi schemes is based on the creativity of the person or persons looking to commit the fraud. There is no playbook available on successful Ponzi schemes for those who commit this type of fraud. A person can conduct an Internet search and reveal Ponzi schemes that were committed in the past, both successful and unsuccessful. Because this information on past Ponzi schemes is so readily available, a person initiating a new fraud will have to create one that is different from past efforts.

No matter the investment information generated to attract the attention of potential investors, the basics of a Ponzi scheme remain the same:

- A large promised return on investment
- A promised short time frame promised to initial investors for a return on their investment
- The promise of little to no risk
- Actual investment return for early participants
- A constant need for new investors

In addition to understanding the basics of a Ponzi scheme, other characteristics to keep in mind are as follows:

- Be aware of an investment opportunity or an actual investment that promises or provides a consistent return. Market conditions change over time, and these fluctuations will cause normal returns to go up and down.
- Many Ponzi schemes attract the attention of potential investors by offering the opportunity to invest in a guaranteed opportunity. The opportunity also comes with little or no risk. With all investments, there is a certain level of risk. The higher the return on the initial investment, the greater the level of risk will be.
- With the offer of a high yield and no risk investment, the person initiating the scheme will hope the attraction will cover their need to provide potential investors with the investment strategies. All investors need to be made aware of planned investment strategies and not believe the potential for a quick and large return adds to the complexity of the overall plan and eliminates

the need for discussion. Individuals initiating these types of scams work to convince the investors of the complexity of the paperwork, that they have their best interest at heart, and that there is no need for detailed discussion.

■ Federal and state securities laws require the proper licensing of investment opportunities. The licensing and registration requirement applies to both the investment professionals and the firms for which they work. Any investment opportunity for which the principals and their firms are not licensed and registered is most likely a Ponzi scheme.

■ The Securities and Exchange Commission (SEC) requires all investments to be registered. All potential investors have a right to look at the company's overall business operation. This is to include the management team, company finances, products, and services. A typical Ponzi scheme will avoid the required SEC registration requirements.

■ Once invested into a Ponzi scheme, the people initiating the fraud will try to convince investors to roll over the investment with the promise of larger returns. This promise is usually made once the investor requests to cash out or has difficulty receiving a payment. If additional investors cannot be generated, the cash available in the scheme will dry up. People already invested in what they perceive to be a Ponzi scheme need to avoid pumping in additional money.

■ Ponzi schemes are frauds and are generated for the sole purpose of making money for those initiating the scam. Anyone looking to make an investment has a right to and should look over all information about the opportunity in writing. If paperwork is provided, it should be free of errors and inconsistencies.

Missing paperwork or written opportunities that contain inconsistencies are signs that the money may not be invested as promised.[5]

As with any investment opportunity or offer of a monetary return, the intended victim must be cautious. At a minimum, it is vital to confer with a family member and discuss the offer or opportunity. Through the promise of large returns, an individual's thought process could be clouded, and bad decisions are possible. It is also recommended that the opportunity be discussed with an investment company contacted by the person considering acting on the money-making offer. A third-party verification is necessary before any money changes hands. When making any type of organization verification, all company phone numbers have to be obtained from directory assistance.

5.3 Pyramid Schemes

Does anybody want to buy a water filter? Most people referencing their knowledge of a pyramid scheme remember the well-known scam of neighbors selling water filters. In that case, the water filters in question provided only the highest quality in filtering ability. Attached to a normal home faucet, these marvel filters turned the ordinary tap water into liquid refreshment. The selling point of the water filter pyramid scheme was not in the sale of the individual items but in the ability to become a licensed distributor. Once a person became an approved representative of the water filter company and authorized to sell individual items, the person also had the distinct opportunity to approve and sell distribution licenses. These licenses were sold to friends, relatives, and coworkers. The additional selling point of this popular pyramid scheme was the opportunity to make a profit from the activity of those they made a licensed distributor.

The attraction of the water filter distribution network relied on the continued ability to recruit new members. The typical process worked as follows:

- One person became a licensed representative of the water filter company. The typical investment was $1,000.
- Their goal or mission from the water filter company was to recruit ten people to become licensed distributors. Each new person recruited was required to pay the $1,000 licensing fee. A small percentage of the licensing fees paid by the ten new recruits was given to the initial representative. The remaining larger percentage generated from the ten new recruits was sent to the parent company.
- The goal for the ten newly licensed representatives was to locate and recruit ten new distributors each. If successful, 100 newly licensed sales representatives were added to the company rolls. For each of the 100 new sales representatives, a small percentage of their $1,000 fee went to the initial license distributor. An additional small percentage also was paid to each of the ten newly licensed representatives. Again, the remaining larger percentage of the money paid by the 100 new sales representatives was returned to the parent company.
- Each new person recruited to become a licensed sales representative had a goal to enlist ten new distributors. And, those ten new distributors are given the same task of identifying and convincing ten additional recruits each to pay $1,000.
- A major selling point to help convince a person to pay the $1,000 fee to become a licensed distributor was that they would receive a percentage of all sales made by their recruits. If their recruits were successful in selling distribution licenses, they also would receive a portion of the money generated.
- For a pyramid scheme to be successful, it is sold on the premise of a bottom-level-entry company. The earlier a person enters the business, the more money the person stands to make. One person (level 1) is hired, and that person hires ten people (level 2). Each of those ten people hires ten new people (level 3). Each of the level 3 people hires ten new recruits (level 4). So far, level 1 has 1,000 employees, level 2 has 100 employees, and level 3 has ten employees. Level 4 employees are given the task of hiring their own new employees. As the levels go higher with new employees, each member of the lower levels receives a portion of the sales made. The initial employee stands to make the most money in the upside-down pyramid.

■ As this scenario shows, individuals entering the business during the formation stages can make money. Others joining the operation during the growth process can also make money if they are productive and recruit new members. Sadly, as the recruitment process grows, there will be more people working for the business than targets left to recruit. Once people decline on the ideal money-making business opportunity, the money flow stops, and the pyramid falls.

■ Early investors might make their principal back, with the founders reaping large profits. All other individuals recruited into the business lose their investment money.

The investment business discussed with the water filter operation is classified as a pyramid scheme. An ideal definition would be the inverted pyramid scheme (see Figure 5.1), which is a business plan that grows from the bottom up, growing ever wider to keep the money flowing. Once the money stops flowing into the business, the weight of the upper levels of the pyramid will cause it to come crashing down.

One analogy can revolve around the life cycle of a shark. A shark is born and begins swimming. As the shark swims through the ocean, the shark needs to keep moving to keep water (from which it extracts oxygen) running over its gills. If the shark stops swimming, it dies.

For a pyramid scheme to be successful and not die, it needs a constant flow of cash into the business. The pyramid scheme is a shark and was most likely initiated by a person with shark-like qualities. For the business to live, it has to constantly move upward with new investors, and the inflow of capital creates the oxygen needed to survive. With the shark and the pyramid scheme, lack of continuous movement means death.

Although a popular form of a pyramid scheme, setting up a business to sell water filters is only one of the many types of multilevel marketing scams. For a pyramid scheme to be successful, there has to be a product to sell, which can be an actual item people might want to purchase. With many pyramid schemes, actual products are sold, and money is made on the selling of the items. From a profitability standpoint of a pyramid scheme, the real money is in the selling of licenses or

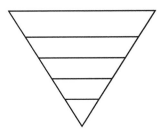

Figure 5.1 The inverted pyramid scheme.

distributorships. The growth of the business depends on the number of new licensing agreements or distributorships sold.

For a pyramid scheme to begin and grow, there has to be a certain level of attraction. Many people are attracted to a new business if they have the opportunity to make money by recruiting friends, relatives, or coworkers into the operation. The attraction grows if the individual is informed that he or she can make additional money if the people recruited are active in attracting new members. Basically, the opportunity to make money is based on the activity level and aggressiveness of those they recruit into the operation: "Make money sitting at home in your pajamas while people you recruited go out and grow the business."

The following are attention grabbers that create the attraction:

■ "A ground-breaking entry-level business opportunity."
■ "Make money at home while salesmen you recruit go out and grow the business."
■ "The more people added to the operation as a result of your initial activity, the more money you can make."
■ "Make large amounts of cash with a low up-front entry fee into a low-risk business operation."

With most frauds targeted toward the consumer or individual, there needs to be an attraction to gain interest. Once the interest level is raised, there is additional discussion on the ability to make money while putting forth a little effort. The enticement of an easy money-making opportunity basically sets the hook, and the fish is caught.

Individuals creating pyramid schemes can easily attract initial and subsequent participants with the enticing information. What information is not disclosed is the continuous need to sell new distributorships and that, without the constant growth, the business or pyramid collapses.

To avoid participation in a pyramid scheme, it is important to develop an understanding of one key point:

■ No matter where or when a person enters the business, it is mathematically impossible to create the level of wealth promised to each person recruited. At a ten-to-one growth ratio that continues at the same pace with each new member, the pyramid will eventually fall when the entire population of the world is recruited into the business. An inverted pyramid that grows larger each day will not be able to support its weight.

Although similar in nature, there are differences between Ponzi and pyramid schemes. Figure 5.2 provides a comparison of these schemes.[6]

	Pyramid Scheme	**Ponzi Scheme**
Typical "hook"	Earn high profits by making one payment and finding others to become distributors of a product. The scheme typically does not involve a genuine product. The purported product may not exist, or it may be "sold" only to other people who also become distributors.	Earn high investment returns with little or no risk by simply handing over money. Often, the investment does not exist or only a small percentage of incoming funds is actually invested.
Payments	Must pay a one-time or recurring participation fee and recruit new distributors to receive payments.	No recruiting is necessary to receive payments.
Interaction with original promoter	Sometimes none. New participants may enter the pyramid scheme at different levels.	Promoter generally interacts directly with all participants.
How the scheme works	Funds from new participants are used to pay recruiting commissions to earlier participants.	Funds from new investors are used to pay purported returns to earlier investors.
Collapse	Fast. An exponential increase in the number of participants is required at each level.	May be relatively slow if existing participants reinvest money.

Figure 5.2   Comparison of pyramid and Ponzi schemes.

5.4 Affinity Fraud

Most people have a feeling or need to belong. This could be as a member of an ethnic community, country club, association, religious organization, and so on. A sense of belonging provides inspiration and allows people to develop a belief they are not alone. Right or wrong, people act and do certain things they might not have done without pressure or support of others. Take a simple activity in an office of pooling money to purchase a large amount of lottery tickets. If everyone is gambling $5 on a multimillion-dollar risk, the attraction is appealing to many. Would these same individuals make a $5 purchase of lottery tickets if they had no personal history of gambling their hard-earned money?

Is their individual decision based on the reward potential of the overall group participants, or is the individual simply caught up in the excitement? Why would a person who does not gamble risk $5 as part of a potential group reward when the person would not make the same risk for themselves? Do these individuals actually believe there is a chance of winning the lottery when the odds are 1 in 150 million? Do they believe their odds of winning actually change if they purchase 5 individual tickets or participate in the purchase of 100 lottery tickets?

If the participants understood statistics, they would know they are not changing their odds of winning if they purchase 5 or 100 tickets. If these same participants do not place the overall odds of winning into their thinking, why risk having to share the prize? If they are going to gamble their hard-earned money, simply make an individual purchase of 100 lottery tickets. The only reason to participate in the office endeavor is if they believe this particular group is going to purchase the actual winning ticket. If not, take a risk on yourself so the winnings do not have to be shared.

Without the excitement and the offer to participate with coworkers, most non-gamblers would not even consider purchasing a single lottery ticket. Their participation in the office lottery ticket purchase comes from the feeling of belonging. They are now a part of something, and the cost of $5 is money well spent.

A basic understanding of human nature and the need to be a part of something bigger than themselves allows people who set up and participate in affinity frauds successful.

Affinity frauds are investment scams that focus more on members of groups, ethnic communities, religious affiliations, and the like. Ponzi and pyramid schemes tend to focus on and target individuals to participate and invest. Affinity schemes also focus on the individual but use the individual's participation or membership in a group or association as a point of attraction. As discussed with most frauds and schemes, there has to be an attraction to gain the attention and interest of potential investors.

As with the nongambler discussion, the only reason the person paid $5 to participate in the purchase of lottery tickets was the attraction of being part of the office group. Many of these same-minded individuals might not become excited if they were offered the opportunity to participate in an investment that required them to act alone. Participating in the low-risk, quick return promise of a Ponzi or pyramid scheme might not gain their attention. These are individual investment opportunities, and the only pressure to participate comes from the person selling the invitation.

With an affinity fraud investment opportunity, a person is not acting alone, and the person can ride the wave of "everybody is doing it." A benefit to the people behind an affinity fraud is the added attraction of peer pressure or encouragement from group leaders.

People who commit affinity frauds will use several methods to gain the trust of group members in an effort to create a growing list of active participants.

5.4.1 Groups Requiring Cash Flow

Many associations, churches, or community organizations raise money through their membership fees or donations. A group can also advertise fund-raising drives, charity auctions, car washes, material sales, and so on. The avenue to raise money will vary based on the needs of the group. The money collected or raised is normally used for building maintenance, meeting space rental, educational materials, management expenses, salaries, utilities, and so on. Typically with groups or associations that operate with a need to have continuous cash flow, the leadership is an ideal entry point for affinity fraud.

An understanding of the basic premise of group affiliation as having a need to belong provides a motivating factor to those committing affinity fraud. If a leader or the leaders of a group buy into the investment opportunities presented, the wheels of a successful affinity fraud scam are set in motion. Individuals who commit affinity fraud will purposely seek out group leaders and present an investment opportunity. The leaders are also persuaded to include all members of their association in participation in a safe-and-secure, high-return investment. Further discussion revolves around the benefit of placing as much money as possible into the investment. Once interested in the investment opportunity, it becomes more appealing with the following sales pitch: "The greater the number of people placing money into the investment, the higher the return, which means more money for continuous group operations."

For most fraudulent schemes, success is based on creating interest and then clouding the thought process. A person considering an investment opportunity will most likely think about the possible end results and not consider the possibility of fraud. A person selling the investment opportunity will use the following phrases to create a path of least resistance:

- "All money invested is secure."
- "This is a low-risk opportunity."
- "Receive a high return on a short-term investment."

Once a person or group leader is sold on the safety and the promised return of the investment opportunity, they become an unwitting participant in the fraud. These individuals are listening to all of the positive information provided and believe they will be a hero to the members of the group. What they are not doing is watching the person behind the curtain.

Obtaining the buy-in of group leaders is the beginning step for a successful affinity fraud scheme. Having group leaders who act as advocates for the investment opportunity makes them unwitting participants in the fraudulent activity.

For example, the main purpose of targeting group leadership for the purpose of committing affinity fraud is to convince members to pay $5 for lottery tickets.

Many successful affinity frauds are successful based on the group dynamic and the need to belong. If an individual group member is presented with an investment opportunity, the individual might choose not to participate. If the same opportunity is presented to the individual by a respected leader of an organization or community to which the individual belongs, the investment becomes appealing. The opportunity becomes appealing if it has been accepted as legitimate by the leadership. Once one member decides to participate in the endeavor, others are quick to follow. The group dynamic effect provides the greatest motivating factor for any individual looking to commit the act of affinity fraud against a group.

5.4.2 Immigrant Groups

Throughout the country, there are pockets of individuals who came to the United States from other countries. Because this country was formed by immigrants and the flood of immigrants passed through Ellis Island, ethnic affiliation determined where many of these new citizens chose to live. Being new to this country and maybe not speaking the language, life in a neighborhood of people from the same country made everyday life easier. Over time, a large majority of newly arrived immigrants assimilated into society. We all became citizens and pursued the American dream. However, to this day, cities all over the country have their ethnic pockets of residents.

These ethnic neighborhoods provide an ideal breeding ground for affinity fraud. Separation from the larger community and possible language barriers can hinder the flow of information. Many residents of these ethnic areas interact on a daily basis with other community members. Most shopping is conducted within the community with residents patronizing the stores and restaurants of their friends and neighbors. Residents of these ethnic pockets also attend the same church, keeping the daily interaction within the community.[7]

Sadly, some people who commit affinity fraud will target neighborhoods with residents of their own ethnic background. Residents of these ethnic communities are more likely to accept people with a similar background. The easier a person can be accepted into a group or community, the faster a level of trust can be developed. Once accepted as a member of an ethnic community, it becomes easier to sow the seeds to grow interest in an investment opportunity. As with the cash-based groups discussed previously, the person presenting the investment opportunity will most likely work to gain the trust of community leaders.

Individuals targeting ethnic groups for the purpose of committing affinity fraud do not have to rely on convincing people to pay $5 for lottery tickets. People living in ethnic-based communities have already developed the sense of belonging. All that is needed to persuade community residents to place their money in an investment is trust.

Having the same ethnic background actually operates in favor of the person committing the fraud. Major selling points to the community are as follows:

- An investment opportunity is provided to people with the same ethnic background.
- An investment opportunity is provided to fellow countrymen.
- There is interest in helping the financial stability of a community where they share the same ethnic affiliation.
- People are only allowed to invest in a great opportunity that shares a cultural history.
- Trust is created based on ethnic affiliation. "I would not ask my fellow countrymen to participate in a risky endeavor."

Once the trust level is created and the investment opportunity presented, many members of an ethnic community can fall victim to affinity fraud.

5.4.3 Religious Affiliation

With immigrant groups targeted for affinity fraud, the individual committing the fraud will look to gain the trust of community members. The same holds true for criminals who use the religious affiliation angle. The goal of those targeting religious groups is to target the religious leaders in an effort to have them spread the word around the congregation. In addition, individuals looking to use the religious affiliation angle can actually be members of the same religious organization. Having common knowledge of the activities and discussions related to the religious group makes it easier to gain the trust of all members.

To commit an effective affinity fraud based on religious affiliation, the con artist has to gain the trust of the group leader or a few congregation members. There has to be a belief created early on that the person presenting the opportunity has the best interest of the religious group at heart. Having the backing of the group leader is a major selling point for the members of the association. The ability to show a religious connection is also another major selling point to other group members early in the process. No matter the initial angle used to gain entry into the religious group, the goal is to develop a level of trust.

As discussed with elderly fraud in Chapter 8, many successful scams are completed based on establishing an initial level of trust. Once the religious leader or key members show a level of trust in the person and the process, other members quickly fall in line. After a trust level is established, the domino factor takes over.

To prevent victimization by affinity fraud scams, the following information has to be understood and followed:

- The goal of individuals looking to have a successful affinity fraud has to be initial buy-in from group leaders or trusted members. To add credibility to the scam, actual payouts are made to early participants. Even though the early participants receive a payout, it does not mean the investment process is working. The money used to pay the initial investors comes from individuals making a late arrival to the process. These payouts are made to the early investors with the hope that they can provide testimonials of an actual return on their investment. If group members can convince others of the legitimacy and actual return on their investment, more people will participate in the process. Eventually, the entire investment scam falls apart, with few group members receiving any type of return.[8]

■ No matter what group a person is associated with, an offer to use personal money in an investment opportunity has to be treated as an individual decision. Selected group members are provided with a return on their money, with the purpose of having them sing the praises of the offer to other members. All group members have to make decisions on their own and not base a participation decision on the recommendations of other group members.

■ With many successful frauds, victims make quick decisions based on the high-pressure tactics used. These high-pressure tactics involve a discussion surrounding a need to act quickly to benefit from the high return percentages. Other individuals are targeted with a high-payout opportunity with a limited entry window. Many are led to believe that if they wait to make an investment decision, they could lose out on the high promised returns.

■ With any investment opportunity, everyone should distance themselves from a person offering a guaranteed return. As with all investment opportunities and other money-making endeavors, there are no guarantees.

■ People working in the affinity fraud arena will also entice targeted individuals with a low- or no-risk guarantee. In the investment world, the terminology involving a no-risk opportunity is a clear warning sign of a fraud attempt.[9]

■ Never make an investment decision without receiving anything in writing. Individuals looking to commit investment fraud typically do not provide anything in writing; legitimate companies provide written documentation. Potential investors need to receive a prospectus or other written information detailing the entire investment process, including the associated risks and how a person can remove his or her money based on a decision to exit the process.[10]

■ For any individual or group considering an investment opportunity, it is vital to seek outside counsel. This can be from an attorney, an accountant, a financial planner, an advisor, or at the least a trusted friend who has no personal involvement in the offer or opportunity. Like a college student who needs to have an additional set of eyes proofread a paper, an investor has to have the offer reviewed by another.

■ Anyone considering an investment opportunity should contact their state securities agency or administrator. The agency can be used to obtain information on the salesperson and the firm involved and to determine if both are actually licensed in the state.[11]

■ With a majority of fraud attempts, many targeted individuals are initially contacted through an unsolicited e-mail. E-mail phishing (Chapter 11) is a popular method used to gain the interest of potential victims. Any offer presented through an unsolicited e-mail has to be approached with caution.

5.5 Investment Opportunity Advance Fee Letters

Advance fee fraud is detailed in Chapter 9, and sample advance fee letters are provided in Appendix B. Individuals committing advance fee fraud are now using terminology referencing investment opportunities in an effort to attract the attention of potential targets. Instead of promising a large monetary payout to the targeted individual, newer versions of the fraud are asking people to work in an investment partnership. The money that will be used in the partnership currently resides in a foreign bank, and investors are needed to move the money to the United States.

The following is a sample introductory letter received via an unsolicited e-mail:

From: David Hunt <david_deverehunt@yahoo.co.uk>

To: Recipients <david_deverehunt@yahoo.co.uk>

Subject: [BUSINESS] Re-investment Funds

Dear Prospective Partner,

I am writing to you on behalf of Akis Tsochatzopoulos. My name is Mr. David Hunt and I am a top management executive at UBS Investment Bank. Our bank website is www.ubs.com.

My friend Akis Tsochatzopoulos has presented a subtle offer which will need the help of a partner like you to complete successfully. Akis Tsochatzopoulos is in a difficult situation and he must immediately relocate certain sums of money out of the UBS Investment Bank in Athens, Greece. More so, this must be done in such a way that it must not be tied to Akis Tsochatzopoulos.

The sum is currently deposited in the name of an existing legal entity. Your role will be to

[1]. Act as the original beneficiary of the funds.
[2]. Receive the funds into a business/private bank account.
[3]. Invest/Manage the funds outside of Greece.
[4]. Value of funds: $47.2 Million US Dollars.

Everything will be done legally to ensure the rights to the funds are transferred to you. If you agree to partner with Akis Tsochatzopoulos, he will compensate you with 20% of the total sum. Should you prefer I re-contact you with more express facts, you can send me your

[1]. Official Full Names:
[2]. Company or Personal profile:
[3]. Daytime Telephone No:

> Kindly ensure to reply me via my private and confidential email address: david.hunt@qq.com for further details, terms and agreement.
>
> Sincerely,
> David Hunt

The goal of the introductory letter is to attract the attention of the recipient with the promise of participating in an investment opportunity using a large amount of money. The goal of the individuals sending the introductory letters is to have the recipients provide the requested personal information. Once the personal information is provided to the sender, the recipient of the introductory letter is advised he or she is an acceptable candidate to participate in the investment opportunity.

After the targeted individual believes he or she is participating in a legitimate investment opportunity, requests for up-front fees follow. Reasons provided to the newly recruited investment participants to provide up-front money are to pay processing fees, cover unforeseen tax issues, and so on. Once the initial payment for an up-front fee is made by the victim, additional requests for more money follow.[12] Up-front fee requests are made until the person or group providing the money realizes they are the victim of a scam.

Another variation of this type of investment opportunity fraud involves the sending of a good faith payment. The targeted victim or group is actually sent a good faith payment in the form of a money order or cashier's check. Unfortunately, the person sending the good faith payment made the check out for an amount larger than the payment amount promised.

To correct the overpayment and allow the recipient to keep their good faith payment, they are instructed to deposit the check into their personal or business/group bank account. After the check is deposited, a request is made to have the amount of the overpayment returned to the contact individual, operating out of a foreign country; the overpayment amount is to be sent via a wire transfer to the contact. Within days after sending the overpayment amount via a wire transfer, the actual check provided and deposited into the victim's bank account is returned as counterfeit. This leaves the targeted individual or group out the amount returned via a wire transfer.

To prevent becoming a victim of an investment opportunity advance fee fraud, individuals or groups need to adhere to the following prevention measures:

- Use caution when receiving an unsolicited e-mail promising an investment opportunity as part of an international business.
- Never provide any type of up-front fee in order to receive a promised payment of a large monetary amount.
- Ask the question: "Why was I [or this association] selected to become involved in this opportunity?"

- Never provide any personal or business-related information as part of answering an unsolicited investment opportunity e-mail.
- Never deposit a check into a personal or association bank account that was sent as a good faith payment.
- Never send money via a wire transfer to any unknown individuals.

5.6 Prime Bank Note Fraud

Prime bank note fraud is a type of investment fraud that operates in the international arena. Prime bank note fraud has also been successful in defrauding countless victims around the world, including individuals and organizations. The financial losses as a result of successful prime bank note fraud are in the billions of dollars. Prime bank note fraud or prime bank investment fraud also goes by the following names:

- Prime bank debentures
- Prime bank guarantees
- High-yield trading or roll programs
- Standby letters of credit
- International Chamber of Commerce (ICC) 3039 or 3034 letters of credit
- Guaranteed bank notes
- Discounted US Treasury securities
- International Monetary Fund (IMF)–backed securities[13]

Successful prime bank note fraud schemes work to entice potential investors to participate in investments that purchase and trade prime bank financial instruments. These financial instruments are traded in clandestine overseas markets and offer a large return on investment. Many individuals victimized by this scheme were offered monthly returns of 20% to 200%. Potential investors were also provided a guarantee of no risk.[14]

In an effort to add legitimacy to the investment opportunity and to ease the suspicion of the targeted individuals, the following information is provided:

- The investors have special access to programs that are generally reserved for financiers on Wall Street, Geneva, London, as well as other world financial centers.
- Potential investors are provided with documents that appear legitimate but are also complex and sophisticated.
- There is a promise of high returns and no risk on their investment.[15]
- The financial instruments are traded, issued, endorsed, and guaranteed by the World Bank, IMF, Department of Institutional Integrity (INT), Operations Evaluation Department, Department of the Treasury, ICC Federal Reserve Bank, or an international central bank.[16]

Potential investors are also advised of the extreme level of secrecy of these types of investment opportunities, which makes providing the names of client references impossible. These potential investors are also informed of the uniqueness of the investment opportunity, basically that the investment opportunities are by invitation only and reserved for special clients.[17]

Once potential targets become attracted to the prime bank note fraud, they are informed the US Treasury Department

- Backs or approves of these programs
- Has a "secret trading room"
- Must approve the humanitarian projects connected to these schemes
- Has purchased securities for investors to guarantee against loss
- Has a way to pool investor funds to buy and sell securities "just like the Rockefellers"

> NONE of these assertions are true: It is illegal to engage in fraud in the offer or sale of a security. Under most circumstances, it is also illegal to sell securities that have not been registered with the U.S. Securities and Exchange Commission. A security includes the following items: "note," "stock," "bond," and "debenture" and more general terms such as "investment contract" and "any interest or instrument commonly known as a 'security'." Designating such instruments as "loans" does not change their legal status as securities. *SEC v. W.J. Howey Co., et al.*, 328 U.S. 293 (1946)[18]

When it comes to recognizing prime bank note fraud, the US Treasury Department, Office of the Inspector General, provides the following warning signs:

- Name-dropping
- Buzzwords
- Excessive secrecy
- Overreliance on authentication
- Excessive disclaimers
- Unwarranted appearance of professionalism
- Big player behind the scenes
- Too high yields
- Lack of transactional basis
- A secondary market where these investments can be laid off quickly and profitably
- Flawed documentation[19]

Individuals looking to attract the attention of potential investors for prime bank note fraud will use many industry terms in notifications, offers, and other documentation. Many of these terms have no meaning or are misused in their terminology.

The goal is to confuse the first-time investor. The US Treasury Department provides the following list of terms used in prime bank note frauds:

- Noncircumvention
- Nondisclosure
- Good, clean, clear, and of noncriminal origin
- Blocked Funds Investment Program
- Prime Bank Trading Program
- Federal Reserve approved
- Treasury approved
- Roll program or bank debenture roll program
- Irrevocable pay orders
- Prime bank debentures, notes, guarantees, letters of credit
- Fresh-cut paper or bank debentures, bank paper
- High-yield investment program (HYIP)
- ICC 3034 or 3039 letter of credit
- Off balance sheet program
- Prime bank debenture trading
- Prime bank instruments, notes, guarantees, trades, or letters of credit
- Prime European Bank letters of credit
- Prime World Bank debentures or financial instruments
- Prime insurance guarantees
- High-yield debenture trading, financial programs, asset management programs
- High-yield promissory notes or bank notes
- Guaranteed bank notes
- Intermediate bank notes
- ICC 500 or 600 Bank Debenture Instrument
- IMF standby letters of credit (SLCs)
- IMF-backed securities, bill of exchange, bill of equity, or backed bonds
- Discounted US Treasury obligations, renting or leasing of Treasury securities
- Blocking of assigned Treasury securities
- "Limited edition" or de facto Treasury securities
- US dollar bonds, federal notes, medium- or mid-term notes or bank notes
- Blocked funds letters or investment programs, documentary letters of credit
- Irrevocable pay orders, collateral first debentures, money center bank
- Seasoned bank debentures
- Private placement programs
- Private trading programs
- International certificate of deposit (ICD)
- Irrevocable bank purchase order (IBPO)
- Irrevocable Corporate/Confirmed Purchase Order (ICPO)
- Irrevocable prime bank commitment
- Zero coupon L/C[20]

The US Treasury Department also provides the following list of prime bank note fraud phrases:

- Secret trading program
- Banks or Federal Reserve will deny involvement in these programs
- Noncircumvent/nondisclosure agreements
- Funds are "good, clean, clear, and of noncriminal origin"
- Funds pooled together for minimum trade amounts of $10,000,000 or $100,000,000 (sometimes listed as "Ten [10] Million USD" and the like)
- Interest rates guaranteed from 6% to 100% to 1,000% each month
- Trades with only the top ten, twenty-five, or fifty banks in the world, such as Barclays or Credit Suisse
- Program backed, approved, or sanctioned by the Federal Reserve Bank (FED or FRB), the IMF, the ICC, or the Treasury Department
- "Trader," "facilitator," or "broker"
- Only five to ten traders in the world have access to this program; trader will conduct forty trades each year.
- Percentage of the yield will go to charity, social programs, or humanitarian efforts
- US government agencies deny existence of these programs because government does not want your money to leave the United States
- US government agencies try to seize the funds for themselves
- "Due 1, 5, or 10 years and 1 day"
- "108" bank-to-bank certificate, which guarantees the principal plus 8% annual interest
- "Funds of noncriminal origin are legally owned by or assigned for the participation in a specified high-yield asset management program"
- Principal guaranteed or secured by letters of credit: "The funds will remain in a bank account that only you are signer on. These funds will be used as collateral."
- Offshore trust accounts/tax-free interest
- Can obtain proceeds through Visa debit cards
- Remove from legitimate pension accounts and send funds to self-directed pension companies who collateralize the funds with a note and are then invested in prime bank instruments
- Facilitator has access to the world's top trader
- "Trader," "trading bank," "exit buyer"
- The way all banks or big banks make their money
- Trades sometimes referred to as "tranches"
- Only a select few are invited to participate in the trading program
- Originally established by the elite families, such as the Rockefellers, Gettys, Rothschilds, and Carnegies
- Fractionalize or collateralize the funds
- Fractional banking laws

- Hypothecation with insurance companies ($1.2 million needed for insurance company to "hypothecate" $100 million needed for the trade)
- Investment periods quoted on contracts would be "ninety banking days," "one year and one day," or "five years and one day"
- Program developed to level out the yo-yo syndrome in the banking industry
- "The information contained in this document is for information purposes only and is not intended as a solicitation or an offer to sell any form of securities."
- Invested funds fully secured by a bank-endorsed guarantee
- "Cash" wire transfer
- C&F ASWP (cost and freight/any safe world port)
- Comfort letter
- "Conditional" SWIFT (Society for Worldwide Interbank Financial Telecommunication) payment
- CUSIP (Committee on Uniform Securities Identification Procedures) number
- Discounting L/Cs (letter of credit)
- "Trades are specifically established at a term of 1 year and 1 day, so they do not have to appear on the bank's balance sheet."
- Foreign bank advice
- Irrevocable, divisible, assignable, transferable, fractionable, revolving, confirmed

L/C Payable 100% at Sight

- Key-Tested Telex (KTT)
- Market to buy or sell L/Cs
- Proof of funds
- Proof of product
- Ready, willing, and able (R, W, & A)
- Soft probe
- 2% performance bond
- Preadvise issued by bank
- Bank responsible commitment of funds
- A claim that the "promoter" has a steady business relationship with a large international bank
- A refusal to give "full disclosure" of all involved
- The expression *mandated agent*
- Standby letter of credit[21]

The Federal Bureau of Investigation (FBI) provides the following list of warning signs and tips to protect individuals from becoming a victim of prime note bank fraud:

- Think before you invest in anything. Be wary of an investment in any scheme referred to as a "roll program" that offers unusually high yields by buying and selling anything issued by "prime banks."

- As with any investment, perform due diligence. Independently verify the identity of the people involved, the veracity of the deal, and the existence of the security in which you plan to invest.
- Be wary of business deals that require nondisclosure or noncircumvention agreements that are designed to prevent you from independently verifying information about the investment.[22]

Notes

1. Further chapters in the book detail the various frauds directed at consumers and individuals. Discussion is provided regarding how the potential victims are targeted and the opportunities made available.
2. Biography.com. Charles Ponzi. 2014. http://www.biography.com/people/charles-ponzi-20650909 (accessed June 9, 2014).
3. US Securities and Exchange Commission, Ponzi schemes. http://www.sec.gov/answers/ponzi.htm (accessed June 9, 2014).
4. Biography.com, Ponzi.
5. US Securities and Exchange Commission, Ponzi schemes.
6. Ibid.
7. US Securities and Exchange Commission, How to avoid affinity fraud. http://www.sec.gov/investor/pubs/affinity.htm (accessed June 10, 2014).
8. North American Securities Administrators Association, Affinity fraud: beware of swindlers who claim loyalty to your group. http://www.nasaa.org/7157/affinity-fraud-beware-of-swindlers-who-claim-loyalty-to-your-group/(accessed August 15, 2014).
9. Ibid.
10. Ibid.
11. Ibid.
12. Once a person provides the initial up-front payment, the person now has a financial interest. After a financial interest is generated by the individual committing the fraud, the victim is led to believe the promised money is within reach. The money is within reach after payment is made for another unforeseen expense.
13. US Department of the Treasury, Prime bank note fraud. http://www.treasury.gov/about/organizational-structure/ig/Pages/Scams/Prime-Bank-Investment-Fraud.aspx (accessed September 2, 2014).
14. US Securities and Exchange Commission, How prime bank frauds work. http://www.sec.gov/divisions/enforce/primebank/howtheywork.shtml (accessed September 2, 2014).
15. US Department of the Treasury, Prime bank note fraud.
16. US Securities and Exchange Commission, How prime bank frauds work.
17. Ibid.
18. Ibid.
19. US Department of the Treasury, Prime bank note fraud.
20. Ibid.
21. Ibid.
22. Federal Bureau of Investigation, Common fraud schemes. http://www.fbi.gov/scams-safety/fraud (accessed September 3, 2014).

Chapter 6

Organized Retail Fraud/Theft

6.1 Organized Retail Crime/Fraud

Retail locations provide a great opportunity for individuals who want to commit fraud or theft. These crimes can range from the simple taking of a candy bar to a loss of thousands of dollars in merchandise from organized retail fraud schemes. The theft of a candy bar affects the bottom line of the retail location. Organized retail crime/fraud can affect the bottom line of the retail location through losses in inventory. With the larger crime of organized retail crime/fraud, the merchant is not the only victim. In addition to the loss suffered by the retailer, individual consumers can be follow-up victims.

With a majority of fraudulent activity, the individuals who want to commit the fraud develop a scheme and find a victim to target. If the fraudulent activity is successful, the person committing the activity receives the desired monetary outcome and the targeted victim suffers a loss. The crime of organized retail fraud has the merchant as the initial victim, with a follow-up victim of the consumer who purchases repackaged and out-of-date consumables. The following is a list of popular items targeted by organized retail crime/fraud operators:

- Electronic merchandise, including cell phones, digital cameras, laptop computers, tablets, GPS (global positioning system) devices, and the like
- Grocery store items, including diabetes test strips, razor blades, batteries, infant formula, high-dollar spirits and wine, and so on

■ Over-the-counter medicines, including diabetic test strips, allergy medication, pain relievers, weight loss pills, smoking cessation products, and more
■ Designer clothing, furs, handbags, and so on
■ Drugstore items, including pregnancy test kits, beauty items, skin lotions and creams, electronic toothbrushes, and the like
■ Kitchen products, including coffeemakers, high-quality mixers, and others

In contrast to the individual candy bar thief, organized retail crime/fraud involves the participation of many. These detailed fraud schemes typically involve the individuals stealing the merchandise (boosters), people who make the items ready for resale (cleansers), and those who actually resell the stolen merchandise (fences).

Beginning with the actual theft of the merchandise, the boosters work using a variety of methods:

■ Enter the store with several individuals who steal merchandise and with other participants who work as lookouts. These lookouts will also create distractions within the retail location to take the employees' attention away from the boosters.
■ Enter the location with actual shopping bags from the store targeted. The boosters fill the shopping bags with merchandise and hope to walk out of the store undetected.
■ Individuals working in organized retail crime/fraud operations will hide out in the store and wait until closing when all employees have left. After the location is empty of employees, the thieves will quickly grab targeted items and depart through emergency exits.
■ Thieves will also participate in smash-and-grab-type operations, for example, ramming a vehicle into the front door of the targeted location, entering en masse, and grabbing as much merchandise as possible.
■ Organized retail crime/fraud boosters will also work with current or former store employees. Employees have been known to provide boosters with items directly from the store inventory or products from the receiving area.
■ Former or current store employees will also assist the boosters by leaving store doors unlocked or providing alarm codes, security information, and management working schedules.[1]

Once the merchandise has been stolen by the boosters, many items go through what is referred to as cleansing or cleaning operations. The goal of the cleaning process is to ready the merchandise for resale. Cleaning operations involve removing any security devices and store-specific labels. Items are also repackaged to give the appearance of coming directly from the manufacturer. With perishable items, cleansers will change the expiration date.

Once the stolen items are cleaned and repackaged, they are ready for resale by the fences. Based on the type of item stolen and repackaged, there are many popular methods used to sell the merchandise:

- Items have been sold at flea market/swap meet–type events.
- Online websites are popular venues used to sell items processed through organized retail crime/fraud operations.
- Items stolen and repackaged in one state are sold or traded to operators in other locations.
- Stolen and repackaged items are also sold to wholesale operations. Stolen and repackaged items are mixed with legitimate merchandise prior to delivering all of the product to wholesale operators.

The goal of those fencing merchandise obtained from organized retail crime/fraud operations is to sell the products to the general public. With many items sold either through the Internet or via other locations, the consumer is receiving a product for their money. Unfortunately, some of the popular items stolen during organized retail crime/fraud operations carry expiration dates.

Consumers purchasing many over-the-counter medications through Internet auction websites run the risk of consuming dated products. The risk of internal harm increases with the purchase of infant formula that is outdated and repackaged with a current expiration date.

Organized retail crime/fraud is not limited to the stealing of merchandise from retail locations. Other crimes or frauds committed by organized groups involve the unauthorized taking of consumer credit card information. The credit card information is then used to purchase merchandise, which is later resold.

Ringleaders generally enlist the support of younger individuals currently working in the food service industry. Restaurant employees will use handheld skimming devices[2] (Figure 6.1) to capture the credit card information or simply copy the appropriate card information while the card is out of sight of the consumer (see Chapter 10 for a discussion of prevention measures when using a credit card in a

Figure 6.1 A handheld skimming device.

restaurant). The credit card information (account number, user name, expiration date) is later used to make unauthorized purchases or it is transferred to counterfeit credit cards.

Once the ringleader obtains the desired number of credit card account numbers, the information is used to purchase gift cards or merchandise. The gift cards purchased with fraudulently obtained credit card information can be used as cash when needed to conduct a wide variety of transactions. Merchandise purchased with the stolen credit card information is later returned to the store for cash or the items are sold on Internet auction websites (see Chapter 11 for additional discussion of these websites).

Organized retail crime/fraud schemes can also take place from a less-complex standpoint and involve small groups of individuals or family members. With these smaller organized retail crime/fraud operations, the goal is to sell or trade the stolen merchandise. Typically, stolen items are traded for drugs or sold through yard/garage sales.

6.2 Retail Merchandise Fraud

Individuals who operate outside the large organized retail theft/fraud groups also participate in various forms of stealing merchandise from retailers. These can be outright thefts of merchandise, as well as use of various forms of deception to obtain items without proper payment. The goal of the individuals working to commit the varying types of retail merchandise fraud is monetary gain at the expense of the retailer. The following are tactics used to commit retail merchandise fraud:

- In the same fashion as those participating in organized retail theft/fraud, individuals enter a retail location and steal merchandise. Many of the tactics used to remove the merchandise from the retail location mirror those of the organized groups. The goal of the individual thief is to sell the stolen items using the Internet, trading them for drugs, or retaining the items for personal use.
- Merchandise borrowing has been the topic of televised sitcoms over the years. *Merchandise borrowing* is the simple purchase of a product for a specific use and then returning the item at a later date. A popular fraud is the purchase of a large-screen television to watch the Super Bowl. After the big game, the television is returned to the store where it was purchased. Other popular items purchased in merchandise-borrowing frauds are expensive clothing and high-dollar electronic items. The events that utilize the temporary purchase of high-dollar items vary.
- Retailers can fall victim to customers purchasing an item and later returning the same piece a few days later. The reason provided for the return is that the item purchased was broken, with the breakage discovered when the

packaging was removed. To provide quality customer service, retailers routinely accept the return of items related to such customer claims.

With this type of fraud, the customer visits the retailer with the intent of purchasing a specific item. The need to make a specific purchase is based on the customer having already purchased the same item. During their normal daily activities, the item was broken. In an effort to have the broken item replaced for free, the customer makes another purchase. The new item is placed in their home, and the broken item is repackaged and returned with a valid receipt.

■ Individuals will also engage in making the legitimate purchase of an item. Once the purchase is complete, the item is placed in one of the retailer's shopping bags. The customer then exits the retail location and places the purchased item in his or her vehicle. The customer reenters the retail location with the shopping bag. Once in the same retail location, the customer shoplifts the same item purchased and places it in the shopping bag. With the same item in hand, the customer uses the receipt provided from the first purchase to complete a return.[3]

■ The Internet provides many services to consumers. Many websites provide legitimate services; others sell items that can be used for fraudulent purposes. One of these fraudulent purposes involves the selling of fake receipts. Fake receipts are used to make returns for items that were initially stolen or shoplifted from the retailer.[4]

■ Price arbitrage involves the purchase of similar items with different pricing, one more expensive than the other. The customer later attempts to return the cheaper of the two items and collect a refund for the higher-priced piece of merchandise. This is also a popular scheme with retailers that offer "buy one, get one free" specials or sell items at a discounted price. Either way, the purpose is to return one of the two purchased items or the discounted piece for the full return price.[5]

Many retailers across the country have liberal return policies in an effort to provide quality customer service. It is hoped these retailers have conducted a cost/benefit analysis to determine the presence of positive sales compared to fraud-related return losses.

In an effort to prevent fraudulent returns, the following tips are helpful:

■ Retailers can implement a timeline for item returns. The return timelines can be for a set number of days after the purchase.
■ Initiate a restocking fee policy for returned items. The restocking fee can be a set percentage of the purchased item.
■ Use extreme caution when processing an item return request within an hour or two after the initial purchase.

■ Inspect items returned for breakage for actual wear. Also, make sure all parts of the broken item are in the original packaging. Retailers can also establish a swapping policy. Instead of providing a refund for the broken item, swap it for one that is in good condition.

■ Provide a return amount for the original purchase price at the time of the sale.

■ Establish an original receipt return policy.

6.3 Coupon Fraud

Typically, manufacturers' coupons are clipped from newspapers or magazines or downloaded from legitimate business websites. Once clipped from the paper or printed, the legitimate coupons are redeemed at various retail locations. Based on the intent of the item's manufacturer, coupons can be issued for a 10% to 20% savings, for example, on the item purchased. Manufacturers can also issue coupons in a promotion to buy one item and get one free and in a push to try a new product for free.

The manufacturer initiates the production of a coupon; these coupons are distributed to the consumer via newspapers, magazines, and online sites. Once the consumer obtains a legitimate coupon, the following can occur:

■ The goal is for the consumer to purchase the exact item described on the coupon.

■ During the purchase, the retailer will deduct the coupon amount from the actual item sale price.

■ To collect for the amount deducted from the item sales price, the retailer sends the collected coupons to the manufacturer.

■ The manufacturer sends the retailer the actual coupon amount redeemed.

■ If the item had a $1 sale price and the coupon was for $0.20 off, the consumer is charged $0.80 by the retailer. After the sale, the retailer asks the manufacturer to send the retailer the $0.20 deducted from the original sale price of the item.

With coupon fraud, manufacturers, retailers, and consumers can all become victims:

■ Manufacturers can be providing money back to the retailer for coupons redeemed but not legitimately issued.

■ Retailers can be denied payment from the manufacturer for redeeming coupons not legitimately issued to the consumer.

■ Consumers can be victimized by coupon fraud by purchasing bogus coupons through Internet auction websites.

Modern technology (computers, printers, and software) allows individuals to create new or copy existing coupons. The intent of those creating fraudulent coupons is to pass these items to consumers. Based on the operating procedures of those creating the fraudulent coupons, varying methods are used to solicit the consumers to purchase what they believe are legitimate manufacturer coupons:

- An individual can receive an unsolicited e-mail that offers the recipient the ability to purchase manufacturers' coupons at an extremely discounted price.
- An individual can receive a phishing-type (Chapter 11) text message offering the recipient the opportunity to purchase manufacturers' coupons at an extremely discounted price.
- Individuals are also alerted, via an unsolicited e-mail or text message, to the opportunity to bid on packages of manufacturers' coupons. This bidding process takes place on Internet auction websites (Chapter 11).

No matter the method used to attract the consumer's attention, the coupons provided were not legitimately issued by the manufacturer. Believing they have purchased legitimate coupons, consumers will attempt to conduct retail transactions and receive the value of the coupon presented. When the fraudulent coupons are presented to the retailer, they can be either honored or denied. Based on the training level used to educate the employees on identifying fraudulent coupons, these items may or may not be processed.

To properly identify legitimate manufacturers' coupons as compared to fraudulent ones, the following information can be used by both the retailer and the consumer:

- Never purchase or process manufacturers' coupons that do not have a Universal Product Code (UPC) (discussed in a separate section further in this chapter).
- Use caution when purchasing and processing manufacturers' coupons that do not require a purchase for redemption.
- Do not purchase or process a manufacturer's coupon that has a face value more than the sale price of the item.
- All legitimate manufacturers' coupons have small-print wording that stipulates the conditions of use. Do not purchase or process manufacturers' coupons that do not contain condition-of-use wording.[6]

6.4 E-mail Coupon Offers Delivering Malware/Spyware

Coupon fraud is also being coupled with cyberfraud via unsolicited e-mails in phishing-type attempts (see Chapter 11 for detailed discussion of e-mail phishing and Chapter 12 as it relates to downloading unauthorized malware/spyware). Unsuspecting individuals are receiving unsolicited e-mails offering service-related coupons that are used by consumers. The types of coupons offered are in constant

From: Free Coupons for Oil Change Discounts EuL90tB@46rjgge.changeoillocal.com>

To:

Subject: Free Oil Change Coupons - Click Here 0832

Figure 6.2   Sample coupon advertisement sent via unsolicited e-mail.

demand, and the offer to receive these types of coupons can quickly attract the attention of the recipient. Refer to Figure 6.2 for a sample coupon advertisement that was received via an unsolicited e-mail.

Individuals receiving these types of unsolicited e-mail-related coupon offers are asked to click on the advertisement so they can locate a service representative near them and download valuable coupons. By clicking on the coupon offer, the recipient is opening up his or her computer to the unauthorized downloading of malware/spyware software. This software can be used to commit identity theft (see Chapter 10 for a discussion of identity theft types of fraud) by giving unauthorized individuals access to information and documents stored on a personal computer.

Organizations, especially small business operations, can be susceptible to this type of fraud if associates use a company computer while attempting to download coupon-related offers.

To protect individual and business-related systems and information, these types of unsolicited e-mails should be ignored.

6.5 UPC/Bar Code Fraud

A popular fraud in years gone by was for a person to enter a retail establishment and take a low-dollar price tag from an item and place it over the price tag of a higher-priced item. After making the price tag switch, the individual proceeds to the register and hopes to check out without the deception being noticed.

In today's world of computer technology in the retail community, a large majority of retailers now use scanners to determine the price of an item. Items for retail sale are all marked with what is referred to as a bar code or UPC (Figure 6.3). Contained within the bar code is the item name and sale price. To process the item for retail sale, the cashiers simply run the bar code over a scanner that generates the now-familiar beep. Once the scanner reads the information related by the bar code, the sale price and item description appear on the register display screen.

As referenced previously with price tag switching, individuals are now creating or switching item bar codes. With bar code switching, the intent is to be able to pay a lower price for a high-dollar item. Instead of switching a simple price tag, individuals committing bar code fraud use one of several methods:

1. Enter a retail establishment and make a purchase of a low-dollar item. Once the individual gets the item purchased back to their residence, they remove the bar code and return to the same retail location. The individual will locate a similar, but higher-priced, item and place the removed bar code over the existing bar code of the higher-priced product they wish to purchase.

   With this type of scam, the person making the bar code switch typically looks for a busy cashier, with the idea that the cashier will not notice the low price of a normally high-ticket item.

Figure 6.3 Example of a Universal Product Code (UPC).

2. In line with the process outlined, a small-dollar item is purchased. Once the purchaser returns to his or her residence, the existing bar code is scanned into a computer. Using the correct size label paper, the scanned bar code is printed. After successfully printing the lower-priced item's bar code onto label paper, the individual returns to the retail location and makes the switch. (Printed labels have an adhesive backing and can be placed over an existing bar code to provide a professional appearance.)

3. As discussed throughout this book, there are numerous websites that offer many options to the consumer. The ability to generate bar codes through the Internet is an option for consumers. With the bar code information for a low-priced item, anyone can visit one of these websites and create a UPC label. Once these labels are printed, the individual committing bar code fraud can place them over high-dollar items they wish to purchase.

4. Consumers also have the option of purchasing personal computer software that generates bar codes. Once the software is loaded, these individuals can print a wide variety of bar codes.

Retailers looking to prevent bar code fraud need to place their frontline defenses into the education of their sales associates. Retailers need to train their sales associates on item pricing and that they need to actually look at the bar code for signs of tampering. In addition, the sales associates need to ensure the information displayed for the bar code scanned is consistent with the item presented for purchase.

Retailers also have options of employing greater technology-based prevention measures in an effort to combat bar code fraud. These options include generating location-specific bar code labels that contain some type of unique markings that make them harder to counterfeit. Retailers can also use a radio-frequency identification (RFID) labeling system. The information contained in the RFID labels communicates directly with an electronic reader[7] and will ensure items are sold at their desired price.

Both of these prevention measures offer a greater level of protection against bar code fraud. They also come with a greater cost factor to implement and operate. Because of the related cost factor, retailers need to conduct a cost/benefit analysis: Do losses caused by bar code fraud outweigh the cost factor of implementing the latest prevention technology?

6.6 Gift Card Fraud

In the past, a person wanting to give another person a gift certificate to a local restaurant had to get into a car and drive to the desired location. A gift certificate could normally be purchased for a set amount, usually in the $25, $50, or $100 range. The person receiving the gift certificate could spend the entire amount or a portion thereof. Based on the establishment where the gift certificate was tendered, the unused portion was returned in cash or a reissued gift certificate for the remaining balance.

The paper gift certificate has been replaced by gift cards the size of an ATM card. These gift cards can be purchased at grocery stores, drugstores, home improvement locations, and so on. The various retail outlets that sell gift cards offer the choice of a wide variety. Gift cards for sale can be offered for such places as restaurants, home improvement stores, retail locations, drugstores, and more. The individual purchasing a gift card also has the option of selecting the amount. Gift card amounts are typically $25, $50, and $100.

Individuals looking to commit gift card fraud have developed numerous tactics to victimize consumers and retailers:

- As discussed throughout this publication, consumer credit card information is used to commit varying types of fraudulent activity. The crime of gift card fraud is not immune to the overall crime of credit card fraud. Individuals will obtain a consumer's credit card information (see Chapter 10 and Chapter 11) to create counterfeit credit cards. These counterfeit credit cards are then used to purchase varying types and amounts of gift cards from retail locations. These gift cards are later sold through Internet auction websites (see Chapter 11 for a detailed discussion of these websites).

- Individuals not wanting to go through the process of obtaining the credit card information of unsuspecting consumers can obtain gift cards in a simple manner. As noted, gift cards are sold in the name of numerous retail operations and for varying dollar amounts. Most retail locations have a central display area or racks showing the many different types of gift cards for purchase. These gift cards are not under lock and key because they have no actual value until activated. Gift cards are not activated until they are purchased.

  With the easy access to display racks and the gift cards similar in size to a credit card, they are easy to steal. Individuals typically enter the various retail locations and steal inactivated gift cards. Once out of the store, the thieves record the card numbers and personal identification numbers (PINs). Once this information is obtained, the gift cards are returned to the display racks.

  The thieves wait for the stolen and returned gift cards to be purchased by an unsuspecting customer. After the compromised gift cards are purchased, they are also activated. Once activated, the thieves use the gift card information to make purchases online. Their hope is to use the balance on the gift card prior to use by the consumer who purchased the item for legitimate purposes.

  (In an effort to prevent fraud on gift cards sold, manufacturers are adding prevention measures to the actual cards. One measure is to cover the card number and PIN with a substance that is removed by the consumer after purchase. Consumers and retailers need to remember, the same technology used to create the protection measures can also be used by those committing various types of fraud. Gift card manufacturers are not the only ones who can place a scratch off substance over the gift card number and PIN.)

■ Individuals involved with organized retail crime/fraud can also have an end game of obtaining active gift cards. Sticking with the initial operation of these organized groups, the first step is to steal merchandise. Instead of going through the repackaging process, the merchandise is returned to the retail establishment in exchange for gift cards. These activated and fraudulently obtained gift cards are later used by members of the fraud group, traded for drugs, or sold through Internet auction websites.

■ As previously discussed, creating fraudulent UPC information is a common method to commit retail fraud. The same practice is also used to commit gift card fraud. An individual will make a legitimate purchase of a store's gift card. Once in possession of the gift card, the individuals committing the fraud will create identical UPC stickers containing the information from the legitimately purchased gift card. These UPC stickers are then placed over the existing codes of gift cards on the display rack at the location of the original card purchase.

Once the gift cards containing the bogus UPC sticker are purchased, the card amount is activated on the original gift card purchased. By placing the fraudulent UPC stickers on numerous gift cards ready for purchase, a large amount of money can be activated on the legitimately purchased card.[8]

Gift card fraud is not unique to individuals operating outside the retail location. Various types of gift card fraud are also popular with store employees:

■ Throughout a normal business day, customers will use a gift card to make a purchase. The gift card can cover the entire amount of the purchase or a portion of the sale price. Typically, sales that require the customer to use another payment to cover the entire transaction amount end with the zero-balance gift card being left at the register in hopes that it will be thrown away.

Employees who want to commit gift card fraud will retain the zero-balance cards. These zero-balance gift cards are later used for what is referred to as the *switch*. When a customer makes a legitimate purchase of a store gift card, the zero-balance card is switched with the one purchased by the consumer. The store employee now has an activated gift card and the customer takes home a card with a zero balance.[9]

■ Employees will also conduct gift card fraud with what is referred to as *laundering*. This process involves an employee and two store registers. The employee will make a purchase of a $50 gift card. Prior to closing out the sale, the employee will use the recently activated $50 gift card to purchase two $25 cards at a different register. After completing the sale for the two $25 gift cards, the transaction is voided. The employee will then use the two $25 gift cards to complete the original purchase of the $50 card.[10]

To prevent employee gift card fraud, retail locations should never allow the same associate to be logged on to two registers at the same time. Retailers also need to track the number of customer complaints of receiving zero-balance cards. If the store has a high volume of complaints, the store needs to look for a pattern of which associates were working the cash registers where the consumer made the gift card purchase. Typically, the zero-balance gift card sales will originate from one or two associates.

Retailers also need to create a central and secure location for associates to place zero-balance gift cards left behind by the customer. Store policy should dictate all zero-balance gift cards be immediately deposited into the secure receptacle. Store managers should also conduct spot checks around store registers for the accumulation of zero-balance gift cards that have been left behind.

Consumers need to employ the following measures to avoid becoming a victim of gift card fraud:

■ Never purchase gift cards from an online auction website. The gift cards sold could be fraudulent, have a zero balance, or not contain the full face value of the card.

■ Select a gift card for purchase that is located at the back of the rack. Individuals who have replaced gift cards on the rack will typically place them in front so they are first to be purchased.

■ Prior to purchasing a gift card, inspect both sides of the card for tampering. If the PIN can be seen, the gift card most likely has been tampered with.

■ When purchasing a gift card at the register, make sure to maintain eye contact with the cashier and keep the card in your sight. Customers should make it a practice to physically hand the gift card to the cashier and immediately request possession of the card after it is scanned. The gift card purchased should be treated like a personal credit/debit card used in a restaurant. Never let the card out of your sight.

■ Make sure to get a receipt from the cashier for any and all store purchases. The receipt can be used as proof of purchase if the gift card has a zero balance.

■ Never provide any personal information to the cashier as part of the gift card purchase process. Dishonest employees will attempt to convince the customer that his or her personal information is required to register the gift card.

    Consumers can choose to register a gift card through the store's website. This process is not conducted at the store register.[11]

6.6 School Impersonation Fraud

Individuals are using the good name of a school, school district, or school official to make fraudulent purchases of merchandise. The merchandise is purchased by using fraudulently obtained line-of-credit information and targeting retailers that specialize in medical equipment, computer/office supplies, industrial equipment, and pharmaceuticals.

To complete this scam, individuals are contacting retailers directly through the retailer's customer service call center or via e-mail. By using social engineering tactics,[12] these individuals are able to obtain information about purchasing accounts of a targeted school. In addition, purchasing account information is obtained through the school's or school district's website.[13]

Once the purchasing account information is obtained, the retail location is contacted directly. Using the purchasing account information, individuals involved with this scam make large purchases of computer equipment, laptops, routers, ink and toner, medical supplies, and so on.

After the order is completed, the retailers are supplied with an address for shipping. The variations on the shipping process are as follows:

■ The items purchased are mailed directly to the school by the retailer. The retail location is provided the true address of the school the caller claims to represent. Once the items have been shipped and received, the school is contacted by a person claiming to be a representative of the vendor. This individual advises the school that the product was shipped in error and provides a domestic address for a return of the merchandise.

    Many of these addresses provided are drop-house-type locations, and the residents of these locations are part of the scam. Once the returned merchandise is received at the drop house, it is repackaged and mailed to an overseas address.

■ The items purchased are shipped to the address of a person who is unwittingly involved in a work-at-home reshipping fraud scam (see Chapter 9 for a discussion of reshipping fraud). The victims of the reshipping fraud scam receive the merchandise, repackage the items, and ship the packages to a supplied overseas address.

■ Items are also initially shipped to individuals unwittingly involved in a romance fraud scheme (see Chapter 7 for a discussion of romance schemes). Once the merchandise is received by the romance fraud victim, it is repackaged and mailed to an overseas address.[14]

Another variation of school impersonation fraud is by e-mail spoofing (see Chapter 11 for a discussion of spoofing). Retailers are contacted via e-mail by individuals claiming to represent a local school. The sender addresses appear to be from the educational institution but lack the .edu extension. Some of the bogus e-mail addresses used are as follows:

■ purchasing(at)ucdavised(dot)us
■ purchasingdept(at)unlav-edu(dot)org
■ purchase(at)uchicagoed(dot)us[15]

The intent of those using the e-mail spoofing angle of school impersonation fraud is to conduct the same type of unauthorized purchases from unsuspecting retailers. The items purchased and shipping methods remain the same. The only difference is in the method of contact.

In an effort to prevent school impersonation fraud, the following prevention information needs to be understood:

- Retailers receiving any merchandise orders by e-mail or through their call centers need to contact the school or school district before shipping the product. The actual order needs to be verified as legitimate and authorized by the school or school district.

  Once the unauthorized merchandise is shipped as part of a school impersonation fraud, the retailer is the one who suffers the loss.
- Retailers need to develop an understanding that all educational e-mail addresses have the extension .edu. Many of the fraudulent variations used contain a bogus extension as previously discussed and do not have the .edu extension.
- Retailers need to ensure the school address provided is the actual location of the school. The retailer can visit the school district's website. School district websites will provide the actual mailing addresses of all of the schools in their district.

6.7 Sports Memorabilia Fraud

Many citizens across the country have a hobby of collecting various items. Young girls collect dolls, teenage boys are into sports trading cards, and many sport enthusiasts like to obtain items signed by professional athletes. Individuals who make a hobby of collecting sports memorabilia have many options available for purchasing these items:

- Signed items can be purchased through sports memorabilia websites.
- Various sports memorabilia organizations host autograph-signing events. Typically, individuals seeking autographs from athletes are charged an event entry fee and additional fees for individual signed items. The autograph fees vary per the item signed and the athlete doing the signing.
- Various charity operations, sports venues, local golf tournaments, and so on offer autographed sports memorabilia in silent auctions. A majority of these events rely on donated items, and the money collected through sales is typically given to a charitable cause.
- Collectors can purchase signed sports memorabilia through various sporting and trading card retail locations across the country.
- Collectors can purchase signed sports memorabilia through various sports bars across the country.

- Collectors can purchase signed sports memorabilia through Internet auction websites.
- Collectors can purchase signed sports memorabilia through classified advertisement websites.
- Collectors can purchase sports memorabilia through flea markets and yard sales.

Based on the venue the collector chooses to make a sports memorabilia purchase, the risk of purchasing a fraudulent item varies. Venues that offer the collector the opportunity to approach the athlete and have the item signed in their presence provide a low risk of fraud. At the other end of the spectrum, items purchased through a classified advertisement website or a neighborhood flea market have a high risk of fraud.

In an effort to avoid becoming a victim of sports memorabilia fraud, collectors need to develop detailed understanding of the tools and methods used to provide authentic-looking signed sports memorabilia:

- Athlete signatures are going to vary based on the item signed and the situation surrounding when the material was signed. With this stated, a person's signature is not going to be exactly the same each and every time. Individuals looking to purchase items autographed by their favorite athlete need to be aware of the autopen.

  The autopen is a machine that traces an original signature; at the same time, a separate arm with a pen places the traced signature on another document or item. Typically, signatures signed with an autopen have an abrupt start and stop, which are caused by the writing instrument being placed on the item at the beginning of the signature and stopping again at the end of the signature. A normal signature begins without a pressure mark and trails off at the end.

  Multiple signatures created using an autopen will be exactly the same. A normal individual's signature will closely resemble their other signatures, but the signatures will not be exactly the same.[16]
- Signatures can be easily forged either by tracing a legitimate signature or by using a carbon copy of an original signature.
- Signatures can also be an outright forgery of an original.
- Athletes have also used administrative staff or clubhouse personnel to sign items. These are individuals who can sign items with a signature that closely matches the original signature of the athlete.[17]
- Preprinted signatures are also used to create the image of an original. A preprinted signature is a copy or reproduction of an original signature.[18]
- Certificates of originality are provided to the buyer of many signed collectables. Individuals who want to make a purchase of signed sports memorabilia need to understand these documents can also be fraudulent. Quality printers can make any document appear legitimate.[19]

Industry experts use several tools to determine the legitimacy of signed items. Handwriting experts also use several tools to determine the authenticity of a signature. The purpose of this section is not to detail the many tools available to determine or possibly determine a signature's legitimacy. This analysis is best left to the experts. The purpose of this section is to inform the reader that sports memorabilia fraud exists.

Individuals working to commit sports memorabilia fraud hope to make a financial gain by selling items they claim to be legitimate. Individuals who want to purchase signed sports memorabilia operate on the hope their money is used to buy a legitimate item. To ensure the legitimacy of signed sports memorabilia, items should be purchased from a reputable organization or at events where the athlete signs the item in their presence. The purchase of legitimately signed sports memorabilia is ultimately based on the source. Buyers need to ask themselves: "Can this source be trusted?"

6.8 Access Device Fraud

All fifty states have laws prohibiting the unauthorized use of access devices. Based on the state, the actual elements of access device fraud vary. No matter the entity, access devices include

- Credit cards
- Debit cards
- ATM cards
- Gift cards
- Reloadable gift/credit cards
- Any type of card containing an account number

Many of the fraudulent activities discussed throughout this book are conducted with some type of access device. In an effort to provide information on what is access device fraud and the related elements, a discussion is provided and is taken from federal statutes.

According to federal law (18 US Code § 1029), the following relate to fraud and related activity in connection with access devices:

(1) The term "access device" means any card, plate, code, account number; electronic serial number, mobile identification number, personal identification number, or other telecommunications service, equipment, or instrument identifier, or other means of account access that can be used, alone or in conjunction with another access device, to obtain money, goods, services, or any other thing of value, or that can be used to initiate a transfer of funds (other than a transfer originated solely by paper instrument);

(2) the term "counterfeit access device" means any access device that is counterfeit, fictitious, altered, or forged, or an identifiable component of an access device or a counterfeit access device;

(3) the term "unauthorized access device" means any access device that is lost, stolen, expired, revoked, canceled, or obtained with intent to defraud.

According to federal law (18 US Code § 1029), concerning fraud and related activity in connection with access devices, the elements of access fraud are as follows:

(a) Whoever—

(1) knowingly and with intent to defraud produces, uses, or traffics in one or more counterfeit access devices;

(2) knowingly and with intent to defraud traffics in or uses one or more unauthorized access devices during any one-year period, and by such conduct obtains anything of value aggregating $1,000 or more during that period;

(3) knowingly and with intent to defraud possesses fifteen or more devices which are counterfeit or unauthorized access devices;

(4) knowingly, and with intent to defraud, produces, traffics in, has control or custody of, or possesses device-making equipment;

(5) knowingly and with intent to defraud uses, produces, traffics in, has control or custody of, or possesses a telecommunications instrument that has been modified or altered to obtain unauthorized use of telecommunications services; or

(6) knowingly and with intent to defraud uses, produces, traffics in, has control or custody of, or possesses—

(A) a scanning receiver; or

(B) hardware or software used for altering or modifying telecommunications instruments to obtain unauthorized access to telecommunications services, (5) 1 knowingly and with intent to defraud effects transactions, with 1 or more access devices issued to another person or persons, to receive payment or any other thing of value during any 1-year period the aggregate value of which is equal to or greater than $1,000

Notes

1. Finklea, K. M., Organized retail crime. http://fas.org/sgp/crs/misc/R41118.pdf (accessed August 30, 2104).
2. Handheld skimming devices are typically a few inches long and about an inch wide and an inch high. The devices are used to swipe the magnetic stripe of the credit card to capture the account information. Once this information is obtained, it can be used to make unauthorized purchases or transfers to counterfeit credit cards.
3. Rittman, T., Nine tactics consumers use to make fraudulent returns. http://www.chainstoreage.com/article/nine-tactics-consumers-use-make-fraudulent-returns (accessed August 22, 2014).
4. Ibid.
5. Timberlake, C., Don't even think about returning that dress. http://www.businessweek.com/articles/2013-09-26/return-fraud-clothing-and-electronics-retailers-fight-back (accessed August 21, 2014).
6. Montaldo, D., What is coupon fraud? http://couponing.about.com/od/groceryzone/a/couponscams.htm (accessed August 29, 2014).
7. Bosner, K., Fenlon, W., How RFID works. http://electronics.howstuffworks.com/gadgets/high-tech-gadgets/rfid.htm (accessed August 30, 2014).
8. Internet Crime Complaint Centers (IC3), Scam alerts, July 18, 2013. http://www.ic3.gov/media/2013/130718-1.aspx (accessed August 31, 2014).
9. Gregory, J., Four ways to prevent gift card theft. http://www.entrepreneur.com/article/229526 (accessed August 31, 2014).
10. Ibid.
11. Scambusters.org, New gift card scams: eight tips to protect yourself. http://www.scambusters.org/giftcard.html (accessed August 30, 2014).
12. From a security perspective, social engineering is the basic art of getting unsuspecting individuals to provide confidential information. The information gathered is typically used for fraudulent purposes and is usually part of a complex scam. http://resources.infosecinstitute.com/phishing-and-social-engineering-techniques/
13. Internet Crime Complaint Center (IC3), African cyber criminal enterprise members using "school impersonation" scheme to defraud retailers. http://www.ic3.gov/media/2014/140904.aspx (accessed January 13, 2015).
14. Ibid.
15. Ibid.
16. Spectrum Sports Collectibles, Sports autograph fraud, fakes, forgery and types of fake autographs. http://www.spectrumsportscollectibles.com/fake-sports-autographs.html (accessed September 10, 2014).
17. Ibid.
18. Ibid.
19. Ibid.

Chapter 7

Frauds Targeting the Individual

7.1 Introduction

Every day, people visit the local convenience store, grocery store, gas station, and other places to purchase lottery tickets. With the scratch-off tickets, the odds of winning a few dollars are normally around even money. A person spending a dollar on a scratch-off lottery ticket has about a 50% chance of winning their investment back. With the scratch-off lottery tickets, the odds of winning the larger cash prizes decreases because there are fewer winning tickets available for sale. Normally, only one or two grand prize tickets are printed for sale, and the odds against winning increase.

People also have the option of purchasing random draw lottery tickets; the odds of winning the grand prize decrease as the number of balls to be drawn increases. The larger multistate lotteries have even higher odds against winning. These lotteries require a person to select five numbers that have to be drawn from a pool of eighty balls. The winner also has to pick one number that has to be drawn from a pool of around forty balls. This places the odds of winning the million-dollar prize at over 100 million to 1 or greater.

No matter the odds placed on the various options available for a person purchasing lottery tickets, individuals line up every day to take the risk. The risk taken is based on the potential for winning large amounts of money. A common theme spoken by these risk takers is: "Well, someone has to win."

Also driving the desire for a person to take a risk on reaching an almost-impossible goal is how many of these games are marketed. Lottery officials spend around 10% of money collected through ticket sales on advertising. The advertising provides a daily barrage of information on current jackpot amounts to entice people to make a purchase. The lottery advertising reaches people daily through television or radio commercials, daily newspapers, online pop-up advertisements, and billboards lining the streets and highways. It is hard for a person to go through a day without knowing the payouts for the current lotteries operating in their state.

When making an analysis of why people purchase lottery tickets, the thinking comes down to the chance of winning a large amount of cash for a low investment. When comparing the thinking of a typical person making a lottery ticket purchase and an individual committing a fraud against the individual, it comes down to the payout. The person purchasing a lottery ticket has a dream of obtaining a large amount of money. The person committing a fraud against the individual also has a dream of obtaining a large amount of money. The person committing the fraud can also deliver the average lottery participant the promise of a chance to obtain a large amount of money.

Lottery officials can reach a large audience of potential players as a result of money collected through ticket sales and allocated to the marketing budget. People looking to defraud the average citizen do not have the ability to advertise on most media outlets used by the lottery officials. A person will not receive information on an individual fraud scheme by watching television or listening to the radio. This person will receive information through unsolicited e-mails, social media notifications, and the mail.

The marketing of individual fraud schemes is directed as a personal opportunity. For some, it is more appealing to receive a personally directed e-mail presenting a financial opportunity versus a chance to win the lottery grand prize with the opportunity shared with everybody. Lottery participants can also reflect over the years and realize the amount of money spent on lottery tickets—thousands of dollars spent with little or no return on investment. They can also look back on their individual motivation for continuous purchasing of lottery tickets as rationalizing that someone has to win. When looking at the potential of a financial opportunity personally directed to them, the thinking is that "I can win."

It is unsure if people who purchase lottery tickets are also past victims of fraud or if a person responding to an e-mail offering a money-making opportunity purchases lottery tickets. Looking at the odds of winning a large lottery prize, a person can wonder why the investment should be made. It can also be questioned regarding why a person becomes involved in an endeavor that leads to fraud and a financial loss. With the lottery, a person should have an understanding of their odds of winning prior to making the ticket purchase. With a fraudulent opportunity, the offer can become so appealing, rational thought is discarded.

Every person has a rational explanation regarding why they choose to act in a certain manner or participate in a financial opportunity. With frauds targeting the individual, participation is driven from the offer received. No matter the method of delivery, the goal is to develop an immediate level of interest. The information provided to raise the initial interest level varies according to the fraud scheme, but the goals are the same.

Many people who become victim to an individual fraud also unwittingly seek the opportunity to participate. Based on the individual need, a person can look for information through an Internet search engine or query an online classified advertisement website. Certain key words that are entered during the online search for a seemingly innocent request can lead to contact with people who want to commit fraud. Requests for information on the Internet can be like drops of blood in the water: The sharks begin to circle.

Whether the process begins by responding to an unsolicited e-mail or answering an advertisement or an information request sent via the Internet, the wheels of fraud are set in motion.

7.2 Fake Check Schemes[1]

No matter how popular the use of online shopping, online bill paying, ATMs (automatic teller machines), debit card transactions, and so on, physical paper checks remain a part of society.

- Small businesses prefer to pay their employees with a weekly check versus using a payroll-processing firm.
- Some people are not comfortable conducting financial transactions online.
- Some elderly individuals do not develop an understanding of modern technology (i.e., computers and the Internet).
- Stories of computer hacking are causing people to revert to conducting financial transactions using paper checks.

The daily use of the still-popular paper check is not limited to paying employees or making retail purchases. Increasing numbers of people are receiving fake or counterfeit checks as part of what are referred to as fake check schemes. The reasons are varied why a person receives a fake or counterfeit check. With fake check schemes, the recipient receives the item as a part of what appears to be a legitimate business transaction. The check recipient is requested to deposit the check into his or her personal account. Once the check is deposited, the recipient is asked to send a portion of the check amount to the sender. Many of these requests might appear suspicious to some, but successful fake check schemes exist. Some are discussed next.

7.2.1 Foreign Lotteries

Many people enter foreign lotteries because they received an unsolicited e-mail from what appears to be a legitimate operation. People will also search the Internet in a desire to play foreign lotteries that are advertised as a safe and secure alternative to domestic lotteries. The promise of large prizes with better odds for the contestant provides an attraction. No matter how a person becomes involved with a foreign lottery operation, the results are similar.

A person is informed that he or she has won a foreign lottery with an appealing prize amount. Along with the prize notification, the targeted individual is mailed a check as a small portion of the total prize. The check is sent with instructions for the recipient to keep a portion of the check as part of the prize and the remaining amount is to cover the associated fees.

Unfortunately, the recipient is informed the associated fees were calculated incorrectly, and the check was issued for a dollar amount that is larger than the prize percentage provided and the fees. Typically, the check amount is made for a dollar amount that is thousands of dollars over the prize percentage and fee.

To correct the error and ensure future payment of the total prize, the lottery winner is instructed to deposit the cashier's check in their personal bank account. Once deposited, the winner is instructed to send via wire transfer the portion of the check that is greater than the amount of the prize percentage and fees promised. The recipient is provided with the wire recipient's name and location and a sense of urgency to complete the wire transfer.

The check deposited is counterfeit and charged back by the bank against the account holder. No additional lottery winnings will ever be received, and the individual caught in the fake check scheme is out the money wired.

7.2.2 Overpayments

Selling personal items through classified ads in the newspaper or an online classified ad website is a popular method of making money. Another selling venue is online auction sites where a seller can actually sell an item for more than the initial listed amount, and sometimes potential buyers will make a purchase bid that is greater than the item listed for sale. No matter the chosen method used to sell unwanted property or other items of value, the potential for fraud exists.

Whether a person is selling an old car, furniture, electronics, or rare breed puppies, initial contact with a sense of urgency is made by the potential buyer. No matter the item for sale, the potential buyer shows an interest in making the purchase immediately. The only problem presented with completing the sale is that the potential buyer is from overseas and has yet to open a US bank account. Luckily, the potential buyer is in possession of a third-party check[2] or paycheck from a former employer.

The check the buyer requests to use to purchase the advertised item is for an amount larger than the asking price. To entice the seller to agree to take a third-party check, an offer is made to pay more than the asking price of the item being sold. Once an agreement is made, the third-party check is proffered for payment.

Because the amount of the check is greater than the total amount paid for the item purchased, this leaves an overpayment. The seller is asked to make a wire transfer of the overpayment amount. The buyer provides a name and location for the wire transfer. Unknown to the seller at the time of making the wire transfer, the third-party check is fake or counterfeit. Once the bogus check is returned, the seller takes a loss on the item sold as well as the amount wired for the check overpayment.

7.2.3 Home Employment

Work-at-home opportunities are advertised in local newspapers, on Internet job boards, on bandit signs (Figure 7.1),[3] and on various community and college bulletin boards. Prospective candidates are also recruited via unsolicited e-mails. The job opportunities advertised contain information on positions that require no experience but offer high pay. These advertisements will quickly gain the attention of someone who wants to make money working from home. The requirement for little to no experience and the offer of high pay provide an advantage of those committing the fraud. A typical person answering a job advertisement clouds his thinking by focusing on the minimal experience requirements and enticing pay offer rather than the potential risk.

Figure 7.1 Bandit sign.

The only method available to contact the prospective employer is via a phone number provided in the advertisement or listed in the e-mail. Typically, all communication is conducted between the perceived employer and the applicant/future employee via the telephone or e-mail.

Once contact is made, the applicant learns the facts and requirements of the position, such as those that follow:

- The hiring firm is an international corporation.
- The international firm is beginning business operations in the United States.
- The job offers the applicant an opportunity to become one of the first US employees in a business with huge growth and expansion potential.
- The international organization has not opened any bank accounts in the United States.
- The functions of the jobs offered vary, but requests are made to have the new associate process business-related checks until bank accounts can be opened in the United States.
- Because the international organization has yet to open bank accounts in the United States, the new employee is asked to deposit checks through his or her personal account.
- With each check sent to the new employee, the employee is requested to deposit the item and deduct his or her fee from the check amount.
- The remaining balance of the check, minus the employee's fee, is to be sent via a money transfer to the main office.

In addition, the new employees are asked to assist their new company in processing deposit items prior to any actual work being performed. The new associates are led to believe they are assisting their new employer and that their effort will not be overlooked as the company grows. Unfortunately, all checks mailed to the employee are fake and will eventually be returned to the bank where they were deposited.

Once returned to the depositing bank, the check amounts are charged back against the new employee's account. The individual or new employee is out all of the money wired to the perceived international office.

Fake check schemes, as part of work-at-home offers, are not limited to the processing of checks for an international employer. Individuals are also recruited for work-at-home positions that require check processing for domestic employers.

A popular work-at-home scam involves recruiting candidates via unsolicited e-mails. The e-mailed job opportunity gains the recipient's attention by offering a position that requires no experience for simply processing rent payments for landlords. The job description lists the only duties as receiving rent payments from the tenants, keeping track of payments received/processed, and sending the payments to the landlord. The following is a sample unsolicited e-mail pertaining to a work-at-home scam:

From: Cole Man <contact.coleman@remax.com>

To: Recipients <contact.coleman@remax.com>

Subject: Re: Work with us!

Hello,

We are seeking qualified individuals for the position of data entry and processing of rent from tenants. Previous experience is not required.

Duties

1. Sending rent to Landlords,
2. Receiving rent from customers
3. Processing rent, remittance and record keeping.

Salary: 10% from each received rent payment processed on the same day you receive it Interested candidate should provide full name, address, city, state, zip code and phone numbers for full details about this position.

Regards,
Michael Coleman
colemanrealestate1@gmail.com

On the surface, the opportunity outlined could appear as a simple and profitable money-making endeavor. The e-mail recipients fail to realize the underlying job requirements and financial costs.

Once the individual is hired, he or she is asked to process a transaction that will eventually become part of the individual's everyday job duties:

■ New employees are mailed a check to be processed.
■ The employee is asked to deposit the check into his or her personal bank account.
■ After depositing the perceived rent check, the new employee is told to keep 10% of the check amount and wire transfer the balance to the landlord.
■ Unfortunately, the check received and deposited is counterfeit.

What makes this scam successful is that the new employees are led to believe the check and deposit activity will be part of their daily job duties. For each rent payment processed, they are to receive 10%.

For the individuals committing this rent payment scam, the goal is to recruit as many new hires as possible. Knowing the scam will be discovered a few days after the perceived rent payment is deposited, the activity of each new hire is limited.

Victims of this work-at-home scam are out 90% of the check amount they deposited into their personal bank account and wire transferred to an individual they believe is a legitimate landlord.

7.2.4 Prevention Measures

The fake check schemes previously discussed are some of the most popular variations that convince a person to deposit bogus checks into their personal bank account. Additional variations exist and are based on the creativity of the individual initiating the scam. The basic premise is to have a person believe the opportunity presented is legitimate. The goal is also to cloud the thinking of the new employee by offering a better-than-expected financial return and providing fake or counterfeit checks that appear to be legitimate.

Prevention measures and warning signs against falling victim to fake check schemes are as follows:

- Never deposit checks into a personal bank account at the request of a new employer.
- Never accept a third-party check as payment for anything.
- Question why it is necessary to make an immediate withdrawal of the deposited check's amount.
- Opening a bank account in the United States is a simple process that takes about an hour. (Many victims are drawn into the scheme by using their personal bank account because their potential new employer claims to be having trouble with the time required to open an account in the United States.)

7.3 Mortgage Fraud

The idea of home ownership is part of the American dream. Most people would rather make a monthly payment that adds equity to an investment and not have their money go toward a rent payment. When it comes to purchasing a home, the buyer has to select a mortgage company and negotiate the interest rate and length of the loan. Mortgage periods can range from fifteen to thirty years, and the interest rate is usually based on the credit history of the person or persons seeking the loan. Once the home purchase process is complete, the new residents begin making their monthly mortgage payment. During the initial years of making mortgage payments, a larger portion of the payment goes toward the interest generated on the loan. As the years go by, the percentage of the monthly mortgage payment directed toward the loan interest decreases. With less of the mortgage payment amount going toward paying down the interest on the loan, more money is paid against the actual loan amount (principal). The more money going toward and lowering the loan amount, the greater the amount of equity the homeowner develops.

Home equity is important for the homeowner if the owner decides to sell the house to upgrade or to refinance the loan to lower the monthly mortgage payments. Also, the greater the amount of equity a person has in a house, the better protected the person is in a housing market downturn. When it comes to the equity a person has built in their home, it is vital an individual works to protect this investment.

The goal of people looking to commit mortgage fraud is to steal the equity amount a person has built up in their home by having the legitimate homeowner unknowingly transfer ownership. Other mortgage frauds have the homeowners pay for services they never receive or make monthly payments their mortgage company never receives.

7.3.1 Ownership Transfer

Television and radio advertisements are rife with companies claiming they can help homeowners lower their monthly mortgage payment. Within the home mortgage refinance community, many of these companies offer a legitimate service. There are also companies that advertise refinancing services through unsolicited e-mails, social media notifications, and bandit signs. The main difference between the legitimate refinancing agencies and those looking to commit mortgage fraud is the level of attraction generated. By offering a homeowner the ability to obtain a substantially lower interest rate than one offered by a traditional refinancing company, the lending process has taken a turn down the path of least resistance.

The legitimate mortgage companies offer to refinance a home loan based on current market conditions of lending rates and the bond market. The interest rates offered to those looking to refinance with the legitimate lending organizations are the current market condition rates.

In an effort to attract the attention of homeowners considering refinancing, special interest rates are offered. These special interest rates are below what the homeowner can receive from a legitimate lending institution. As the case with many frauds, the purpose is to cloud the thought process of the targeted individual. The goal is to get the target to think of the end game results and not the process. A person refinancing a home with a legitimate organization will most likely not come across anything suspicious in the paperwork process. With many mortgage fraud schemes, the paperwork process varies from the norm, but the financial opportunities are greater. Those committing mortgage fraud have their targets focus on the end game financial benefit and not the person lurking behind the curtain.

Within the packet of papers to sign in an ownership transfer mortgage fraud, one of the documents is a deed. Once the deed document is signed, the ownership of the property is transferred to the individuals committing the fraud or to a related company.[4] No matter who the home ownership is transferred to, all equity in the house is lost.

With a legitimate lending agency, all refinancing documents are discussed in detail and explained to the homeowner prior to signing. To have all the documents signed in an ownership transfer mortgage fraud, the homeowner is told whatever the homeowner needs to hear to obtain the much lower interest rate. Forms are traditionally rushed through the process with little explanation to those signing the documents.

Any homeowner looking to refinance should research the lending agency, including verification from the Better Business Bureau. Most legitimate lending organizations do not solicit customers via random e-mails on social media sites or bandit signs.

7.3.2 Loan Modification Fraud

With many frauds, the customer contact methods differ from those of organizations offering a legitimate service. As previously mentioned, legitimate home lending and mortgage companies will advertise their services through mainstream venues. Individuals looking to refinance or modify their existing home loan could hear the name of a mortgage company on the television and research the organization through its website. With a person looking to conduct any type of home refinancing procedure, the focus has to be on identifying organizations and performing their own research, such as by verifying the operating history of the loan company, checking valid references, and contacting the Better Business Bureau for any complaints against the finance organization.

Individuals looking to commit loan modification fraud will contact potential victims through unsolicited e-mails, social media websites, and outdoor advertising. The main focus of these advertising venues is to attract people by offering a simple modification process and guaranteeing success with lower-than-average interest rates. The goal is to attract attention and gain a level of trust by distracting with the old shell game: pay attention to the simplicity and cost-saving promises and do not be concerned about the legitimacy of the company offering loan modification services.

A benefit to individuals looking to commit loan modification fraud is the existence of homeowners facing foreclosure. A homeowner placed in a somewhat panic-filled situation of the loss of the family residence can be attracted to false promises that offer hope. The offer of a guaranteed satisfactory resolution to their home loan dilemma can provide a tipping point in what should be an otherwise-rational decision.

Once a homeowner agrees to conduct business with what they believe to be a legitimate finance organization, the promises and requests made should act as warning signs:

- The requirement for an up-front fee that can guarantee the loan modification. The fees vary between $1,000 and $5,000.
- The guarantee to stop the foreclosure process.

- The guarantee the loan can be modified or successfully refinanced.
- The promise of a 100% money back guarantee.[5]

Legitimate home loan financial organizations do not require an up-front fee to guarantee successful refinancing or mortgage modification. Any person looking to refinance or modify an existing home mortgage needs to understand the warnings signs and do their own due diligence. A legitimate home financing company will not seek customers via unsolicited e-mails or through social media websites.

7.3.3 Your Home Mortgage Has Been Sold

Mortgages on private homes are sold between companies as a normal course of business. The homeowner receives a letter from their old mortgage company informing the homeowner of the sale. In addition, the company purchasing the mortgage will also send a letter to the homeowner informing the owner of the transaction. In a mortgage scam, the homeowner will only receive a letter from the company claiming to be the new owner of the home mortgage.

In the letter, the homeowner is informed of the sale or transfer of the home mortgage and information on where to send future payments. If the individual receiving the home mortgage transfer letter believes it is legitimate, the individual will begin sending monthly payments to the bogus company. Unfortunately, their legitimate mortgage holder believes the homeowner has stopped making monthly payments.

Typically, the homeowner who falls victim to the scam is not alerted to the victimization until receiving actual notification of default from the legitimate mortgage holder.

Federal law requires mortgage companies to send hello and good-bye letters in the event of a loan transfer. The company selling the mortgage has to inform the homeowner of the sale. The company purchasing the mortgage also has to inform the homeowner of the purchase.[6]

7.3.4 Lease Buyback Agreements

Homeowners facing possible foreclosure, financial issues, or the possibility of missing a mortgage payment could search the Internet for a remedy. People committing mortgage fraud are aware that financial issues in the home continually arise and are ready with the cure. Homeowners who look for financial relief through an Internet search fulfill the act of desperation requirement necessary to cloud the thought process and lay the foundation for fraud.

Mortgage fraud becomes successful by offering the homeowner a means to keep their home. A popular method used on homeowners facing financial problems is a lease buyback agreement. The homeowner is presented with a document that appears legitimate and makes the promises or affects the homeowner as follows:

- The homeowner is convinced of the need to sign a quitclaim deed to temporarily transfer ownership of the home to avoid foreclosure.
- By signing the quitclaim deed, the homeowner can continue to live in the house and eventually repurchase the home.
- The signing of the quitclaim deed works to stop the foreclosure process.
- It is necessary to temporarily transfer ownership, which allows the homeowner to stay in the home by paying monthly rent.
- The homeowner is attracted by the offer of paying rent that is lower than the current monthly mortgage payment.

The unfortunate result of homeowners signing a quitclaim deed is that they actually transfer the rights to the property. Based on those committing the mortgage fraud and the amount of equity in the home, the end results vary:

- The new property owner could choose to sell the house, forcing the victim to move out of the home.
- The individuals committing the fraud can let the homeowner pay rent until the bank forecloses on the property.[7]

With either method, the homeowner loses whatever equity they had in their family home. A homeowner should never sign a quitclaim deed in an effort to resolve mortgage payment issues.

7.4 Scare Tactic Frauds

CASE STUDY 7.1

Vicki Victim was spending a relaxing Sunday afternoon watching television. Suddenly, her cell phone rang, and the individual on the other end of the call was a person claiming to be from the local sheriff's office. Ms. Victim was informed by the sheriff's deputy that he was in possession of an arrest warrant. The warrant was issued in the name of Vicki Victim, and she was being charged with failure to appear for jury duty. To avoid the deputy serving the arrest warrant and taking Ms. Victim to jail, she was informed she could pay the fine. The deputy told Ms. Victim that the fine for failure to appear for jury duty was $500 and had to be paid by the end of the day. If no payment was received by the Sheriff's Department, she would be arrested.

Panicked, Ms. Victim asked the deputy how she could pay the $500 fine. Ms. Victim was instructed to purchase a prepaid card in the amount of $500. After purchasing the prepaid card in the amount requested, she was instructed to call the deputy back at the phone number provided. Ms. Victim made the card purchase and contacted the deputy. She was instructed to provide the code numbers on the back of the prepaid card to the deputy.

A common fraud targeting individuals involves using an authority figure or institution to have the unsuspecting victim pay a fine or fee. The threat of arrest by a member of the local Sheriff's Department can persuade some that their freedom could be in danger. Being provided the option of paying a fine versus being arrested can spell relief to a person believing they could have overlooked a jury summons.

If a target victim believes there is a pending arrest, they can easily be convinced their troubles can be dismissed by paying the fine amount requested. By purchasing a prepaid card and providing the code numbers to a third party, the dollar amount of the card can be spent by the person committing the fraud.

To make these types of scare tactic frauds successful, the target victim has to be provided with a story that could actually apply to them. Many people are not 100% accountable for all the mail they receive on a daily basis and could possibly overlook a jury notification.

Another popular scare tactic is to contact a potential victim and claim to be a representative of the Internal Revenue Service (IRS). Most tax-paying citizens have an understanding of the power of the IRS and fear their tax accountability being called into question. Individuals using the IRS as part of their scare tactic fraud have added a fraction of believability to their claim and eventual monetary demand. Victims contacted by a person claiming to be from the IRS are normally informed of the following:

- The individual on the other end of the conversation is an agent of the IRS.
- Their previous federal income tax returns have been audited.
- Discrepancies in their federal tax filings have been discovered.
- The discovery of the federal tax filing discrepancies has resulted in a large fine.
- If immediate action is not taken on the part of the victim to pay the federal IRS fine, he will be arrested.
- The victim will be arrested at his home and placed in handcuffs in front of his neighbors.

The success of the IRS-based scare tactic fraud relies on keeping the conversation with the victim about the power of the federal government and the IRS, the constant threats of immediate arrest, and public embarrassment in front of their neighbors. The individuals conducting the scare tactic fraud also provide an area of relief to the target victim by offering the opportunity to pay the fine.

The telephone conversation with the target victim all revolves around the topic of immediacy:

- You will be arrested today.
- You will be placed in handcuffs today.
- You have to pay the fine today.

As with the story of Ms. Vicki Victim, the fine payment methods are the same. The target victim is instructed to purchase a prepaid card; with the IRS threats, the dollar amount to place on the card is normally around $4,000 to $5,000. To satisfy the payment of the fine, the victim is asked to provide the card code numbers to the caller.

To avoid becoming a victim of scare tactic frauds, the awareness and prevention methods are as follows:

- Initial tax issue notification from the IRS will normally come via a mailed letter. The same is true if the taxpayer is being audited.
- The IRS allows the taxpayer to provide documentation in their favor if there is a question of tax filing or payment issues.
- Arrest warrants are not served over the phone.
- A criminal fine comes as the result of a hearing or trial.
- Verify the person calling actually works for the law enforcement office or government agency. Use directory assistance to obtain the phone number of the office or agency you are calling. The individuals committing the fraud will provide a phone number to a drop house where there are people waiting to verify the legitimacy of the caller.
- Once the codes on a prepaid card or gift card are provided to a third party, these individuals can drain the monetary amount of the card.

Individuals seeking to use scare tactics to gain the attention of the targeted individual are also using e-mail notifications. These e-mail notifications can be an attempt to have the target pay a monetary amount to avoid the trouble identified in the body of the message and subject line. These can also be part of phishing attempts (Chapter 11) in an attempt to have the targeted individual open attached files. By opening the attached files, the recipient could be opening their personal or business computer to the unauthorized installation of malware and spyware.

No matter the intent of the individual sending a scare tactic e-mail, recipients need to employ the same prevention measures as previously discussed and those in Chapter 11 for preventing becoming a victim of phishing attempts. The following is an actual scare tactic e-mail sent with the goal of having the recipient believe they were suspected of a crime:

From: Court Agent <custsupport445@capeannlawyers.com>

Date: Wednesday, August 27, 2014 9:47 AM

To: jyoungblood5@cox.net

Subject: Notice of court attendance

Attachments: PlaintNote_5584_copy.zip (76.5 KB)

As a defendant you have been scheduled to attend the hearing in the Court of Oceanside.

Hearing date: 14 September 2014
Hearing time: 11:00 a.m.
Hearing subject: illegal use of software

Prior to the court thoroughly study the plaint note in the attachment to this mail.

Sincerely,
Court agent,
Abigail Mason
Open Attachment PlaintNote_5584_copy.zip

The goal of the person sending this scare tactic e-mail is to have the recipient open the zip file attachment. Keeping in line with many unsolicited advance fee letters sent through e-mail, the recipient should be able to notice the unprofessionalism of the wording. At no time should the recipient of any scare tactic e-mail open the provided attachment; also, court appearance notices are not delivered via electronic communication.

7.5 High-Dollar Item Street Sale Fraud

A large portion of fraudulent activity geared toward an individual is based on someone having a lucky day or being offered a unique opportunity. A person offered the opportunity to purchase high-dollar/brand-name speakers and other electronic equipment can fall into the unique opportunity category. Across the country and for many years, people have attempted to sell substandard stereo equipment while operating out of a vehicle.[8] The particulars of this type of fraud are as follows:

- Victims are typically walking to their vehicle in the parking lot of a bank or retail location.
- The individuals attempting to sell the substandard equipment are normally driving a large van with no back windows.
- The pitch is made to the targeted individual for an opportunity to purchase high-quality speakers at half the price or lower.
- The rationale provided for offering a low sales price for high-dollar stereo equipment is an overpurchase. The target is informed the salespeople are on their way back to the warehouse and do not want to return with excess product. Adding to the need to sell the product at a discount, the target is informed the warehouse boss will be mad, and the salespeople could be fired for returning with excess product.

- Once the attention of the target is obtained, the target is shown brochures of the merchandise they are led to believe they have the opportunity to purchase.
- The target is also shown the boxes in the back of the van, marked with a brand name that produces high-quality stereo equipment.

The goal of the individuals selling the substandard stereo equipment is to complete the sale without having to show the actual product. Individuals purchasing stereo equipment in the parking lot from the back of a van have received substandard equipment or speaker shells that have no internal parts.

To avoid becoming a victim of this type of fraud, the warning signs are as follows:

- Being approached in a parking lot and offered the opportunity to purchase high-quality stereo equipment.
- Being offered the purchase opportunity at a great discount.
- The use of high-pressure tactics that lead the target to believe the salespeople will be fired for returning to the warehouse with excess product.
- A need for cash-only sales.
- A reluctance to show the actual product offered for purchase while showing flashy brochures to the target.
- Not being provided with contact numbers of the salespeople or a phone number for the home office.

7.6 Debit Card Fraud

A person can use a credit or debit card in similar fashions. When using a credit card, card owners have to sign their name to complete the transaction. With a debit card, card owners can either enter a four-digit personal identification number (PIN) or treat it like a credit card transaction and sign their name. Expenses generated from credit card transactions appear on a monthly account statement. The credit card holder can choose to pay the amount owed in full or make a smaller minimum payment. When conducting a transaction with a debit card, the amount of the purchase is deducted directly from the account holder's checking account.

If a consumer discovers a fraudulent charge on a credit card statement, the consumer can dispute the charge. As a result of the fraudulent credit card transaction, the account holder is not responsible to make a payment toward the purchase amount.

Because debit card transactions are directly deducted from the account holder's checking account, the individuals do not have the luxury of waiting until the end of the month to dispute any unauthorized charges. Although the debit card account holder is not responsible for the fraudulent transaction amount, the unauthorized deduction of money from a personal checking account can cause immediate financial hardships.

Unauthorized deductions from a personal checking account can cause previously written checks to bounce or authorized monthly debit charges to be denied. Many consumers have their utility bills and monthly mortgage payments debited directly from their checking account. If the account balance is unexpectedly depleted, these authorized payments can be rejected by their bank. The same holds true for small business owners who as a normal course of business use a debit card that is attached to their main income depository account. Unauthorized debits from a small business account can cause weekly payroll checks to bounce.

7.6.1 Skimming

A popular method used by individuals committing debit card fraud is to use what is called a skimming device. Skimming devices are attached to ATMs and pay-at-the-pump terminals at gas stations. The use of skimmers is not limited to the ATM or gas pump; they can be placed on any machine where a debit card is inserted to conduct a transaction. The devices are created to look like part of the machine that accepts debit card transactions. The devices are placed over the slot where the debit card is inserted. Once the debit card is inserted into the skimming device, the account data are compromised. All account holder data is contained on the black magnetic stripe on the back of the debit card.

Along with placing a skimmer device on any machine that accepts debit card transactions, a small PIN camera will also be used to capture the PIN. Once the PIN and account holder information is captured by the skimming device, it can be used to make all types of unauthorized purchases. The account information can be transferred to the magnetic stripe of a counterfeit debit card and used for ATM withdrawals and in-store purchases. The debit card information can also be used to make unauthorized purchases on the Internet.

Individuals committing debit card fraud by using skimming devices typically prefer to target ATMs not connected physically to the financial institution. These are remote ATMs in parking lots or other locations that are not constantly monitored during the normal course of business. The same theory holds true for the rationale behind placing skimming devices at service stations. There is no constant level of traffic, and the person placing the skimming devices can monitor the activity from a parking lot.

Consumers can protect their account information from being captured by skimming devices based on the following:

- Avoid using independent ATMs that are not linked to a major financial institution.
- Avoid using stand-alone ATMs.
- If using a debit card to purchase gas, pay for the transaction through the cashier.
- If using an ATM or other machine that accepts debit cards, look for signs of tampering around the slot where the card is inserted.

7.6.2 Internet Purchases

Consumers who use debit cards to make product purchases have to be aware when making purchases on the Internet. By opening the wrong e-mail attachment, malware/spyware could have been placed on the consumer's computer (refer to Chapter 12 for additional discussion of malware and spyware). Malware, short for malicious software, can be used to capture private information from a person's computer. This unauthorized software can also be used to capture account information data when online purchases are made. Any individual using a personal computer to make purchases through the Internet needs to purchase and install antimalware/spyware programs.

It is also necessary to make sure to use a secure website prior to making any online purchases. The Uniform Resource Locator (URL) is the line of data used in the website address. To make sure the website is secure, the URL has to contain the letters HTTPS. By using HTTPS, the activity is encrypted and secured. Not all websites use HTTPS, so consumers need to check the address bar prior to making any online purchases from their personal computer.

With the popularity of free Wi-Fi hot spots, more and more people take a laptop with them to surf the Internet while away from home. Many of these locations are not secure, allowing others in the area to tap into the consumer's activity. All Internet activity conducted while operating on an unsecure network allows unauthorized individuals to hack in and access personal information. To protect sensitive bank account information (debit cards), online purchases should not be made when using a free Wi-Fi hot spot.[9]

7.6.3 Debit Card Purchases at Restaurants and Bars

Consumers use a personal or business debit card to make purchases at various retail locations on a daily basis. A majority of the time, the consumer has the ability to swipe their debit card at the register or checkout location. After swiping the debit card, the consumer confirms the transaction amount and enters their PIN. During the transaction, the debit card does not leave the consumer's eyesight.

Using a personal debit card to pay for a meal at a restaurant or drinks at a local bar is a common practice. Patrons easily hand over their debit card to settle the check. Unfortunately for the consumer, the debit card is out of sight for a period of time. A large percentage of the time, the card is returned and the transaction is conducted as a normal course of business. For an unsuspecting consumer, it takes one instance of the restaurant/bar employee stealing the debit card information while the card is out of the sight of the holder.

As discussed in Chapter 2, people will apply for a position and be hired for the sole purpose of stealing or committing fraud. With the high employee turnover rate in the food service industry,[10] some restaurant operators need to fill positions quickly. Having a need to hire new employees to wait tables and serve bar patrons on a continuous basis could limit the detailed level needed to conduct a satisfactory applicant verification or background check.

Consumers who use their debit card in a retail location where it has to be taken out of their sight for a period of time need to be aware of the potential for the sensitive account holder information to be compromised. The following prevention procedures can be utilized when confronted with having to allow a debit card to be removed from sight to process a transaction:

- Pay for the meal or service with cash.
- Use a gift card or a prepaid debit card to pay for the meal or service.

Protecting an individual debit card from unauthorized use for fraudulent purposes is based on the security level the cardholder wishes to employ. A debit card holder can choose to place their transaction activity on the path of least resistance by

- Making Internet purchases through unsecure websites that do not use HTTPS in the URL
- Not checking for tampering to look for skimming device placement on ATMs and other devices that require the debit card to be inserted to complete a transaction
- Giving their debit card to a third party to complete a transaction, removing the card from their sight for a short period of time

7.7 Charity Scams and Fraud

Giving to those in need is a part of human nature for a large majority of the population. Some people choose to donate their time by volunteering to work in a soup kitchen. Others prefer to provide a monetary amount in financial support of the charity. No matter the method of providing support to a charitable organization, those at the receiving end are appreciative of the assistance.

With any operation for which something of monetary value changes hands, there are those looking to exploit the situation for fraudulent purposes. Individuals committing charity fraud will use the good name of well-known charitable organizations, as well as look for financial gain through recent disasters.

Legitimate charitable organizations have been known to advertise on the television and radio in search of donations. This is especially true when working to support the victims of a natural disaster. After natural disasters, charitable organizations advertise how donations can be made via sending a certain text message to a select phone number. In addition, many charity business operations solicit donations directly through their website.

No matter the method used to collect donations by a reputable charitable organization, legitimate-appearing tactics are used by those looking to commit fraud in the name of giving:

■ Using the good name of a legitimate national charitable organization and going door to door to collect donations. These individuals will claim to work directly for the represented organization and manufacture counterfeit documents and name tags to make their representation appear legitimate.

■ Using a recent natural disaster and going door to door to solicit donations. These individuals will also claim to represent a national charity organization or use a like-sounding name of the charity. A popular method used to add credibility is to mention the names of neighbors on the street who donated to the cause.

  There are many free websites that offer to provide the names of residents living on a certain street.

■ Using the untimely death of a local student to help provide financial support to their family. Almost every local school (junior high, high school, and college) has some type of social media web page for current students and alumni. These school pages can be used to inform the members of a tragedy involving a current or previous student of the school. Information can be provided to the web page members of a current fund drive and donations solicited that will be provided to the student's family.

  Individuals looking to use charity as an angle for fraud in the event of a local student's untimely death have also been known to obtain the school's e-mail list for current students and parents. A parent receiving a personally directed e-mail referencing a fund-raising drive in the name of a classmate of a son or daughter can work to add credibility to the scam.

No matter the method used to gain the attention of an individual to solicit money in the name of a charitable cause, due diligence is necessary before any money changes hands. In the sad world of people stealing money in the name of a good cause, it is unfortunately up to the potential donor to make sure they are working with a legitimate organization or representatives:

■ Legitimate charities do not work in a pressured environment or insist on immediate donations.

■ Individuals going door to door to solicit donations on behalf of a legitimate charitable organization will provide information on the charitable organization and its cause.

■ Documentation is provided to the resident about the charitable organization.

■ Potential donors are invited to visit the website of the charitable organization and to make a donation at their leisure.

The potential warning signs of charity fraud are as follows:

- Receipt of an unsolicited e-mail from a well-known charitable organization requesting a donation for a particular recent national tragedy. Major charitable organizations do not send unsolicited e-mails seeking donations. Some might send an e-mail to a person who has made previous donations through the organization's website.
- The use of high-pressure tactics to persuade a person to make an immediate donation.
- The individual collecting for a charitable cause informs the potential donor there is a minimum donation amount. Legitimate charities are grateful for any donation amount.
- People going door to door to collect for a charitable cause use the names and addresses of neighbors on the street, who they claim donated a certain amount. As mentioned, anyone can obtain the names of household residents through many white page–type websites.
- A request to make a charitable donation to a well-known national charitable organization through a foreign bank.

The following information needs to be reviewed by any individual considering making a charitable donation:

- Never give cash to anyone conducting door-to-door solicitations. If a decision is made to make a donation, it should be made through the organization's website.
- Do not provide a check to anyone collecting for a charitable cause. If the person is using subterfuge in an effort to collect money, the routing and account numbers on the check can be used for counterfeiting.
- Most collection drives in the name of an accident victim are established through a local financial institution and bank branch.
- Sadly, natural disasters occur around the world: floods, earthquakes, hurricanes, and so on. Individuals who want to commit a charity scam will use a natural disaster to solicit donations from caring citizens. To ensure the donated money will be directed to relief efforts, contributions should be made through nationally trusted charitable organizations.
- A popular charitable cause used to obtain donations from unsuspecting individuals is to claim a fund drive is being made for the fire or police department. Many people are happy to support their local police and fire departments, which makes the use of their name for charity fraud a popular choice. Anyone wishing to make a donation to the police or fire departments should contact their offices directly to determine if there is an actual fund drive and where contributions can be made.

- Caution has to be used when responding to a solicitation request through an e-mail. Attempts are made in the e-mail to use like-sounding or actual names of valid charitable organizations. Links are provided directing the e-mail recipient to visit the official website of the organization they claim to be representing. Unfortunately, the e-mail link goes to a bogus look-alike website.[11] (Refer to Chapter 11 for a discussion of website hijacking.)
- Verification of a legitimate charitable organization can be made through the Better Business Bureau or Wise Giving Alliance.

7.8 Fund-Raising Website Fraud

When donating money to a charity, a person has to use sound judgment and due diligence prior to making a contribution. Unscrupulous individuals will take the good name of a charitable organization and solicit donations for the purpose of fraud. These same individuals will also exploit a local or national tragedy in an effort to commit fraud based on a person's generosity. The typical methods used to commit charity fraud are unsolicited e-mails, social media websites, and going door to door.

Growing in popularity are websites where an individual can create a personal web page in an effort to solicit donations from the general public. These websites offer easy signup, page generation assistance, and a central money collection location. The actual need or cause for the fund-raising campaign is based on the individual creating the web page:

- A child's hospital expenses
- Upcoming wedding
- Unexpected death of a family member
- House fire
- Homeless food drive
- Memorial fund
- Lost or missing child
- Educational fund

There is no limit to the reasons for a person to solicit donations on the many fund-raising websites. The individual creating the web page, based on the individual money-raising cause, can provide a detailed backstory and include pictures. The individual can set a target goal for the amount of money to raise and a time frame in which to achieve the monetary goal. The individual fund-raising web page can also be linked to contact lists on a person's social media website.

Depending on the fund-raising website, the fees charged vary and are normally based on a percentage of the amount donated. Individuals making a donation through the fund-raising website are offered various options: writing a check, using a credit/debit card, using an online payment system, and so on.

These fund-raising websites are or have been developed with the best intentions and are a good source for a person to generate donations for a cause. Success stories through the various fund-raising websites are numerous and are 100% aboveboard. Many of these fund-raising websites allow visitors to link to the website of major charitable organizations.

Sadly, individuals looking to make money through the donations of good-hearted citizens have discovered another opportunity for fraud. Individuals who want to commit fraud will create a web page that is not for a legitimate cause in an effort to collect donations. To add legitimacy to the cause, fraudulent fund-raising websites have also been created. With a fraudulent fund-raising website, the individual campaigns listed are not legitimate, and all money donated will be used for fraudulent purposes. The following needs to be taken into account by anyone looking to make a donation through a fund-raising website:

- Is the fund-raising website accredited through the Better Business Bureau?
- Are the pictures posted on the web page related to the fund-raising cause?
- Are the fund-raising goals relevant to the reason for seeking donations?
- Are people actually making donations to the specific fund-raising drive?
- Can a physical address of the fund-raising website be located?
- Does the fund-raising website have a contact phone number?

Fortunately, legitimate fund-raising websites will take down a web page if fraud is discovered or suspected.

7.9 Internet Prescription Fraud

Purchasing products over the Internet is becoming an increasingly popular method of shopping. Company websites provide detailed descriptions of the products they sell, competitive pricing, and the ability to make purchases from home. In an effort to compete with shopping malls, the big box stores, and other retail locations, many companies selling items over the Internet offer free shipping to save the consumer money. Shoppers are also able to make purchases over the Internet for items they might feel embarrassed about buying over the counter. Individuals are also able to purchase prescription and over-the-counter drugs through Internet websites and can have the medications shipped to their home.

There are many legitimate websites that operate in a legal environment and offer a safe, private, and convenient method of purchasing medication. To verify the integrity of prescription drugs and over-the-counter medication purchased through the Internet, the following guidelines are recommended:

- To sell medication through an Internet website, the pharmacy has to be state licensed. This requirement applies to pharmacy websites located in the United States.
- Make sure the Internet pharmacy has a licensed pharmacist to answer customer questions.
- Make sure the Internet pharmacy requires that a prescription be issued by a licensed medical professional.
- Use caution when corresponding with an Internet pharmacy that attempts to sell prescription medication via an unsolicited e-mail.
- First-time customers of an Internet pharmacy should use caution if there is no requirement to complete an online questionnaire.
- Verification of an Internet pharmacy should be made through a state board of pharmacy or the National Association of Boards of Pharmacy. A customer needs to make sure the Internet pharmacy has a valid license and is adhering to state quality standards.
- Proper research needs to be completed by the consumer prior to providing an Internet pharmacy with personal information, such as Social Security number, medical history, personal health information, and credit/debit card information.
- Make sure the Internet pharmacy provides security and privacy policies on its website.[12]

As mentioned, there are many legitimate Internet pharmacy websites that fill subscriptions and provide medication approved by the Food and Drug Administration (FDA). However, there are also what is called "rogue websites" that operate illegally and sell potentially dangerous drugs. These unapproved medications have not been checked for safety and effectiveness. Medications reviewed by some of these rogue prescription websites have been known to contain the wrong ingredients or have too much or too little of the active ingredients. In addition, some drugs have been known to contain ingredients dangerous to the health of an individual.[13]

CASE STUDY 7.2

The FDA purchased and analyzed several products that were represented online as Tamiflu (oseltamivir). One of the orders, which arrived in an unmarked envelope with a postmark from India, consisted of unlabeled, white tablets. When analyzed by the FDA, the tablets were found to contain talc and acetaminophen, but none of the active ingredient oseltamivir.

For example, the FDA also became aware of a number of people who placed orders over the Internet for one of the following products:

- Ambien (zolpidem tartrate)
- Xanax (alprazolam)
- Lexapro (escitalopram oxalate)
- Ativan (lorazepam)

Instead of receiving the drug they ordered, several customers received products containing what was identified as foreign versions of Haldol (haloperidol), a powerful antipsychotic drug. As a result, these customers needed emergency medical treatment for symptoms such as difficulty in breathing, muscle spasms, and muscle stiffness—all problems that can occur with haloperidol.[14]

Medications sold through some online websites have been proven not to meet minimum quality standards. Consumers need to be aware of the following information as it pertains to medications purchased through rogue websites:

- The strength of the medication may not be consistent. Pills have been known to be too strong, too weak, or too old.
- The safety standards required by the FDA for manufacturing the drugs cannot be guaranteed.
- The medication was not approved by the FDA for human consumption.
- Unapproved medications can have dangerous side effects.
- Medical professionals work to ensure all the medications they prescribe can be taken by a patient at the same time. When purchasing multiple prescriptions through a rogue website, they are not verified for compatibility.
- It is possible medication sold through rogue websites was not stored in the proper manner. There have also been incidents of labeling issues and improper packaging for shipping.
- Last, some medications shipped by rogue websites have been counterfeit.[15]

To ensure the legitimacy and trustworthiness of the Internet pharmacy website, ascertain the following:

- The Internet pharmacy is located in the United States, showing it is governed by strict FDA standards.
- The Internet pharmacy website is licensed by the state board of pharmacy in the state where it operates. A list of the state boards can be obtained through the National Association of Boards of Pharmacy.®
- The Internet pharmacy provides a licensed pharmacist to answer consumers' questions.
- A telephone number is provided for the Internet pharmacy for contact purposes.
- To obtain medication from an Internet pharmacy website, a subscription from a licensed medical professional is required.[16]

Another way to check on a website is to look for the National Association of Boards of Pharmacy's (NABP®) Verified Internet Pharmacy Practice Sites[CM] seal, also known as the VIPPS® seal.

This seal means that the Internet pharmacy is safe to use because it has met state licensure requirements, as well as other NABP criteria. Visit the VIPPS website to find legitimate pharmacies that carry the VIPPS® seal.[17]

Signs of an unsafe Internet pharmacy website are as follows:

- A person can purchase medication at a much lower price than through a traditional pharmacy.
- A person has the ability to purchase prescription medication without a prescription.
- There is no contact information available on the Internet pharmacy website.
- The origin of the medications cannot be verified.
- The wrong medication is shipped.[18]

Internet prescription fraud not only creates a financial loss for the individual, but also can lead to serious health consequences. Strict due diligence needs to take place on the part of the consumer if a decision is made to purchase any type of drug or prescribed medication through an Internet pharmacy.

7.10 Mystery Shopping Fraud

In the retail world, there are many organizations that hire the services of companies that provide mystery shopping. For varying reasons, an organization wishes to know if employees are ringing all sales through the cash register. Mystery shopping is also conducted to determine if certain procedures are being followed in accordance with company policies. It is possible for an organization to solicit the services of a mystery shopper on an independent basis. Most mystery shopping activities are acquired through an organization that specializes in providing these services.

The organization hiring the services of a mystery shopping operation will provide the store locations to shop and exactly the type of transaction to be conducted. The transactions can range from entering an establishment to make a small purchase or one that requires additional time and observation.

A legitimate mystery shopping operation will either provide the associate with the money required to make the transaction or have procedures in place to reimburse them for the purchase. If the person has to travel for the shopping activity, the legitimate shopping firm will pay a set amount per mile traveled; most times, the individual is allowed to keep the purchase. Most mystery shoppers work on a part-time basis, receive any necessary training from the hiring organization, and do not have to pay up front for hiring expenses or certifications.

With the work-at-home scam previously discussed, becoming a mystery shopper can sound like the way to an easy job. Many fraudulent mystery shopping operations will advertise that their workers have the ability to set their own schedule while working with the public in many different business settings. There is also the offer to make a lot of money for little work.

Many fraudulent mystery shopping jobs are advertised in newspapers or through the Internet via unsolicited e-mail notifications (see Figure 7.2). The offers are appealing to the applicant because of the promise of easy money and fluidity

Hello,

My name is James Holmsend, Human Resources Manager of Conundrum Shoppers LLC.

We're a mystery shopping company that conducts secret shopping evaluations throughout the US, South America and Europe. We are looking for 60 qualified shoppers to conduct secret shopping evaluations in the US. We need individuals such as yourself to work about 4hrs a week, performing secret shopping activities. This is a part time job paying between $500–$800 per week.

We assign secret shopping assigments and after evaluation, the shopper sends in a report or comment about the events that happened during the visit. The information should be objective only and should contain only the facts about the visit. The shopper is provided funds for the request of service, he nee you do not need to pay any amount to start or even invest a cent of your money into shopping. We will be providing all the funds needed. You are paid a flat fee of $120 for successfully completing an evaluation. The mystery shopper/Evaluator acts like any normal customer, you will be discrete about the evaluation, that's the only way it can be efficient.

Once you accept an assignment, your report must be completed and submitted within 24hrs hours after the visit to the evaluated Company or Business. Your job will be to evaluate and comment on customer service ranging from speed of service delivery, environmental neatness, attitude and manner of approach from the employees and your subjective opinion of service delivery from the business as potrayed by the employees. This report will be turned over to me directly and I in tum will collate this and the result of the survey, delivered to the business.

Our services are rendered when businesses perceive a declined in service utilization, what worse time for any business than the present recession within the country. Your Identity must be confidential and secret just as the job specifies (MYSTERY SHOPPER). Your fee is a flat $120, for every evaluation assignment. Transportation allowance is provided in the amount of $30, this will bring running costs and allowance to $150. You would be provided with the service location to evaluate as soon as you accept the position.

Please read the descriptive above carefully, sending me the infos below means you are very willing and ready to start work, I don't tolerate time wasters and ghost evaluators.

Show ONLY your continued interest by sending me the following...

Full name(s)...
Full Physical Address... City, State and Zip...
Contact Numbers(CELL** & Home)... Email addresses (If you use more than 1)...
Age...
Current Occupation...

James Holmsend, Human Resources.
jamesholmsend@me.com Conundrum Shoppers LLC

Figure 7.2   This is an actual unsolicited e-mail that was received by a person who became an eventual victim of mystery shopper fraud. The grammar and spelling errors in the e-mail are exactly as received by the individual who responded with the information requested.

in scheduling. The applicants are also informed that once they apply for a job as a mystery shopper, they are guaranteed a job. In a legitimate business world, there are no guarantees.

Once initial contact is made by the prospective employee to the bogus mystery shopping firm, basic contact information is requested. After the applicant provides personal information (name, address, phone number, age, e-mail address, occupation), the applicant is normally informed within a few days of being hired as a mystery shopper (see Figures 7.3 and 7.4). Once certified as a mystery shopper, the individual is notified of his or her first assignment (see Figures 7.5 and 7.6).

A popular mystery shopping scam and one that sounds legitimate to the newly hired shopper is to investigate a money-processing company. Two popular organizations are Western Union and MoneyGram. Both companies offer the service of wiring money from one person to another. A wire transfer takes place when a person enters a location and provides the amount of cash to be wired, the location or office where the money is to be sent, and the name of the recipient. A small percentage fee is charged by the wiring company.

The individual or individuals committing wire transfer fraud will tell their shopper there is a contract with the parent organization to test the operating practices of their field offices. The shopper is told to conduct a wire transfer, but the shopper will not have to provide any up-front money. The mystery shopping firm advises the shopper that the firm is sending them a cashier's check or money order to deposit into or be cashed against their individual bank account.

On receipt, the mystery shopper is asked to deposit the check or money order into their personal bank account or actually cash the check. If the check is deposited, the shopper is advised to immediately withdraw a percentage of the check amount and use the cash to make a wire transfer. The mystery shopper is told the remainder of the check amount is theirs to keep for conducting the wire transfer.

The amount left over after withdrawing a large percentage of the check is appealing to the newly hired mystery shopper. Having the ability to make a few hundred dollars for a simple transaction has the mystery shopper looking at the potential money made versus the possibility of depositing or cashing a fraudulent item.

If the counterfeit item is deposited into the personal financial account of the mystery shopper and a percentage of the check is withdrawn in cash, all the shopper has to do is to visit a wire transfer establishment as directed by the hiring firm. The shopper is told the geographic location of the receiving wire transfer company and the recipient who is to receive the transferred money. A typical individual who believes they were actually hired as a mystery shopper will make the deposit and withdrawal and transfer the money without thinking twice.

Days after the wire transfer is complete and the newly hired mystery shopper is waiting for the next assignment, the check or money order is returned to the bank. The reason for the check or money order being returned is that it is a counterfeit item. The amount of the counterfeit item is charged against the bank account of the mystery shopper. The total amount of the counterfeit check is withdrawn from

------- Original

Message -------

From: James Holmsend

To:

Subject: Re: RE:MSPA opening

Hello,

Received your application. I am happy for the level of interest shown and information supplied You appear to be a good match for an evaluator. I would like to congratulate you as you've been chosen as one of I0 evaluators for Conundrum Shoppers LLC. I hope your addition to the fold will bring another edge and an heightened perspective to our surveys.

To begin your Mystery Shopping career, we are going to be evaluating two(2) out of these three(3) businesses to stait with, we'll be evaluating.

WALMART STORES INC, SEARS & WESTERN UNION COMPANIES.

These are independent companies being evaluated privately and independent of each other. We're particularly concerned about the customer support, a random customer is treated to, while visiting another WalMart store, Western union location or Sears. As well as the service quality delivered when visited.

These companies are not the only ones we work with, but I'll be limiting your evaluations to these companies alone for the next couple of weeks. I would like you to find the closest locations of these businesses....

LOCATE THE NEAREST LOCATIONS TO YOU ONLINE.

1. **WESTERN UNION MONEY TRANSFER.**
2. **WALMART STORES.**
3. **MONEYGRAM MONEY TRANSFER.**

When you find the nearest locations, send me their exact Names, Phone and Address.

These are well known businesses and finding the closest location to you, should only be a matter of minutes when you visit their respective websites.

Your first assignment, will be scheduled for sometime this coming week. I will give you a 12–24 hour notice before we proceed. At Walmart, you will be required to make a purchase equivalent to, but not more than $20.00.

(FUNDS TO EVALUATE WITH WILL BE DELIVERED TO YOUR RESIDENCE IN THE FORM OF MONEY ORDERS; THIS MONEY ORDERS WILL CONTAIN YOUR PAY,

Figure 7.3 This is actual follow-up information received by an individual who responded to the unsolicited e-mail requesting applicants for open positions as mystery shoppers. Introductory information is provided about the first mystery shopping assignment.

CONUNDRUM SHOPPERS LLC

119 Cherry Street, Seattle WA 98104. 206–203–1715

www.conundrumshoppers.com, Email: info@conundrumshoppers.com

TO WHOM IT MAY CONCERN

Please accept this letter as confirmation that you have been accepted and employed with Conundrum Shoppers LLC as a secret retail evaluator. To carry out independent surveys of retail outlets specified within your local community.
You:

- Hold the title of Retail Evaluator.
- Conduct timely retail surveys and submit timely reports.
- Will make retail surveys and collate customer service reports.
- Earn a wage of $120 on every survey carried out paid on evaluation day without bonuses.
- Works on a part time daily basis of less than 4hrs per day. (**Work Hours is Subjective to your hours**)

If you have any questions or require further information, please do not hesitate to contact me at jamesholmsend@me.com.

Sincerely yours,
Survey Evaluations.
James Holmsend
jamesholmsend@me.com
CONUNDRUM SHOPPERS LLC.
www.conundrumshoppers.com

Figure 7.4 This is an actual confirmation letter sent to an individual who eventually became a victim of mystery shopper fraud. At the time the letter was mailed to the recipient, a phony website was established and e-mail was sent in the name of Conundrum Shoppers LLC. Individuals committing mystery shopper fraud will establish a phony business name and contact information that can be confirmed by the applicants. After using the business name and contact information for a short period of time, the accounts are closed, and new company names are developed. Notice the verification the recipient is provided with the title "Retail Evaluator."

the bank account of the mystery shopper. This includes the cash amount withdrawn for the wire transfer and the profit amount that was promised to the mystery shopper for completing the transaction.

If the cashier's check or money order was for $1,000 and the mystery shopper was asked to withdraw and wire transfer $800, their bank account is actually charged for the total $1,000 amount of the deposited item, including the $200 profit they believed they would receive for conducting the mystery shopping activity.

Subject: Evaluation

Delivery

Good Morning,

Today is evaluation day, a lone money order in the amount of $970.20 has been mailed out to you yesterday for delively today. It will cover all evaluation costs and proceedings. I have also emailed instructions, on how to negotiate your first evaluation and how to complete it, every step of the way. The instructions email was sent with Subject "First Evaluation", check you INBOX AND SPAM FOLDERS.

A survey sheet will come with this money order, you can either fill in your report on the survey sheet and scan back to me or simply type it out in an email, as my email contains the same set of questions on the survey sheet.

If for any reason you do not have the evaluation instructions in both you Inbox and spam/junk folder, email me back immediately so I can resend ASAP. We have a 48hr deadline for submission of reports.

Good Luck with your evaluations today, the more evaluations you can handle the better and the more you make.

James Holmsend,
Conundrum Shoppers LLC

Figure 7.5 Notification of an upcoming mystery shopper assignment.

Legitimate mystery shopping companies do not require their employees to pay an up-front fee to receive certification. The legitimate firms also do not require their employees to use their personal financial accounts in the process of conducting mystery shopping activities.

Simple prevention measures can be employed to avoid becoming the victim of a mystery shopping scam:

- Use caution when sending a résumé for an advertised mystery shopping job that was posted in a newspaper's help wanted section or was received via an unsolicited e-mail. The personal information in the résumé can also be used against the applicant for the purpose of identity theft.
- Never use a personal bank account to deposit checks as part of a mystery shopping assignment.
- Never withdraw money from a personal bank account for the purpose of making a wire transfer as part of a mystery shopping assignment.
- Do not fall for the guaranteed job promise in a mystery shopper job ad.
- Never pay an up-front fee to obtain any type of employment.
- Do not pay an advance fee to obtain certification as a mystery shopper.
- Do not pay an advance fee for the ability to access mystery shopping opportunities in your geographical location.

Subject: First Evaluation

PLEASE READ CAREFULLY, ANY QUESTIONS. DO EMAIL ME, WILL BE ON MY PC ALL DAY I am sure you have located the nearest locations of these two(2) businesses to you. WE FINALLY PROCEED WITH EVALUATION TODAY.

WALMART STORES I NC & THE WESTERN UNION COMPANY...

Your first assignment is scheduled for today. FUNDS TO EVALUATE WITH WILL BE DELIVERED TO YOUR RESIDENCE VIA UPS MAIL. You will be receiving a money order.

When you do receive the money order for $970.00. Cash it at your bank, THE BANK ONLY. It should be cashed on the spot. After cashing deduct evaluation costs as enumerated below.....

The Money order will cover the evaluation of both businesses to be evaluated this morning as well as your payment for assignment.

The total deductions will come to...

WALMART & WESTERN UNION EVALUATION

Your pay $150.00

Items to be purchased $20.00 @ Walmart Transportation allowance $30.00

Total Deductions = $200.00

Cash the check, after cashing deduct $200.00 from the total on the Money Order The balance is what you will be evaluating western union with, the money will be wired to a local sampling co-coordinator in Philippines in my care as James Holmsend. He will be evaluating WU and a local H&M over there as well. Whatever you buy at Walmart is yours for keeps and will not be returned to anyone.

AT WESTERN UNION... You will be evaluating Western Union by wiring the balance after deductions to the details below...

Name: City: State: Country: Zip:
JAMES HOLMSEND
Cebu Manila Philippines 4200
http://us.mgl.mail.yahoo.com/dc/launch?.gx = l&.rand = Ogijkoa9hul pj 11/9/2010

Figure 7.6 Notification of the first mystery shopper assignment. *(continued)*

Print Page 2 of 2
SPECIFY PAYOUT IN US DOLLARS.

AT WALMART... You will purchase anything of your choice within a $20.00 budget, whatever you buy is yours for keeps. Be sure to take note of the 12 questions asked below, as evaluation is based on them.

Once the evaluation is complete and the money's sent. Please send me the following info, along with your report of the evaluation...

a. Your full names and address exactly how you wrote it on the Western Union slip.
b. The receiver's name exactly how you penned it down on the Western Union slip.
c. The total amount sent (Amount receivable by the receiver).
d. MONEY TRANSFER CONTOL NUMBER MTCN. (This is the 10 digit number for receiving funds, it is not the receipt number)

These questions below are what you will base both evaluations on.

You will be very attentive to the following things. Evaluate both businesses based on these questions.

1) The exact address and location of the store evaluated
2) The name of the cashier that attended to you.
3) Your time of arrival at the venue.
4) Your time of departure.
5) How long the transaction took?
6) Any other area you think Walmart/Western Union should improve on?
7) The General Sanitation level?
8) How clean was the rest room?
9) Would you return to that particular store?
10) What you feel about the customer service?
11) How would you rate the overall experience on a scale of 1–10?
12) How tedious was the checkout process?

Remember, you're a mystery shopper. You are EXPRESSLY FORBIDDEN to disclose this information to anyone, related to the evaluated business. (In store or out of the store)...

Your report will be turned over to me and me alone, THIS EMAIL ADDRESS ALONE, its for survey collation, jamesholmsend@me.com

Figure 7.6 (continued) Notification of the first mystery shopper assignment.

7.11 Romance Schemes

The ability to pull off an individual fraud scam is based on the creativity of the person working to commit the crime and the gullibility of the targeted individual. Over the years, there have been numerous successful romance schemes that relied on the naïveté of the target. These successful scams were also delivered by individuals who possessed the believability and deceptiveness.

When analyzing the success of romance schemes, it is easy to see the creativity involved. Analyzing these frauds from the perspective of the victim, many professional and nonprofessional individuals cannot fathom how the fraud was successful.

Many of the fraud schemes discussed throughout this book are based on the growing popularity of technology. Computers and electronic communication have introduced a growing list of venues that are available to generate and commit new fraud scams. One of these new venues for fraud was created after the rollout of online dating websites. Many of these websites actually work to bring singles together, and some have high marriage success rates.

Unfortunately, a positive also brings out a negative. With the birth of online dating websites, creativity spawned the romance scheme.

Successful romance schemes can begin on any of the numerous online dating websites:

■ Fake profiles are created on these legitimate online dating websites.
■ As a result of these profiles, contacts are made. On the part of the person setting up the profile, the goal is to commit fraud. On the part of the person connecting with the fake profile, the goal is companionship.
■ With successful online dating schemes, the individual who created the fake profile immediately moves the relationship away from the introductory stage. The scammer quickly informs the person looking for companionship of almost-instant deep-felt feelings—an almost-immediate connection.
■ The scammer works to take the communication away from the message centers of the online dating website. Communication between the scammer and their target moves to e-mail, text messaging, social media, and phone communication.
■ The goal of the scammer is to have the target believe a meaningful relationship has developed over a short time frame. The scammer will send victims inexpensive personal gifts in an effort to build the belief they have been swept off their feet.

Once the foundation has been established, the scammer takes the relationship to the next level. This level involves having the target send money or assist in other requested services:

■ The target is led to believe their love interest (scammer) has fallen ill and needs money to assist with medical expenses.
■ The target is led to believe their love interest is currently out of the country and has fallen on hard times. The person needs financial assistance to return to the United States.

- The target is led to believe their love interest has had a close family member fall ill or on hard times. This is followed by a request for financial assistance.
- The target is asked to assist with a business endeavor of the scammer. The scammer convinces the target that the scammer and the scammer's business partners are having trouble getting supplies shipped out of the states to their overseas business operation. The scammer involves the unwitting target in a reshipping fraud. Reshipping fraud involves having stolen items or items fraudulently purchased sent to a domestic address. The items are then repackaged and mailed to an overseas address (see Chapter 9 for details on reshipping fraud).
- The target is convinced by the scammer that the scammer has an offshore business endeavor but does not want to process a check drawn on a US bank. The victim is asked to deposit a check the scammer mails to them. Quickly after depositing the check into his or her personal account, the victim is asked to wire transfer the money to an offshore location. Typically, after the money is sent via wire transfer, the check is returned as counterfeit.
- The target is convinced to become involved in a money-laundering scheme using personal bank accounts. The victim is led to believe the financial activity is legitimate and involves legal issues with offshore business operations.

The goal of those committing online romance schemes is to have the victim participate in one of the previously discussed requests. If successful, the victim is asked to provide the following:

- Personal credit card information that can be used to cover the requested expenses.
- Personal bank account information that can be used to cover the requested expense.
- Personal information to assist the scammer in setting up offshore bank accounts as part of a lucrative business opportunity. The victim is led to believe he or she will receive some of the business profits.

Online romance schemes can simply be avoided by following the analogy of "it seems too good to be true." Finding true love in a brief time frame is a true rarity. Any individual asked to provide any type of financial assistance to a person they met through an online dating website needs to consider the following:

- Have they met this person face to face?
- Can love be generated through electronic communication?
- Why is this person I have never met asking for financial assistance?
- Are the requests being asked of me legal?

Notes

1. A fake check is false on all counts. The company name on the check is not a legitimate business, and the bank account and routing numbers on the bottom of the check are fictitious. A counterfeit check contains the name and account number of a legitimate organization, along with the correct bank routing number. Counterfeit checks are not printed with the permission of the organization whose name is on the face of the check.
2. A third-party check is a check issued to one person. The person the check is made out to endorses the back of the check and gives the check to a second person for whatever reason. The new holder of the endorsed check uses the item as payment and endorses the check to a third person or third party. The third person can then deposit the check into their bank account. With overpayment scams, a popular reason for having a third-party check is that the check holder just sold his or her car. The individual now wants to use the money (check) made from selling the car as payment on another vehicle.
3. Typical bandit signs are signs eighteen by twenty-four inches made of corrugated plastic. The signs are attached to a metal or wood stake and inserted in the ground. Bandit signs are normally placed at road intersections and exits from shopping area parking lots.
4. Da Costa, P., Five mortgage frauds. http://abcnews.go.com/Business/top-mortgage-scams-avoid/story?id=20178540#5 (accessed June 14, 2014).
5. Ibid.
6. Ibid.
7. Ibid.
8. A majority of these types of frauds take place where the individuals selling the equipment operate out of a white cargo van.
9. Profis, S., Six ways to use public Wi-Fi hot spots safely. http://www.cnet.com/how-to/6-ways-to-use-public-wi-fi-hot-spots-safely/ (accessed June 16, 2014).
10. In 2013, the employee turnover rate in the restaurant and accommodations industry was 62.6%. During the same year, the employee turnover percentage for the remaining private sector was 42.2%. National Restaurant Association, Economist's Notebook: hospitality employee turnover rose slightly in 2013. March 20, 2014. http://www.restaurant.org/News-Research/News/Economist-s-Notebook-Hospitality-employee-turnover (accessed June 21, 2014).
11. Fraud!org, Charity scams. http://www.fraud.org/scams/general-fraud/charity-scams (accessed June 21, 2014).
12. Food and Drug Administration, The possible dangers of buying medicines over the Internet. http://www.fda.gov/forconsumers/consumerupdates/ucm048396.htm (accessed June 25, 2014).
13. Ibid.
14. Ibid.
15. Ibid.
16. Ibid.
17. Ibid.
18. Ibid.

Chapter 8

Frauds against the Elderly

8.1 Introduction

One of the easier groups of individuals to target for fraudulent purposes is the elderly. A simple search of the Internet with the topic of "fraud against the elderly" will reveal many stories about lost life savings or how an eighty-year-old grandmother was victimized in an advance fee fraud or lost money as a victim of fraud to a person they trusted. Criminals who commit fraud against the elderly or elder fraud do so because there is a lower-than-average percentage rate of getting caught. Elderly victims of fraud often do not report the crime, fail to provide an accurate account of the case details, or have personal reasons for not coming forward with their financial loss to family members for fear of having restrictions placed on their individual freedom. From the criminal perspective, all that is needed for elder fraud is to develop a level of trust and create a financial opportunity.

Remembering when I was much younger and with my grandfather in North Carolina, he often used the phrase: "He is a person you can trust." As I went through childhood and on to adulthood, it became apparent that many elderly individuals based their faith in others on establishing a level of trust. This can be a trust level based on years of an ongoing relationship or having a respect for those in a position of authority, either in law enforcement or in an official government position.

> **CASE STUDY 8.1**
>
> My grandparents lived in a three-bedroom house on a 180-acre farm in western North Carolina. They had another elderly individual who worked the farm with my grandfather; this individual stayed in the back room in their house. Their house was located about a quarter mile off the main two-lane roadway and was accessed by a single-lane, long, winding dirt driveway. The closest neighboring house was quicker to reach by walking as the crow flies than by driving.

One day, two individuals drove onto their property in an official-looking vehicle; both wore clothing that bore a shirt patch indicating they were officials from the Henderson County Tax Office. Both presented identification as being from the county tax office and stated that their visit was to reassess the square footage of the house for the purpose of lowering the property tax payment. These were then individuals in a position of authority with an additional benefit of a financial opportunity.

The phony tax assessors stated they needed to measure the rooms to obtain the proper square footage. One of the individuals quickly went to work in the front rooms and got my grandparents and the helper involved in holding and reading tape measures. While the four of them were busy with the measuring, the second individual was in the unoccupied rooms pocketing cash and other valuables. Once the measurements were taken and the promise was made that my grandparents would receive a new property tax bill in a few weeks, the individuals bid farewell. Later in the day, the thefts were discovered.

On a visit to North Carolina a few months later, I learned of the incident and theft from my grandparents, who wondered if the connections I had in law enforcement could secretly help recover their lost valuables and cash. I also found out that afternoon that the incident was never reported to the local authorities, with the reasoning of possible embarrassment if the information ever got out in the local community.

The incident with my grandparents contained the necessary factors for successful crime/fraud against the elderly: trust and opportunity. A level of trust was developed along with a financial opportunity. What is better than two individuals from the official county tax office offering to lower annual property tax amounts?

The threats of elder fraud can come from various groups of individuals, ranging from relatives, caregivers, to complete strangers. From the trust and opportunity aspect, the elderly individual creates the trust level in the person committing the fraud, and the fraudster creates the opportunity. The level of trust can be built instantly through the perception of dealing with a person of authority and respect (police officer, nurse, county official, company representative, government official, church officers or ministers, etc.) or over time through neighbors, friends, relatives, and so on.

8.2 Protecting against Fraud by Caregivers, Relatives, and Other Individuals of Trust

As a family member ages, a choice may have to be made by the person's children or other younger relatives to place the individual in a nursing home or move them into the younger individual's house. The choice can also be made to obtain some type of in-home assistance or part-time caregiver for a grandparent, aunt, uncle, or other elder individual. It is rare to sit through an evening in front of the television or listen to the radio for a period of time and not listen to an advertisement for a company offering in-home assistance for an elderly family member. These organizations are numerous, and all claim to employ the most trusted level of caregivers who have gone through an extensive background check.

A large percentage of these organizations are in business with the best of intentions and have a focus of providing the best service to their customers. Most businesses offering a service to the general public need to hire employees. As mentioned, these in-home care organizations have their employees go through varying types of reference and background checks. The level of new hire scrutiny can and should be checked by the individual looking to hire a caregiver through one of these agencies.

Individuals can also offer services to the elderly; these individuals do not work directly for an agency or an elder care service company. The methods of marketing their services vary and can range from using social media advertising websites to word-of-mouth referrals. These individuals claim to have obtained various types of health care or medical credentials and to have performed these types of services for varying numbers of years. In addition to years of service and certifications, many come with prior reference information.

When it comes to employing or working in the home health care industry, the requirements for caregivers vary by state. Currently, there are no national in-home caregiver requirements or standards, and the industry is not regulated by the federal government.

Ideally, having an elderly relative living close to a son or daughter is an ideal circumstance for ensuring the relative's safety and financial well-being. Many times, this is not the situation, and a widowed parent chooses not to move from a family home or leave the town where they have lived for a majority of their lives. This decision could be for reasons of comfort or not wanting to move away from friends and neighbors. Having an elderly relative living in a different town can raise the potential of them becoming a victim of fraud. It is hard for the younger out-of-town individual to help monitor relationships and financial activity of a parent, grandparent, aunt, uncle, or other elderly person.

To help lower the concern over an older relative living in a different town, a son or daughter, niece or nephew, or other concerned relative can hire or suggest the older family member obtain some form of in-home care. This care can be a person hired to assist with daily household chores, to provide some type of medical attention, to provide a chauffeur service, or to provide companionship. The hiring of someone to provide in-home care for an older relative, more times than not, is a good idea and actually aids in the day-to-day life of these older individuals. History has also shown there are those in the home care industry that pursue this line of work to commit elder fraud, and there are others who work with the elderly for years and a change in circumstances provides the opportunity or need to commit fraud. The changes leading an otherwise professionally operating caregiver to commit elder fraud are the following:

- Changing financial situation and a sudden need for money
- Having a feeling of being unappreciated for their work by other family members

- Obtaining knowledge of the assets of the person in their care
- Convincing themselves only a small amount will be taken and not noticed
- Easy access to obtaining assets from the elderly person while covering their tracks

Protecting an elderly family member from becoming the victim of fraud at the hands of an in-home caregiver can take place along the path of least resistance. By placing roadblocks along the path to your relative's front door and providing enough detours in the way, the relative can be moved from the path of least resistance. As with many types of fraud, those looking to commit elder fraud will look for an easier target. When hiring in-home care through a professional agency or obtaining the services of an independent caregiver, make sure to use as many of these prevention tools as possible:

- Develop an understanding of requirements for working as an in-home caregiver in your state.
- Ensure the individual sent by the agency meets the state requirements.
- If hiring an independent caregiver, make sure the person meets the state requirements.
- If professional certifications are required by your state to work as a caregiver, make sure the individual sent by the agency or independently hired has the required credentials.
- If using a professional company to hire a caregiver, make sure the company has liability insurance.
- Do not take the word of the professional agency that the caregiver's references have been verified. Obtain the reference information from the individual sent to your relative's home and verify their work history. Have the caregiver provide the name and address of their references. The person obtaining the services of a caregiver should use directory assistance to obtain the phone numbers.
  A person looking to commit elder fraud will provide the phone number of a person involved in the scam, who will verify the credibility of the caregiver.
- If hiring an independent caregiver, have them provide references and verify them. Again, obtain the phone numbers through directory assistance.
- Be careful using social media websites when looking for a professional care provider.

In addition to utilizing as many of the prevention measures as possible when hiring a caregiver for an elderly individual, a process of education needs to take place. The elderly family member needs to be provided with a list of dos and don'ts on the information they should share with a caregiver and should make sure to protect financial information:

- Never leave bank account information out in the open.
- Never leave credit card statements out in the open.

- Never leave any personal financial-related documents out in the open (investment information, mortgage documents, etc.).
- Avoid discussions with a caregiver about financial status, bank account balances, and so on.
- Avoid discussing negative family issues with a caregiver. A recent dispute with a family member can be used by a person looking to have the elderly individual believe the caregiver has the older individual's best interest at heart.
- Contact a family member for discussion prior to providing a response to any kind of request for financial assistance made by a caregiver.
- Protect the Social Security number from disclosure to anyone.

CASE STUDY 8.2
Stories of the elderly being victims of fraud are many, and I had the opportunity to witness several of these incidents when working in bank security. I remember receiving a call from a branch manager, who was concerned about an elderly widowed lady who had been coming to her branch for years. On this particular afternoon, the lady was requesting to take a large amount of cash from her savings account. For safety purposes, the branch manager advised the withdrawal could be better protected if she placed the funds in a cashier's check. When the elderly woman insisted on obtaining cash, the branch manager became concerned and called my office.

After talking with the elderly woman, it became clear she wanted to give the cash to a younger woman who she believed to be a niece who needed the money for rent and food for her baby. On further discussion, the widowed woman indicated she met the younger woman earlier in the day when she presented herself as a family member.

Hungry for companionship, the older woman quickly accepted the younger woman on face value and enjoyed the time they spent together that morning. After convincing herself the younger woman was a relative and needed family support, the widow was eager to help. Luckily, an aware branch manager, who had received consumer fraud training presented by the security department, noticed a red flag and aided in preventing the older woman's loss of money. Even though the financial institution would not have been responsible for the monetary loss, protecting an unsuspecting customer from becoming a victim of fraud is a valuable aspect of customer service.

The information discussed in Case Study 8.2 does not represent a unique situation, but one that takes place across the country on a daily basis. The elderly potential victim chose to explain her need for withdrawing a large amount of money as assistance to help a family member. She almost became a victim by allowing a trust level to be created by a younger person offering companionship.

Different from the hiring of a person working as a companion in the home of an elderly relative, younger individuals will recognize an older person in their neighborhood and develop a friendship with the sole reason of committing elder fraud. Many elderly people living alone go through each day with little outside interaction and welcome someone who shows concern for their well-being and who likes to engage in conversation.

Once a relationship is established between the elderly person and the perceived concerned younger neighbor, a foundation is built between the two with trust as the base. Once the trust level is built, the younger person can begin to slowly engage in conversations with the elderly person about financial issues; the purpose is to gain knowledge of the types of assets available and where they are housed.

Gaining financial knowledge of an elderly individual is not always generated through conversations but sometimes by having unlimited access to the residence of the target. After many conversations and the development of a level of trust, the younger person might offer to assist the elderly individual around the house with the laundry, cleaning, cooking, and so on. By being able to move around the residence of the elderly individual, the newly trusted friend can easily obtain information on the financial assets available. Once the fraudster learns whether there is money in various banking accounts, stocks, savings bonds, and so on, a plan is hatched to extract the assets.

In addition to a trusted caregiver or new companion, an elderly person can become the victim of fraud from a family member. Many times, this family member has a relationship with the elderly relative and for varying reasons decides to defraud the relative for monetary purposes. The money from the fraudulent activity by a trusted family member can be taken outright in a large amount or in smaller amounts with the hope of covering the activity. No matter the amount taken, the elderly relative falls victim based on the trust and opportunity factors.

Younger family members, for varying reasons, choose to steal or defraud older relatives. The reasons are many; some are as follows:

- The younger relative has developed a financial need through a drug habit.
- The younger relative has developed a large amount of debt.
- The younger relative is pressured by friends and is easily influenced.
- The younger relative is influenced by fellow gang members.
- The younger relative needs money to pay for expenses as a result of a recent arrest or vehicle accident.
- The younger relative develops a feeling of being owed money for having to look after an elderly family member.
- The younger relative needs quick cash to cover gambling debts.

Individuals, not family members, looking to commit fraud against an elderly individual also have a variety of reasons. These could be financial need or drug-related costs, or the individual is just a professional thief. Whatever the motivation to commit elder fraud, it is important to develop an understanding of the methods used by caregivers, relatives, or other individuals of trust.

8.3 Protecting against Fraud Committed by Strangers

Complete strangers also have an advantage in coming into the lives of elderly individuals to commit fraud. A much quicker trust-based relationship is developed between the complete stranger and the elderly person when there is a need or opportunity in the elder individual's life for some type of benefit. This benefit is most likely based on a financial foundation when an opportunity is offered to the elderly person for financial gain, cheaper goods or services, investment opportunities, inexpensive travel, and so on. The trust level is now built in a short amount of time in the mind of the elderly individual, even though their thinking is clouded by opportunity. The person or persons committing the fraud are well aware of the various types of opportunities, although fraudulent, that are quickly attractive to an elderly person.

8.3.1 Financial Institution/Bank Account Fraud

A person committing any type of fraud related to the bank accounts of an elderly person will work to plant the seed for the need to place the fraudster's name on bank accounts. The elderly individual is convinced that he or she needs help with making deposits, writing checks, paying bills, receiving the proper interest rates on savings accounts, and so on. Many times, the older person has a hard time leaving the house and taking care of personal matters; the offer of help by a trusted person can work to ease the concern of bills being paid on time and the overall security of their financial assets.

To ease concerns regarding the security of their financial assets and timely bill paying, elderly victims are convinced of the necessity to add a caregiver's name to bank accounts. Once a name has been added to a bank account, this individual now has the same transaction authority as the original account holder. The addition of a name and creation of a joint bank account allows either name on the account to write checks, make deposits, transfer funds, and so on. Once the person committing the fraud has his or her name added to the checking and savings accounts, any money in these accounts can be transferred or withdrawn.

Once the elderly account holder acts in an overt manner and willingly adds another person's name to his or her bank accounts, the financial institution is no longer responsible for the account activity. Activity on these types of accounts is treated in the same manner as an account established by a husband and wife. Either person can conduct transactions related to the account, leaving both parties responsible for overdrafts, returned deposit items, and so on.

The goals of individuals committing frauds against the elderly through the elderly individual's bank accounts have the intent of depleting all assets from as many accounts as possible. In an effort to have access to additional funds in the bank accounts of elderly individuals, the person of trust will deposit forged or counterfeit items into the accounts. Once these deposit amounts become available, the money is withdrawn, and the person of trust moves on to the next victim.

With the deposit item scenario, the elderly victim cannot go after the financial institution for the assets withdrawn from the bank accounts. The trusted individual was willingly added to the bank accounts as an authorized signer and had the legal authority to conduct activity as a legitimate account holder. Once the forged and counterfeit checks were deposited into the bank account, a crime was committed. The money withdrawn from the bank account as a result of the balance created by the depositing of bogus items is the result of criminal activity. The crime was committed by a legally recognized account holder of the financial institution. In the eyes of the financial institution, both the signers on the account are responsible for the money stolen as a result of bogus deposit items.

Based on the investigative activities of bank personnel, financial institution policies, and possible police involvement, various outcomes are possible:

- The elderly account holder has to convince bank personnel they were victimized by a person of trust.
- The financial institution can accept the word of the elderly account holder and take the write-off for the money withdrawn as a result of bogus deposit items. If the financial institution accepts the loss, it can refer the case to law enforcement for possible prosecution.
- If the financial institution does not accept the write-off of the withdrawn money, the elderly account holder is responsible for making restitution to the bank. This occurs unless the trusted individual can be located, admits to the crime, and agrees to return the funds to the bank.
- The elderly victim can return the money withdrawn as a result of the bogus deposit items. Once the bank receives this money, the elderly individual is a victim of fraud and can pursue the matter through law enforcement.

In Case Study 8.2, an alert branch manager saved an elderly customer from financial loss. Unfortunately, financial institutions do not have a directive requiring extra scrutiny on bank activities conducted by customers over a certain age. Bank branch personnel do not have a crystal ball to determine if a person being added to the account of an elderly customer has good intentions.

8.3.2 Power of Attorney

A properly executed power of attorney allows one person to act in the best interests of another. On many occasions, family members and other trusted individuals are granted a power of attorney by an elderly individual. The elderly individual granting the power of attorney normally does so based on a level of trust created with a family member or someone perceived to be acting with his or her best interests at heart.

Individuals looking to obtain a power of attorney for fraudulent purposes understand the need for the trust factor. This is true for family members with ulterior motives or an outsider working to defraud an elderly person. There is the need to have the elderly individual develop a level of trust so the elder will sign a power of attorney.

The tactics used to gain the trust of elderly individuals vary, but many revolve around establishing a level of fear. The level of fear is not physically related but is based on a precautionary measure to ensure bills are paid on time and the security of financial assets. As mentioned, many elderly individuals are convinced they need to add a person of trust to their bank account or create a power of attorney.

When adding a person of trust as a signer on personal financial accounts, it is possible an employee of the bank will notice signs of attempted fraud. By creating a power of attorney, this process can be completed online without having face-to-face contact with an attorney. When creating an online power of attorney, the pertinent information is developed through a questionnaire process. Once the necessary information is collected, the required documents are completed and mailed to the individual requesting the power of attorney. After receiving the documents for power of attorney, they are signed by the requesting individual and mailed back to the agency providing the assistance. (In most states, all that is required is the signature from a notary or the presence of two witnesses.)

From a fraud perspective, the online process takes an unbiased and professional individual out of the questioning and rationale process of creating a power of attorney for an elderly person. It also allows for the use of two accomplices to act as witnesses on the signed paperwork.

8.3.3 Home Improvement Fraud

The US Department of Health estimated that 60% of elderly individuals live in homes that are more than twenty years old. Typically, older houses require a more constant level of upkeep and maintenance. For elderly individuals living in older homes, there is an added need for home improvement services. At times, elderly individuals could require construction services to improve walkways and have other accessibility requirements.[1]

It is also estimated that around 30% of scam/fraud victims in the United States are elderly individuals. The rationale surrounding a high level of victimization for elderly individuals could be based on their outward attitude. A large majority of elderly individuals are more open and accepting of others; they are polite and willing to engage in conversations with strangers.[2]

With the increased need for home repairs and an open nature with strangers, elderly individuals are a prime target for home improvement fraud. Within the home improvement fraud world, many scams are used to target elderly individuals. Based on a history of analyzing home improvement frauds, the warning signs are as follows:

- Home improvement and other reputable home-related service companies will go door to door and leave flyers at a resident's front door. Many individuals looking to commit home improvement fraud will actually knock on the door and generate a conversation with the homeowner. The purpose of the conversation is based on selling the homeowner home improvement services.
- Many home improvement scams begin as outlined in the first bullet point: with a knock at the door. The pitch delivered revolves around having just completed a job in the neighborhood. Because these individuals are already in the neighborhood and have leftover material, a special price can be offered on the particular home improvement project. The elderly homeowner is also informed that the home improvement can be completed quickly.
- Requests are made to pay for the entire project up front.
- A request is made to pay for the project in cash.
- High-pressure tactics are used for the customer to make an immediate decision.
- A request is made for the homeowner to obtain any required permits (a possible sign of an unlicensed contractor).
- The customer is enticed with a long-term guarantee on the completed project.
- The customer is not provided with a state-issued contractor license number.[3]

In addition to everyday home improvement scams, individuals will use the aftermath of large storms to con citizens out of money. After a major storm blows through a community, many residents suffer roof damage from high winds or fallen trees. Individuals looking to commit fraud after storm damage will typically show up in the community the day following the storm.

Homeowners are enticed by the promise of a quick repair coupled with attractive repair costs. With this particular home improvement scam, a request is made for full up-front payment, which allows the contractor to begin the job the next day.

These frauds after storm damage typically have two endings:

- Once the full payment is provided, the contractors fail to show up to complete the work.
- The job is completed using substandard material with poor workmanship. (A few months later, the homeowner has to pay even more money to have the work completed in a satisfactory manner.)[4]

To prevent victimization from home improvement scams, the following information has to be understood and these tips followed:

- An agreement should not be made with any contractor who goes door to door offering construction services.
- With any home improvement project, homeowners should obtain at least three bids.

- Make sure the person offering to do any work on a home is a licensed contractor in the state.
- Verify the business has a permanent business address and how long it has been operating.
- With normal contracting projects, half of the total project cost is paid as a down payment. The remaining half is paid on satisfactory completion.
- Consumers need to check references from previous customers. If possible, obtain a reference for a project that was completed at least a year ago. This allows consumers the ability to verify the quality of past work completed and establish a history of operation.
- Consumers should never allow a decision to be based on a short time frame of completion or other pressure tactics.
- Prior to agreeing to have any home improvement project completed, consumers need to obtain a written contract.
- Check with the Better Business Bureau for any complaints against the contracting company.[5]

8.3.4 Telemarketing Fraud

Telemarketing fraud, as detailed in Chapter 9, can be directed at any individual who answers their phone.

Elderly individuals are more susceptible to this type of fraud based on the following:

- Many senior citizens spend a lot of time alone and can be looking for anyone willing to engage in a conversation.
- Elderly individuals are used to making purchases over the phone versus using the Internet.
- Many elderly individuals are on a fixed income and could easily respond to an attractive cost-saving offer of a product or service they require.
- Mobility issues require elderly individuals to rely on others for shopping needs. Having an offer to receive a desired product without having to leave their home can work to cloud the thought process.

Many telemarketing frauds directed toward elderly individuals revolve around high-pressure tactics regarding a need to act quickly and to follow a limited timeline. Popular offers directed toward elderly individuals include the following:

- Free or discounted vacations
- Cheap vitamins
- Low-cost medication and health care products. (Refer to Chapter 7 for a discussion on purchasing health-related products outside a physically standing neighborhood pharmacy.)
- Free prizes

Based on the offer delivered as part of the telemarketing fraud, the loss to the elderly individual will vary. Items offered for purchase are usually never delivered or have substandard quality. With the offer of vacations and prizes, the individual is requested to make some type of up-front payment. Once the payment is made, the vacation or prize is never received.[6]

The effort to protect against telemarketing fraud targeting elderly individuals involves an education process for senior citizens and their family members. The main points that need to be understood in a prevention effort are as follows:

- If it sounds too good to be true, it is.
- Never provide an up-front payment for any product or service.
- Use extreme caution when purchasing health care products over the phone. All medication purchased over the phone should contain the approval of a physician. (See Chapter 7 for a detailed discussion of Internet prescription fraud.)
- Do not concede to high-pressure sales tactics.
- Establish an agreement with an elderly family member to discuss any phone sales offers with relatives prior to making a decision.

8.3.5 Funeral Services, Funeral Home Overbilling, and Cemetery Fraud

Individuals working in the fraud arena will use any approach necessary for monetary gain, and no group of people is immune. Popular fraud scams targeted at senior citizens pertain to funeral services, funeral home overbilling, and cemetery fraud.

With funeral services fraud, complete strangers read the local obituaries and actually show up at the funeral for someone's deceased spouse. Those committing this type of fraud will target the widow or widower and claim that the spouse had an outstanding debt with the fraudster. The goal of the fraud is to approach the targeted widow or widower in their grieving state in an attempt to extort money for fake debts.

Elderly individuals are also targeted by funeral home owners and their representatives, who add costs to the total bill. A popular fraud is convincing the grieving widow or widower that a high-end casket is required for cremation. In actuality, a cardboard casket can be used for cremation purposes.

Finally, disreputable cemeteries will sell plots that have already been sold to other individuals. The goal of the scammer is to have the targeted senior pay for the entire plot up front and for the scammer to disappear before the fraud is discovered.[7]

To avoid becoming a victim of funeral home and cemetery fraud, consumers need to involve a trusted family member or friend in the decision-making process. Purchasing decisions should not be made quickly, and all consumers should obtain a detailed price listing of the services offered.

To avoid becoming a victim of funeral services fraud, senior citizens need to be educated on the process and the various scams targeted toward their age group, especially during their time of grieving.

8.3.6 Grandparent Scams

Individuals looking to commit a grandparent-type fraud will make calls to senior citizens, with the hope of having them believe they are being reached out to by a grandchild. A typical random caller will ask the elderly individual who answers the phone: "Hi Grandma [Grandpa], can you guess who this is?" Typically, the elderly individual will provide a name of a grandchild the caller most sounds like. If this process takes place, the elderly individual has created a fake identity for the caller.

Once the association is made, the person posing as a grandchild will use varying stories, all based on the need for money. The supposed grandchild will inform the elderly individual that they need cash to pay their rent, pay for an unexpected repair, pay off a costly traffic ticket, and so on. No matter the reason given for requiring quick cash, the elderly individual is asked to send the money via a wire transfer.

In an attempt to have the elderly individual complete the request for money and not inform other family members of their intent, the person posing as the grandchild will ask that his or her parents are not told. The scammer indicates that the parents would be really mad at them falling on hard financial times, in contrast to Grandma (or Grandpa), who is always understanding.[8]

8.3.7 Popular Frauds

Elderly individuals are also the targets of frauds or schemes used by criminals across the board. These popular frauds include the following:

- Prize, sweepstakes, and lottery scams in which the victim is targeted through unsolicited e-mails (Chapter 11).
- Internet prescription fraud: Elderly individuals living on a fixed income will search the Internet for cheaper medication. Believing they can save money for needed medication, they can fall victim to Internet prescription fraud (Chapter 7).
- Investment frauds (pyramid and Ponzi fraud and affinity scams) as discussed in Chapter 5.
- Fund-raising and charity frauds as detailed in Chapter 7.
- Mortgage, debt elimination, and loan frauds as discussed in Chapters 7 and 9.
- Automobile repair fraud: Elderly individuals are also popular targets for this type of fraud. Some garages and repair shops will add unneeded expenses to a repair bill or charge for services that were never completed. To keep elderly family members from becoming a victim of automobile repair fraud, it is vital

that a trusted family member or friend is involved in the car repair process. Research should be made on the garage or repair shop prior to making a decision for vehicle service.

8.4 Reverse Mortgage Fraud

Reverse mortgages are a popular method for elderly individuals to benefit from the equity they have built up in their home. To qualify for a reverse mortgage, the homeowner has to be at least sixty-two years of age. Other qualifying factors require the elderly individual to own their residence outright or have a significant amount of equity built up in their home.

With a traditional mortgage, the individual purchasing the home makes a monthly payment to the lender. With a reverse mortgage, the homeowner is paid a monthly payment or issued a line of credit against the equity built up in the home. Basically, the homeowner is borrowing against the equity established in their home.

A major issue with reverse mortgages is the true understanding of the money paid to the homeowner. Eventually, the institution lending the money to the homeowner is going to want to be reimbursed. In simple terms, the institution is going to want its money back.

Individuals taking out a reverse mortgage are not required to pay back the lending institution until the primary homeowner moves out of the house, the residence is sold, or the individual passes away.

With reverse mortgages, there are also certain requirements established by the lender that require the loan to be paid back:

- Death of the homeowner.
- Failure of the homeowner to pay the property taxes and keep the insurance current.
- The sale of the property.
- The homeowner stops using the home as his or her primary residence.[9]

Many elderly individuals who take out a reverse mortgage fall victim to various tactics used by lenders or brokers:

- Not informing the homeowner of the risks and fees associated with a reverse mortgage. Some reverse mortgages are advertised in a manner that lets the homeowner believe they are participating in a money-for-nothing endeavor. With reverse mortgages, there are associated fees, and the money provided the homeowner will eventually have to be paid back.
- As with many frauds committed against individuals, there is the use of high-pressure sales tactics convincing the homeowner of the need for and the benefits associated with a reverse mortgage. This basically is selling the reverse

mortgage as an opportunity that the homeowner cannot pass up and has no strings attached.

■ Not informing the homeowner of the various stipulations involved with a reverse mortgage and what requires repayment. As mentioned, a reverse mortgage has to be paid back if the homeowner dies, moves out of the residence, fails to maintain insurance, fails to pay the property taxes, or sells the property.[10]

A major problem faced by senior citizens concerning reverse mortgage frauds is the lack of knowledge surrounding the entire process and the ability of the person selling the package to convince the homeowner of the need for and benefits of obtaining a reverse mortgage. Seniors are led to believe a reverse mortgage is a no-strings-attached endeavor, and the money can be used to pay for a needed vacation or to purchase high-dollar items. Many elderly individuals who fall victim to reverse mortgage fraud are unable to pay the expenses associated with maintaining the agreement:

■ Keeping up with the various fees associated with the reverse mortgage
■ Paying the expenses related to maintaining the property as a standard of obtaining the reverse mortgage
■ Keeping the property taxes up to date

To prevent senior citizens from becoming trapped in an agreement (reverse mortgage) they do not need, family members and trusted friends need to be involved in any financial decisions considered. Elderly individuals need to be educated on the many requirements and stipulations of a reverse mortgage, especially regarding the related costs and fees and a determination if the homeowner can actually afford a reverse mortgage.

8.5 Elderly-Targeted Work-at-Home Schemes

Many individuals are targeted, via unsolicited e-mails, with the opportunity to make money from the comfort of their own home. The pitch in the unsolicited e-mails is directed to people who are in their home during daytime business hours. An ideal target group for these work-at-home solicitations is retired individuals.

With more and more elderly citizens becoming comfortable with using computers and communicating via e-mail, a work-at-home money-making opportunity can be a made-to-order endeavor for many senior citizens. A popular job opportunity targeted toward elderly individuals is the position of package manager. These positions are advertised as work-at-home opportunities that require no heavy lifting. The package manager duties include receiving items mailed to their house, repacking the material, and mailing the boxes to addresses provided.

From: <amacorpquyqo@usa.com>

To: Administrator jyoungblood5@cox.net

Subject: Good income from home? This is real

Our company is happy to propose this new great vacancy of Package Manager.

This position is designed exclusively for homemakers and the retired. If you are staying at home from 9am through 5pm, this job is ideal for you.

You will have to work with parcels. You will have to receive parcels, repack them and send them to the end addressee. This job is very simple and it is ideally suited for the aged and others who either work from home or are at home during daytime hours.

There will be no heavy packages. Most packages contain toys and clothes.

Enrollment requires no money. You will not have to spend any of your money earning money with us. All work-related expenses are on us.

To work for our company you will have to have a computer with an access to the Internet, a mobile phone and means to print necessary documents.

The amount of money you will be earning depends on the quantity of parcels you will be processing.

During the probationary period people which are employed by us make up to $150/week.

Contact us now bdffhoko@10mail.org

P.S. To qualify, all you have to do is to on site at home from 9am to 5pm.
For those who are unable to fulfill this, this job is not for you.

The material that requires repacking is merchandise that was purchased through various Internet websites using stolen credit/debit card information. The goal of the individuals committing this type of fraud is to have the fraudulently purchased merchandise arrive at the desired destination in new packaging and from an address not related to the fraudsters.

The downfall for the targeted senior citizens involved in this type of fraud is their unwitting participation in criminal activity and an eventual loss of money.

Typical payments for repacking activities involve the issuing of a cashier's check to the individual who believes they are currently working as a package manager.

After completing their first repacking assignment, the elderly individual is provided with a cashier's check that is written for an amount greater than their promised payment. Elderly individuals are asked to deposit the check into their personal bank account and keep their promised payment amount and related repacking and shipping costs. The remaining amount is to be wire transferred to what they believe is the home office. Other variations ask the elderly individual to purchase a prepaid debit card for the remaining balance and provide the card information and personal identification number (PIN) to an individual at the home office. As soon as the prepaid debit card information is provided to the person committing the fraud, it is used to make other purchases of items to be used in future repackaging schemes.

Unfortunately for the elderly person involved in this scheme, the cashier's check is later returned as counterfeit. Once the check is returned, the elderly individual is out the amount of money sent back to the home office and related shipping expenses.

To avoid becoming a victim of work-at-home frauds targeted toward elderly individuals, these individuals should never respond to job offers delivered via an unsolicited e-mail. Elderly individuals considering becoming involved with any type of work-at-home position should verify the legitimacy of the company through the Better Business Bureau or AARP. It is also recommended to discuss the particulars with a trusted family member or close friend prior to accepting a work-at-home position.

8.6 Raising the Awareness of Elder Fraud

Fraud awareness and prevention information is vital for anyone wishing to take their threat level off the path of least resistance. It is necessary for everyone to understand that those who want to commit fraud seek individuals who place the least amount of barriers on the path. The scammers' desires or means of making money are based on committing fraud, and they will work until potential victims are identified. A majority of these victims lack basic knowledge of the various fraud schemes used and the steps necessary to erect the proper fraud prevention barriers.

As it pertains to providing this fraud prevention information to senior citizens, steps need to be taken regarding security, loss prevention, law enforcement, and other individuals whose jobs pertain to fraud awareness and prevention. Security-related professionals should consider volunteering their time to share fraud awareness and prevention knowledge at local senior centers. These same fraud awareness classes can also be offered to residents of local retirement communities. A majority of these retirement communities have association meetings, which provide an opportunity to add fraud awareness classes to their agenda.

8.7 Reluctance to Report

When researching crime data for murder rates on a national or regional basis, the information is easy to find because of accurate reporting standards. Annual statistics can also be obtained for violent crimes, aggravated assaults, and other major criminal activities. The ability for these types of statistics to be tracked can be credited to reporting the incidents to law enforcement.

Statistics on crime against the elderly are harder to track, and accurate percentages of victims involved in crimes against senior citizens are ballpark figures at best. The main reason for a lack of accuracy in reporting and tracking of these crimes is a reluctance to report the incidents on the part of the elder victims. There are various rationalizations and assumptions about why elderly fraud victims fail to report the crimes. With a low level of victim interviews for the category of elderly fraud, logical assumptions have to be made.

As discussed previously in the chapter concerning the details of how my grandparents became victims of theft and fraud committed by individuals representing authority figures, their reluctance to report was caused by embarrassment. Between the crime and my visit, neither the police nor other relatives, friends, or neighbors were called. My grandparents were reluctant to call the police because they felt embarrassed about falling victim to a simple crime. This level of potential embarrassment concerned their immediate community of friends, neighbors, and close living relatives.

My grandparents, as well as other elderly people in their geographic location, operated on their perceived standing in the community. The embarrassment of falling victim to an authority-based trust figure fraud was perceived as possibly causing damage to their community standing. This community consisted of people they came across on a daily basis at the market and saw every Sunday at church. In their minds, a standing in the community could never survive the possible whispers at church.

Community standing is one of many perceived and legitimate reasons for elderly victims not reporting fraud crimes. Another reason for elderly individuals having a reluctance to report being the victim of a fraud is concern over the reaction of their children and other family members. After working for forty years and raising a family, an elderly widowed person or couple takes solace in their independence. With elderly parents living alone, especially if they reside in a different state, their children are always concerned about their well-being. The elderly parents have a wish to continue the perception of being competent enough to live alone. If it is discovered an elderly parent became a victim of fraud and lost a portion of their life savings, there is the thought that they will be forced to move in with one of their children or the dreaded nursing home.

Many elderly individuals also fail to report the crime of fraud to maintain a level of independence. If an elderly individual is forced to move in with family members or into a nursing home, the level of independence is erased. The desire of some elderly individuals could be based on the greater need to maintain their level of independence compared to providing information for the potential arrest and prosecution of the person committing the fraud.

In addition, many elderly fraud victims could develop a fear of retribution for reporting the crime. This could be a perceived threat or an actual threat made by the person who committed the fraud.

The reporting of elder fraud can also come down to knowledge. Many times, the elderly fraud victim does not know who or what agency to provide information on the crime.

Notes

1. Bruce, B., Scams that target the elderly. https://www.americanbar.org/newsletter/publications/gp_solo_magazine_home/gp_solo_magazine_index/scamstargetelderly.html (accessed August 3, 2104).
2. Retirement Industry Trust Association, Senior fraud initiative. http://www.ritaus.org/senior-fraud-initiative (accessed August 3, 2014).
3. Davis, A., Preventing home improvement fraud. http://www.homeadvisor.com/article.show.Preventing-Home-Improvement-Fraud.17322.html (accessed July 10, 2014).
4. Better Business Bureau. Home improvement tips. http://www.bbb.org/acadiana/migration/consumer-tips/2014/03/springtime-home-improvement-tips/ (accessed August 12, 2104).
5. Davis, Preventing Home improvement fraud.
6. Federal Bureau of Investigation, Fraud target—senior citizens. http://www.fbi.gov/scams-safety/fraud/seniors (accessed August 12, 2014).
7. National Council on Aging, Top 10 scams targeting seniors. http://www.ncoa.org/enhance-economic-security/economic-security-Initiative/savvy-saving-seniors/top-10-scams-targeting.html (accessed August 13, 2014).
8. Ibid.
9. Nolo, Reverse mortgage scams. http://www.nolo.com/legal-encyclopedia/reverse-mortgage-scams.html (accessed August 14, 2014).
10. Ibid.

Chapter 9

Advance Fee Fraud

9.1 Introduction

Advance fee fraud, also referred to as up-front fee fraud, is any type of scam in which the victim or victims pay an up-front fee for money, products, services, assistance, and so on. These scams have many forms of initiation, with a high level of attempts. In exchange for promised money or services, the potential or target victims are many, and the methods of contact vary. The individuals committing this type of fraud can work in groups or alone. Their ultimate goal is to select a wide pool of targets.

The methods of contact for a successful advance fee fraud can vary from an actual mailed letter, e-mail, advertisement, potential job announcement, and so on. To gain the attention of the potential victim or target, the fraudster can write a letter to tug at the heartstrings of a person or can seem to offer large monetary payment, help locate a missing child or family member, or aid law enforcement in the capture of a criminal. The individuals committing the various types of advance fee fraud cast a wide net or solicit a wide range or large number of targets. To be profitable, the criminals only need to have success with defrauding a few individuals even though they contact thousands.

Many individuals working as security, loss prevention, or law enforcement professionals will cite what is referred to as a Nigerian 419 letter when referencing many advance fee frauds. This type of scam received its name because it originated in the country of Nigeria, and the former Nigerian criminal code number for theft under deception was 419. Since its inception, this type of crime has moved beyond the borders of Nigeria and is practiced by fraudsters worldwide.

9.2 419 Advance Fee Fraud Letter Scams

The types of letter generated by advance fee scams are now referred to as an advance fee fraud, but many professionals in the financial crimes community still use the 419 terminology. For the purposes of this section, these letters are referred to as 419 letters.

On receiving or looking at one of these letters, most professionally minded individuals will have their Spiderman senses alerted and recognize a problem. Unfortunately, there is a history of recipients who have responded to the requests in the letters, and the hook has been set. Past victims of this type of fraud are not limited to the individual. Many past victims have been business owners and executives, who have actually lost company assets as a result of this type of fraud.

The most current method of delivery of these letters is through unsolicited e-mail, but there are still those delivered the old-fashioned way through the US mail. The most likely targets or recipients have been small business operations, churches, nonprofit organizations, and individuals. However, the target list is not limited to the groups previously outlined.

The letters are written to seek an immediate business relationship with confidentiality vital for all parties to become profitable. The proposed sender of the letter is usually identified as some type of official in a high-up position in the government in the country of origin.

Sample 419/Advance Fee Fraud Letter

MR JINHO LEE. <mrjinholee@undp.org>
(PRIVATE DEAL FROM UNDP PROJECT MANAGER ASIA-PACIFIC)

Greetings?
    Firstly, i must apologies for barging into your mailbox without formal introduction of myself to you, actually, I got your contact information from a reputable business/professional Directory of your country which gives me assurance of your legibility as a person while trying to get a good and capable business person in your country for business and investment purposes, this why without wasting any time i am seeking a decision maker to grab my offering $64,000,000,Yours free! With some simple conditions you will need to follow and work closely with me, you can't say my generous offer of 50% $64,000,000 a once in a lifetime opportunity.
    Have i got your attention?

Let me introduce myself I am the Senior Project Manager with the United Nation Development Program in the Asia Pacific Region with UNDP,I am the person directly responsible to answer to the board of directors to UNDP on monthly meetings, My special role is to evaluate all contract appraisals and the approvals to foreign contractors, As you are aware i am the Senior Project manager ANSWERING TO THE PRINCIPLE DIRECTORS OF UNDP i got sick of answering to stubborn management i decided to deploy early retirement, this is where our deal begins to work for you and me.Under my strict supervision you will be working closely with me directly, I am letting you to my finding, during routine supervision over foreign contracts; i noticed a series of over invoiced contracts that amassed to $128,000,000.00 Here comes the advantage you have, I have successfully secured the sum of $128,000,000 One hundred and twenty eight million US Dollars, I want us to work closely together and enable to transfer the total amount of$128,000,000.00

My question to you is do you want to be a millionaire all you need do is assist me on what is Required you get $64,000,000. Upon the success of the transfer we shall form a partnership and invest my share with yours into blue chip investments, As a result of this obviously i will have to surrender my position with UNDP. Then immediately afterwards make provision to relocate to your country. Now i hope you understand everything is transparent all things my side are perfected at this point all you need is to follow my directives.

Accept the $128,000,000.00 into your business account bearing in mind it is a 50-50 deal.I will require UN undertaking from you that you will not run of with the $128,000,000 Driven by greed. On this basis i will agree to assist you transfer smoothly to your account $128,000,000.00 that at that point in time, call it winnings or compensation is your choice it's the $64,000,000 dollar question.

PLEASE YOU HAVE TO PROVIDE YOUR FULL INFORMATION SUCH AS STATED BELOW;

1) Full Name
2) Full Address
3) Age
4) Sex
5) Home Telephone
6) Mobile Phone
7) Active Email Account

8) Fax Number
9) Business Number
10) Business Address
11) Current occupation status
12) Country of Origin
13) Nationality

Also be informed that this transaction will take us 15 working days to accomplish beginning from When i receive your Data, after you have assumed the position of foreign contractor to UNDP.I will Also file an application in the UNDP headquarters & secure the necessary approval and letter of Clearance. you as Contractor to UNDP in favor of moving this funds to an account that will be Provided by you. This process is 100% risk free as i have set out all the modalities to see that a legalized method is used because then i will prepare all the necessary documents, Please note that utmost secrecy and confidentiality is required at all times during this transaction, Once the funds have been transferred into your nominated bank account we shall share ratio of 50% for me, 50% for you. If you are not interested please delete this proposal, so that i can look for another competent partner to conclude this above mentioned transaction.Should you be interested please send me your full details as stated above.

Your earliest response to this email will be appreciated.

Best Regards

Mr Don Jinho Lee
Senior Project Manager to UNDP

As you can see in the sample 419 letter, the potential to share a large amount of money is appealing, and with the initial contact, there is no mention of a monetary requirement. The initial steps call for the recipient to provide detailed contact and personal information.

Once contact has been made with the target and the target has responded with the initial information, further and more detailed requests are made. The next step for contact with the victim by the perpetrator is to request account deposit information to begin the process for the transfer of funds. The follow-up conversations usually contain the discussion of the money that is to be removed from the country and shared. With the potential to gain a percentage of millions of dollars, many victims easily provide financial institution information.

After obtaining the target's financial account information, which is used to commit additional fraud at a later date, the target is informed of delays in the process. The letter writer claims the process is continuing, but a small payment is required. These small up-front payments become continuous events and can continue until the victim gives up on the process or moves on to another step. The reasons given for the required additional payments can include the need for a tax payment, processing fee, government-accessed payment, or attorney fee. The up-front payments keep increasing as long as the dream of riches are still in the mind of the target. Many times, the victim runs out of money or realizes he or she will never receive the bulk sum of money from out of the country or that they are a victim of fraud.

A final step in the 419 letter process, once the victim has been taken for a sizable amount of up-front fees, is for the victim to come to the country of the letter writer's origin for a face-to-face meeting. Other requests have been made to meet with the victim in a neutral country in a hotel room for the money transfer. Once the victim leaves the United States and travels to a foreign country, the victim is at the mercy of the fraudsters.

Victims of this scam have reportedly endured physical harm or threats and basically been forced to release a larger amount of money or money is extorted from family members for their safe return.

After speaking with victims of 419 letter or advance fee fraud letter scams over the years, some have mentioned follow-up attempts at additional fraud. After the victim has accepted the loss of various amounts of money to those engaged in the fraud, the victim is contacted by one or more individuals claiming to be investigators pursuing criminals committing the type of fraud by which they were victimized. The new fraudsters claim their information was obtained through the investigative process, and they are here to help the victim recover their money. Many times, the hook is set again.

As time goes on, there is no actual investigation, but there are additional requests for up-front money to cover investigative costs. To keep the victim in the scam, the victim is told that the investigators are close to closing the case and the victim's money will be returned. But, to ensure successful closure of the case, more investigative fees are required.

Alternate versions of 419 advance fee fraud letters have also surfaced using well-known names of high-level government officials (numerous examples are provided in Appendix B). The sales pitch is similar to those of years of advance fee letters offering the promise of a large monetary payout. Typical 419 advance fee letters make an initial request for personal information, with follow-up attempts to obtain advance payments and the release of personal financial information.

Newer versions entice the recipient by using the name and official government title of senior officeholders. These letters also make an up-front request for bank account information, including the account and routing numbers. The hope is to have the recipient believe in the legitimacy of the letter sender for a quick transfer of the promised funds. The following example uses the name of the current chair of the Board of Governors of the Federal Reserve System:

From: MRS. JANET YELLEN <janyelnny.frb1822@hotmail.com>

To:

Subject: FROM NEW FEDERAL RESERVE GOVERNOR./ NEW YORK.

Federal Reserve Bank New York
Date: 12th August, 2014.
Ref.: Payment Release Update.
Amount Valued: US$12,800,000.00.

Foreign payment allocation security code (US/A84PRFGN2014)

Attention: Beneficiary,

By means of this message, we wish to inform you that your hour of compensation and actualization has come after our meeting with the United Nations, Bank of America, Central Bank of Nigeria and the Federal Reserve Bank officials, it has been agreed that your real approved funds valued US$10,500,000.00 and the compensation of US$2,300,000.00 (Total US$12,800,000.00) will now be processed and released to your Bank Account through Wire Transfer Department of the Federal Reserve Bank New York.

However, it may interest you to know that after the meeting, with the Bank of America, Central Bank of Nigeria and Office of the Director On-line Account Department have entered into full partnership with the Federal Reserve Bank and your funds Total valued US$12,800,000.00 will now be credited to your Bank Account by the Wire Transfer Department of the Federal Reserve Bank as soon as you make contact with me.

To this effect, you are to contact us with the details below for the immediate release of your funds.

Full Name:........................
Address:.............................
Country:...................................
Telephone:..................................
Mobile:..
Email:..

Bank Name:— — — — — — — — — — — —
Address:— — — — — — — — — — — — —
Account No.:— — — — — — — — — — — —
Routing No.:— — — — — — — — — — — —
Swift Code:— — — — — — — — — — — — -
Account Name:— — — — — — — — — —

Thanks for banking with Federal Reserve Bank New York while we looking forward to serving you with the best of our service.
Thanks and Congratulations in Advance.

Best Regards,
MRS. JANET YELLEN,

Also with the newer versions of the advance fee/419 letters, the senders are focusing on the true scam and using US addresses. In addition, the recipients of these newer version advance fee letters are advised the actual large monetary payouts can be obtained with the assistance of the US government, in the case of the following example, the Federal Bureau of Investigation:

From: MRS.MARINA LUDA <service@newjbt.com>

To:

Subject: CONTACT HIM NOW FOR YOUR $10.5 MILLION USD

Attention:

I am Mrs. Marina Luda, I am a US citizen, 48 years Old. I reside here in Florida USA.My residential address is as follows, 7008 E Hwy 326 Silver Springs FLorida 34488 United States,am thinking of relocating since I am now rich. I am one of those that took part in the compensation in Nigeria many years ago and they refused to pay me, I had paid over $85,000 while in the US, trying to get my payment all to no avail.
So I decided to travel to Washington with all my compensation documents, And I was directed by the Federal Bureau of Investigation Director to contact Barrister Tony Gani, who is a representative of the Federal Bureau of Investigation and a member of the Compensation Award Committee, currently in Nigeria and I contacted him and he explained everything to me. He said whoever is contacting us through emails are fake.

He took me to the paying bank for the claim of my compensation payment. Right now I am the most happiest woman on earth because I have received my compensation funds of $10.5 Million US Dollars, Moreover, Barrister Tony Gani showed me the full information of those that are yet to receive their payments and I saw your email as one of the beneficiaries on the list he showed me, that is why I decided to email you to stop dealing with those people, they are not with your fund, they are only making money out of you. I will advise you to contact Barrister Tony Gani. Kinldy send your personal details to him to prove your identification.

Full Name:
Home Address:
Occupation:
Phone Number:
Age:
Gender:
country:

You have to contact him directly on this information below.

Compensation Award House
Name :Barrister Tony Gani
Email: barristertonygani@yahoo.co.uk

You really have to stop dealing with those people that are contacting you and telling you that your fund is with them, it is not in anyway with them, they are only taking advantage of you and they will dry you up until you have nothing. The only money I paid after I met Barrister Tony Gani was just $355 USD for the paper works, take note of that.

Once again stop contacting those people, I will advise you to contact Barrister Tony Gani so that he can help you to deliver your fund instead of dealing with those liars that will be turning you around asking for different kind of money to complete your transaction.

Thank you and be Blessed.
Mrs. Marina Luda
7008 E Hwy 326 Silver
Springs FLorida
34488 United States

Recipients responding to this newer 419 advance fee fraud letter face a two-prong risk. Requests could be made to the respondent to provide the various types of advance fees as detailed previously. Respondents could provide the advance fees and remain on the hook until they realize they are the victim of an advance fee fraud. These same individuals could see the error in their ways prior to forwarding an advance fee, but they still face a financial threat by providing their personal bank account information.

Victims of the 419 letter advance fee fraud, as with other types of fraud, many times do not come forward and report the crime to authorities. This is because of the fear of additional threats or harm or simple embarrassment. "How could I have fallen victim to such an obvious scam?"

The prevention measures to combat 419 letter fraud are simple: On receiving any type of unsolicited letter through the mail or e-mail discussing the need to form a partnership to share a large amount of money currently in a foreign country, do not respond. Do not provide any type of company letterhead, names, bank information, and so on. The only step needed by the letter recipient is to contact their local police department's financial crimes unit for further guidance.

9.3 Work-at-Home Schemes

"Make $1,000 a week without getting out of your pajamas or leaving your house." This statement sounds too good to be true and was obtained from a flyer attached to a bulletin board. In addition to advertising work-at-home jobs on bulletin boards, a delivery method involves the use of unsolicited (phishing) e-mails (discussed in detail in Chapter 11).

Remember the famous P. T. Barnum statement: "There is a sucker born every minute"? I am not sure if people are suckered every minute, but there are individuals who look for an easy opportunity to make money. Many of the individuals who become prey in these scams might believe the statements: "If it was posted on or sent via the Internet, it has to be true" or "A person cannot post or send anything through the Internet that is not true."

With the wealth of information available on the Internet and the ease of initiating contact with people via e-mail, many people are vulnerable to become the victim of a work-at-home scam. As with the 419 letter scams discussed previously, many work-at-home frauds involve the need for up-front fees or advance fees. These fees are necessary to cover the expense of initial materials needed to get the business going. When the fee requested by the person committing the fraud is forwarded by the person hoping to begin a lucrative home-based business, the victim either does not receive work-related materials or receives items that cannot be used to complete the related job functions. The typical amounts requested to cover the start-up materials usually range between $500 and $1,000.

The types of work-at-home business ventures vary and are always changing. A popular business promoted as one that a person can start and work out of their home is that of a medical bills processor. The future entrepreneur is promised quality processing software and up-to-date listings of potential clients. With this type of work-at-home scheme, the victim normally provides the requested up-front fee needed to cover the cost of work-related material. Other victims request to receive the work-related materials prior to sending the requested payment. In an effort to add legitimacy to the scheme, individuals committing work-at-home fraud will forward medical processing software and name lists. Once received, the software is substandard, and the name listings are inaccurate and out of date. The victim later realizes that he or she paid for material that cannot be used for the desired position of a medical bills processor.

Additional jobs offered to make money while working from home include envelope stuffing, other types of payment processing, product assembly, processing rebates for well-known companies, and so on. All of these and other work-from-home jobs that require an up-front fee more than likely are not legitimate and will result in a monetary loss for the applicant.

When responding to an e-mail or flyer attached to a telephone pole/bulletin board, do your homework on the company offering the job. Research the company name through the Better Business Bureau and try to obtain the names of the company officers and a physical office location. If you are going through a telephonic interview process, ask yourself why there is no face-to-face contact with an official representative from the company. Also, if there is an up-front fee required before beginning work, this is most likely a fraudulent opportunity. Finally, personal information should never be provided through phone or e-mail conversations.

Additional forms of work-at-home schemes actually involve the person applying for the position performing a job-related activity. Typically referred to as reshipping fraud, individuals are solicited to apply for these positions via e-mail notifications. Reshipping fraud schemes typically follow the next scenario:

Reshipping Fraud

Reshipping fraud is a name assigned to work-at-home schemes that solicit victims through job announcements posted on Internet job websites:

- A job announcement is posted with the catch phrase "Work-at-Home Opportunity."
- The work-at-home job opportunity advertises the position using varying names that sound official and that will catch the attention of the job seeker.
- Job titles include reshipping manager, repackaging assistant, processing manager, merchandising manager, and the like.

- Interested individuals who answer the job posting advertisement are asked to provide personal information initially and are forwarded a job application.
- After completing the application, the individual seeking the position is usually hired without a formal interview.
- The newly hired reshipping manager is informed that the job duties include receiving items that are mailed to their residence to be repackaged and mailed to an address provided by the perceived employer. The repackaged merchandise is typically mailed to addresses in eastern European countries.
- The merchandise initially sent to the newly hired reshipping manager is electronic items purchased through legitimate Internet websites. The items are purchased using stolen credit card information. In addition, the reshipping manager is mailed counterfeit money orders. The counterfeit items are repackaged and mailed to the address provided.
- The newly hired reshipping manager is also provided with a check or money order that is provided to cover the postal expenses and salary.
- The items to be repackaged arrive in the same mailing as the payment check or money order. The reshipping managers are advised of the necessity for expediency. They are asked to repackage and mail the items received the same day as received. The purpose of the expediency is to have the items repackaged and mailed before the payment method is discovered to be counterfeit or fraud.[1]

Another popular method used to solicit victims to this variation of a work-at-home scheme sent via an unsolicited e-mail:

From: Jyoungblood <amdeeqes@ravemail.com>

To: Webmaster <jyoungblood5@cox.net>

Subject: Vacancy for you #1894891

Forwarding Agent Opening at Double K Logistics LLC
Payment: $ 13 \ per hour

GENERAL RESPONSIBILITIES:
Your job will comprise picking up packages at FedEx or UPS Service Center, verifying the contents and further forwarding.

For this employment you must be accessible by phone at all times.

You need to perform each order as soon as possible once you get the info about it.

- Coordinate mailings and deliveries (letters and packages from/to our buyers).
- Provide general paperwork and records.
- Run calculations.
- Complete weekly and end-of-month chars to assure results are traced.

Requirements:

- At least 21 years old
- Good communication and teambuilding skills
- Over the top customer service and interpersonal skills
- Great typing, data entry, and computer skills
- Accessible by phone at all times
- Stable PC and internet connection

Background:

We always greet experience of our potential employ-ees, but we also can hire a newcomer who is will-ing to quickly learn all the subtleties of working in our company.

Experience in customer care and sales is highly preferred.

If you are interested send your CV to Danyelledhysm@gmx.com

For work-at-home scams to be successful, the victim is asked to provide an up-front payment to begin the position or is paid with a counterfeit check. Victims are asked to deposit the payment method into their personal bank account. Typically, the check is for a larger amount than the salary amount promised plus expense incurred performing the initial job function. The victim is asked to send the amount of the check that is greater than the salary and job expenses via wire transfer to a designated person and location. The goal is to have the money transferred prior to the check being returned as counterfeit.

9.4 Telemarketing Fraud

The telephone is a popular method of communicating with friends, family, business associates, and so on. Many people use their phones to communicate with businesses to make reservations, purchase items, speak with customer service associates, and so on. The phone has become a common tool of communication and is widely used, with the cell phone replacing traditional in-home landlines. A large percentage of the population has a cell phone, and most take a cell phone with them whenever they leave their house.

The popularity of the cell phone only works to add to the ability of people to fall victim to telemarketing fraud. When stuck at a red light, no matter the city or state, it is almost impossible to look into the other vehicles on the street and not see one person talking on a cell phone. If the driver is not talking on his or her phone, a passenger is busy sending or receiving a text message. The same holds true when observing patrons having dinner at a local restaurant: Many people in the dining area or at the bar are busy with their cell phones. We have become an instant contact society, with little downtime when a person cannot be reached via the telephone. Having an almost-addictive populous reliant on being in constant contact with others produces an increasingly large target audience for people involved in telemarketing fraud.

Criminal elements who want to profit via telephonic communications from fraudulent activity view the popularity of the cell phone in a positive light. As more and more people purchase cell phones and keep the phone with them on a constant basis, there becomes a growing target audience for telemarketing fraud. Based on the individual or individuals involved in a telemarketing scheme, the initial contact promise or selling point will vary. Telemarketers will contact a wide variety of cell phone or landline users on a daily basis and try to sell a number of enticing offers.

The offers can range from free vacation or travel packages, extended warranties, cheap insurance policies, and so on. Not only are individuals offered enticing opportunities, but also they can be contacted to participate in charitable causes, to donate to a local resident's victim fund, or to purchase a specific product. During the initial contact with the targeted individual, the following selling points are presented:

- ■ "You have been specially selected to receive this offer."
- ■ "If you buy right now, you will receive a special bonus prize."
- ■ "There is a limited time frame to purchase [receive] the offer or prize."
- ■ "Only a limited number are available."

The individual making the initial contact has to obtain the attention of the target early in the conversation. The interest can be raised based on being offered an unbelievable opportunity or through a sympathetic discussion on the unfortunate accidental death of a local resident. No matter the method used by the caller, if the fraudster can gain the interest of the target individual, the potential for fraud raises.

To help the person making the telephone call not raise a level of suspicion in the individual targeted, the caller will have the name of the person they are calling. A person answering the phone and receiving an offer that starts out, "You have been selected to receive a free vacation to Las Vegas," might develop a level of disbelief.

If the person answering the phone is addressed by name with the same offer, the call now becomes more personal and believable. The individual or target answering the call and receiving the offer directed to them personally could think in the back of their mind that they could have registered or signed up to receive a special offer.

With the increasing growth of what is available through the Internet or from advancing computer programs, it is a somewhat easy task for criminal elements to match a name with a phone number. National cell phone directory websites can also be accessed to obtain the name of a person associated with a specific cell phone number. In addition, regional name and phone number call lists can be obtained from a wide variety of data collection groups.

To increase the target audience for potential victims of telemarketing fraud, another means of contact is through text messages. Restaurants typically have patrons register their name and cell phone number to receive special offers. This is a good marketing tool, and customers can actually receive quality text message offers from a restaurant or other retail operations.[2] A marketing method that is good for the retail business world can be easily exploited and has now become a contact means for telemarketing fraud.

Any person with a cell phone can now receive that special text message, only reserved for them, for a free vacation offer, discounted insurance, or affordable travel packages. The text message recipient is alerted of the offer and the limited time frame in which to respond. If the person receiving the text message offer does not call back within the allotted time frame with the special offer code, the opportunity will be provided to someone else.

No matter the method used to contact the targeted individual, the goal is to convince the award recipient of a requirement to provide an up-front fee. For a charity or victim fund donation request, the ultimate goal is to have the contacted individual make a payment to the cause. To add legitimacy to the prize or vacation offer or charity drive, bogus websites are created, and the individual is directed to visit the site.

Once the targeted individual is convinced of the legitimacy of the scheme, they are directed to provide a monetary payment. Many options are used to collect money, the advance fees from telemarketing fraud victims. The various options are as follows:

- Placing cash in an envelope and mailing it to an address provided.
- Providing a credit card number, with the promise that only the agreed-on amount will be deducted.
- Placing a certain amount on a gift card and forwarding the card to an address provided.
- Placing a certain amount on a prepaid debit card and providing the account number and personal identification number (PIN) to a designated representative.
- Providing actual bank account information, checking/savings account numbers, and the bank routing number.
- Sending a set amount through a wire transfer to the account number provided.

- Sending a set amount through a money transfer organization to the location and recipient name provided.
- Writing a check for a set amount and having the check picked up by a courier.[3]

Based on the operating procedure of the individual committing the telemarketing fraud, the rate of continued communication with the victim varies. Some individuals are satisfied to receive the requested advance fee and then move on to other targets. Others will maintain contact with the victim and continue promises of delivery as long as additional fees are paid. No matter the advance fee payment method, nothing of benefit is received by the victim.

With most telemarketing schemes, there are warning signs for targeted individuals:

- Winning a prize or contest that was never entered.
- Being able to receive a discounted product through a third party.
- Receiving an offer that is too good to be true.
- Receiving any offer with a short time frame for action.
- Hearing the words "low risk" from the individual initiating contact.
- Being advised there is no need to contact company references.
- Responding to any offer for which the calling number is blocked.

Adhering to the warning provided will allow the contacted individual to be diverted from the path of least resistance. Those not adhering to the warning are offering the least amount of resistance.

The actions of people who are contacted by telemarketers will vary from those who break off contact immediately, to those who go through the warning signs in their head and do not make the requested advanced fee payment. The last category, outside those who follow through and make the advance fee payment, are individuals who need to take verification steps to determine they have been contacted for telemarketing fraud. The additional verification steps are as follows:

- Use a reverse 411 website to verify the location and name of the number calling.
- Use directory assistance to obtain the phone number of any charitable organization.
- Visit the legitimate company website of the charitable organization and do not go through any text message links provided.
- Do an Internet search of the offer provided. Type in the name of the offer with the word *scheme* or *scam*. Most likely, there will be numerous hits on similar telemarketing frauds.
- Ask yourself why you are paying for a "free prize."
- Ask yourself what is the guarantee the promised offer will be received?
- Contact the local office of the Better Business Bureau for advice on continuing with the telemarketing offer. It is most likely that these trained individuals will advise of the potential for fraud.

- Talk the offer over with friends or family members.
- Remember that fund drives for local accident victims are normally established through a local bank.

To further assist individuals who have been the target of telemarketing fraud or to take an additional step off the path of least resistance, the following steps should be considered:

- Visit the national "Do Not Call Registry" and block cell phone numbers.
- Contact the local cell phone carrier's website and determine how unsolicited text messages can be blocked.
- Only provide financial information over the telephone on self-initiated calls for products the phone owner wishes to purchase.
- Realize that offers that are too good to be true are too good to be true.

Unfortunately, there are many daily victims of advance fee fraud throughout the country. Some choose to report the fraud to law enforcement, and others do not. No matter if the crime was reported to law enforcement, people who have committed successful advance fee telemarketing frauds have been known to contact the victim at a later date. The purpose of the additional contact comes from wanting to work with the victim to help them recover their loss. The unsolicited caller will claim to work for an investigative organization, a local law enforcement department, or a federal agency.

The contacted individual and former fraud victim will be convinced the sole purpose of the call is to help recover the stolen money. As the recovery assistance process continues and the past victim is ensured the contacting agency is close to recovering the stolen money, the victim is asked to help pay for investigative costs. As with the advance fees paid as part of the initial telemarketing contact, any additional investigative fees paid are lost money.

9.5 Unsolicited Prize/Sweepstakes Notification Advance Fee Schemes

As technology advances around the world, more and more people communicate via e-mail, text messaging, and various types of social media. A large and growing participation rate in the electronic communication arena has created another avenue for fraudulent activity. A popular attraction for those looking to commit fraud is the large number of younger individuals who use the Internet on a daily basis. A middle-aged business professional would most likely react differently from a teenager checking their e-mail and receiving the information outlined in Figure 9.1.

> Congratulations you have won 1,000,000.00 USD from Publishers Clearing House Online draw that was held today, do email us back Claims Requirements: Name = Address = Mobile-No = Sex = Occupation = Country = Email us back: pchonline-claims@hotmail.com

Figure 9.1 Email prize notification sent for the purpose of committing advance fee fraud.

It is also possible that the teenager notices a potential fraud at first glance, while the business professional sees a financial windfall or the other way around. Either way, there are a large number of these types of e-mails sent every day with an unknown number of respondents. The cost factor associated with sending mass e-mails is minor when compared to the monetary gain generated through fraudulent advance fee prize notification schemes.

E-mail delivery is not the only method used to attract potential fraud victims with prize-winning notifications. Social media websites are also popular venues, with random members informed they were selected as a winner of a large amount of money. To begin the prize collection process, all the recipient has to do is provide the personal information requested to the return e-mail address provided.

What makes this type of advance fee fraud attractive to the recipient is the quality of the organizational names used to indicate those putting on the contest. If people receive an unsolicited e-mail informing them they just won $1 million dollars through a contest operated by their local community center, their interest level would not be piqued. However, it would be different if the sponsoring contest corporation was one of the following:

▪ Publishers Clearing House
▪ Google
▪ Facebook
▪ Twitter
▪ Microsoft
▪ Yahoo

By using a major corporate name that is popular for conducting sweepstakes or a driving force in the Internet or computer industry, the interest level of those receiving the notification is aroused. Unsolicited prize notifications have become a worldwide issue, with all targeted individuals not residing in the United States. Individuals have received e-mails or social media alerts in countries around the world.

With these types of advance fee schemes, the methods of requesting the personal information vary. The target recipient can be provided with an e-mail address to send their personal information and begin the prize award process. Other targets have been provided a telephone number and name of a contact person at the organization's national headquarters. Once the individual makes the phone call to the contact person, the process of extracting personal information has begun.

No matter the method of notification or how the recipient is advised to begin the prize award process, the results are the same. For the contest winner to receive their large cash award, some type of advance fee is requested using a variety of reasons. Based on the claimed home country of the prize-awarding organization and the geographical location of the contest winner, the recipient could be informed of the need to pay a tax to have the money sent from a foreign country.

In addition to requesting an up-front fee for foreign tax purposes, the contest or sweepstakes winner is informed he or she needs to pay the service or handling fees. No matter what the name of the requested advance fee is called, the fee needs to be paid by the winner before the prize money is sent. Based on the amount of the prize and the determination level of the winner to obtain the cash award, the individual committing the fraud will continue to request various named fees for as long as the victim sends the requested monetary amount. No matter how much money is paid in one or more advance fees, the prize amount is never received.

People who commit unsolicited prize/sweepstakes notification advance fee schemes operate within the boundaries of the path of least resistance. Alerted individuals who supply the requested information through the provided return e-mail address or call the telephone number provided find themselves on the path of least resistance. Those who ignore the e-mail or social media notification, remember the following information, or adhere to the following prevention measures will make sure they become a less-attractive target:

- Recipients who do not immediately respond to the prize notification might receive a follow-up e-mail with an attachment that claims to legitimize the contest and award. The follow-up e-mail could be a revenge attempt for not initially responding, and the opening of the attachment could cause a computer virus (refer to Chapter 12 for additional discussion on virus-related software).
- Use caution when responding to a notification that indicates the winner was selected from a list of random e-mail addresses.
- Before responding to a winning contest notification, make sure you remember entering the contest.
- Do not be fooled by the well-known corporate name associated with the contest or sweepstakes.
- Never provide personal information as requested in the e-mail notification.
- Do not call the telephone number provided in the social media notification.
- If a well-known corporate name is used in the contest winner notification, check the legitimate company website. Somewhere on the legitimate website there will be information on any contest the company is sponsoring or associated with.
- Never pay an advance fee to collect a prize amount as the result of a notification of winning a contest or sweepstakes.

9.6 Advance Fee International Lottery Schemes

As discussed with the unsolicited prize/sweepstakes notifications advance fee schemes, the Internet is the favored delivery method used to inform a targeted individual that he or she has won an international lottery. With the growing popularity of social media, the individuals involved in international lottery schemes have also started using social media sites to inform their lucky winners. The common theme is the use of wording that the winner has won a prize in an international lottery. Most likely, the individuals hoping to successfully obtain an advance fee through the lottery scams are operating outside the United States (see Figure 9.2).

The lucky winner is informed via an e-mail of their great fortune and that thankfully organizers of the international lottery located their individual e-mail address, assigned the address with a random number, and entered it in the lottery. The e-mail account holder is notified that the number associated with the account was drawn, and they have won a large cash prize. A typical notification to the recipient could contain the following information: The subject line informs the recipient of the e-mail that he or she has won a varying named lottery. The lottery name usually has an official business name attached to add legitimacy. Names used in the past have been Microsoft, Google, CNN, or another technology-related business (see Figure 9.3).

From: Euro Raffle <1126306019@nku.edu.tr>

To: sgaines1211 @gmail.com

Subject: Re: ATTENTION: AWARD

Attentn: WINNER

We are Pleased to confirmed your E-mail as the WINNER of (2.000.000 EUR(OS)) Held JULY 2014 in Europe. We Randomly select winner's through our Partners Web Directory.
   Send Below Form;

   SEND NAME......
   Contact ADD...
   Home Tel.....
   Cell Tel.....
   Alt. E-mail...
   Quick Reply requested.
   Claims Director
   (Euro Raffle)

Figure 9.2 International lottery scam notification.

From: CNN <info@admin.org>

To: undisclosed-recipients:;

Subject: 2014 WINNER.

Your E-MAIL ADDRESS WON £1,000,000.00GBP IN 2014 CNN AWARD PROMOTION. For claims process, send (Full Name, Mobile Number) to Email: cnnaward783@sbcglobal.net or Call Mr. Paul John Tel# +27780573389 Contact with Reference Number: CNNSA838344

Figure 9.3 Lottery scam appearing to come from a legitimate business.

Following the alert is an official address located in a foreign country, with batch/ serial numbers added to make the lottery and results appear legitimate. In the body of the notification e-mail, the recipient is informed that the drawing took place on the specific drawing date. Information is also provided on the prize amount, along with additional lottery facts and that their specific e-mail address was selected out of 3 million.

The prize-winning recipient is informed to contact the lottery agent, and the alert contains a name and one or two international phone numbers. The winner is told to make sure to provide the batch and serial numbers when calling. The purpose of providing the notification numbers when calling the lottery agent is to let the call recipient know what prize format notification has drawn the caller's response. The e-mail recipient is also alerted of the time frame in which to respond to begin the prize collection process.

The alert closes with a congratulatory message sincerely presented by the president of the pretend international lottery company. To add to the supposed legitimacy of the lottery, no person under the age of eighteen is eligible to receive the prize and will be disqualified.

Once the prize-winning e-mail recipient contacts the lottery agent, the first request is for confidentiality for security reasons. The second request is for the prize winner to provide personal information: name, address, phone numbers, Social Security number (SSN) for tax purposes, and copies of a driver's license and passport. The need to obtain the vast amount of personal information from the prize winner supposedly is for verification purposes and to initiate the money transfer process. If the personal information requested is forwarded, the target is most likely to become a victim of an advance fee fraud (see discussion in this chapter) and identity theft (see Chapter 10 for additional discussion of identity theft).

To add validity to the lottery and subsequent prize, the winner will be directed to official-looking websites. The information on the websites has been known to contain copies of official-looking identification cards of so-called lottery officials, along with legal wording.

Once the target is convinced they are an official winner of an international lottery, the advance fee process begins. When an initial fee is forwarded, the individuals involved in the scheme will request additional payments for as long as the winner is willing to pay. It is up to the person paying the advance fees to realize they have participated in a scam.

With all advance fee frauds, the so-called winner is given numerous reasons to provide fees to assist with the prize payment: initial processing fees, international taxes, fees for transferring money across international boundaries, and so on.

To prevent an international lottery scheme from becoming successful, the following information and prevention measures will take the recipient off the path of least resistance:

- Remember international lotteries are illegal in the United States.
- Never provide personal information in response to an unsolicited e-mail.
- Do not call international phone numbers in response to an unsolicited e-mail.
- Opening provided links in an unsolicited e-mail can result in a computer virus.
- Never physically mail or e-mail scanned copies of a driver's license or passport.
- Do not consider yourself a lucky individual when a person unknown to you attached your e-mail address to a random number and entered it in an international lottery.
- Do not consider yourself lucky if the random number assigned to your e-mail address was drawn from a field of 3 million.
- Never pay an advance fee to collect a prize.

9.7 Advance Fee Loan Scheme

To start a new small business, expand a current operation, or obtain capital to keep a current business operating, the business owner will most likely look at borrowing money. Small business loans are very popular as a method of generating the money required for the needs of a business. Small business owners go through the paperwork process from various financial entities and obtain legitimate loans. Many financial entities receive loan requests from numerous types of business operations across the country, with some applications approved and others rejected.

As mentioned, there are many reasons business owners seek to obtain additional operating capital; many entrepreneurs have a strong belief in their product or idea and need cash to get the idea off the ground.[4] Whatever the reason for seeking a small business loan, the individual or individuals need to keep a clear head and ensure they are working with a reputable financial entity.

Those business owners who apply for a loan through the traditional process and receive a rejection letter might look at alternate means for obtaining the necessary financing. Often, the rejection of a loan application, desperation, or a strong belief in an idea can cloud the thought process of the business owner or entrepreneurs.[5]

Online options offer a popular avenue for seeking the necessary financing after rejection for a business loan. The tiger waits for its prey in this arena.

Fraudulent lending agencies will create websites that provide details of success stories and references from what they refer to as satisfied clients. The applicant is also promised a quick turnaround on receiving the loan, which is advertised at a low interest rate. Once the loan applicant is convinced they have located a legitimate lending agency, the advance fee process begins.

The small business loan applicant is mailed the necessary application paperwork to begin the loan process. All the documentation is generated to look professional, and these documents contain the necessary legal jargon to appear legitimate to the applicant. After the loan applicant completes the loan application paperwork for their current operation or new business concept, they are informed of the necessity of an up-front fee to obtain the loan. The money is typically required for the application- or loan-processing fee.

Another variation of requiring an up-front fee from the applicant is to guarantee the loan or hold the loan open during the loan-processing time frame.

Applicants are also informed of the necessity to pay lending fees that are based on the size of the loan. Based on the amount of the loan applied for, the lending fees can range from $10,000 to $50,000. For many small business operators or entrepreneurs, a $50,000 up-front fee on a $1 million dollar loan might seem acceptable.

Many people reading about and developing an understanding of how or why a small business owner or entrepreneur can become caught up in an advance fee scheme need to develop a relationship with the thought process of the applicant. After being rejected by a bank for a small business loan and perceiving that he or she has a great expansion idea with unlimited profitability, a business owner's rational thinking can become clouded. The same can be said about the entrepreneur who believes he or she has the foundation for a solid business plan and subsequent operation. With this type of thinking and desire, certain levels of desperation can take over.

When looking at the rationale of a business owner or entrepreneur and their desire to obtain additional capital, one must also look at how the thinking can play into the path of least resistance. A rational-thinking business owner who is operating within the parameters of a business operation would scoff at the thought of paying a large amount of money to secure a loan. Entrepreneurs with a million-dollar idea will slowly work through the process of lining up financiers to launch the business successfully. These business individuals deviate from the path of least resistance, and those operating in the fraudulent world of advance fee small business loans are aware of this thinking. The criminals are looking to target the business operator and entrepreneur who stay on the path of least resistance.

From a prevention perspective, anyone in the business world or looking to create a new business based on a groundbreaking idea needs to understand that legitimate financial institutions or lending agencies do not require or ask for up-front fees for processing the loan or for application fees. Strict due diligence needs to take place on the part of the applicant to ensure the lending agency is legitimate; strict time frames for obtaining the loan or the promise of a guaranteed loan should never cloud the thought process.

9.8 Individual Consumer Advance Fee Loan Fraud

Businesses and entrepreneurs are not the only groups of people who are susceptible to or targets for an advance fee loan. Individuals are also the target of advance fee loans, and what makes them attractive to targets is a level of desperation. Many individuals throughout this country experience financial hardships and are in desperate need of money. The need for additional cash flow could come from the loss of a job, unexpected expense, vehicle breakdown, family medical expense, and so on. Whatever the reason for the desperation, the sudden need for a financial infusion of cash can work to cloud the individual thought process.

With limited avenues for obtaining a bank loan or borrowing money from friends or relatives, the next-best option is to seek loan prospects through the Internet. Unfortunately, people who prosper in the individual advance fee loan community are lying in wait to respond to Internet searches for quick personal low-interest loans. Most people who have built, over time, a strong financial footing can take their time and seek a loan from their bank or cash in other financial assets when the need for additional cash arises. The benefit for these individuals is that they have diverted their sudden need for cash off the path of least resistance.

The benefit for those looking to gain a financial windfall in the individual advance fee fraud arena is that they are sought by people whose financial situation has placed them on the path of least resistance. A desperate need for money and a proven advance fee scheme provide the perfect marriage for the fraudster and the person or family in financial hardship.

The typical method of partnering the individual seeking a personal loan and the criminal element looking to defraud people via an advance fee process is through an Internet search. The person seeking a personal loan as quickly as possible will conduct an Internet search and come across a company offering low-interest loans with an approval process that can be expedited. Another selling point that is advertised by the lending company and provides a further hook into the consumer is the promise of not requiring a credit report or credit history verification.

The goal of fictitious lending operations is to use the level of desperation and couple it with attractive bells and whistles. The ability to obtain a low-interest, quickly processed loan without the necessity for a credit check creates the perfect recipe for fraud.

Once all of the ingredients are combined, the communication and documentation process begins, leading the individual seeking the loan to believe the financial hardship will be solved in a short period of time.

Based on the criminal element involved in the consumer loan advance fee scheme, the communication between the two parties continues through e-mail contact or is diverted to telephonic discussion. With either method that continues the lending process, the desperate individual will continue to hear positive information, making them believe they are operating with a legitimate agency.

Once the hook is set, the person seeking the loan is asked to provide personal information: their name, address, phone number, SSN, and so on. The purpose of having the personal information has nothing to do with the lending process and more with the process of further victimization through identity theft (see Chapter 10 for additional information on identity theft).

After the personal information is forwarded and the so-called necessary forms are completed, the only step remaining in the lending process is the small matter of a processing fee. The individual seeking the loan is told that once the processing or application fee is received, the loan amount will be secured and sent to the applicant. Another method of obtaining the up-front fee from the consumer is through an insurance fee that is necessary to hold and secure the loan amount. As with the processing fee, once the insurance fee is received, the loan amount will be in the hands of the consumer.

The methods used to obtain the advance fee from the consumer vary and include using a wire transfer or a prepaid debit card. With the prepaid debit card, the consumer is asked to put the advance fee amount on the card and forward the access code and PIN to the lending agency. Once the advance fee is sent through a wire transfer or collected via a prepaid debit card, the loan never materializes. Contact is broken between the lending agency and the consumer, and the consumer is out the amount of the advance fee.

The prevention measures that should be followed by those seeking an individual loan are as follows:

- Do not try to obtain a personal loan through an Internet search.
- Never provide personal information through phone conversations or seek a loan over the phone.
- Always use directory assistance to obtain telephone numbers for any businessperson you need to contact. This includes looking for a lending agency or any other type of business operation.
- Never provide credit card numbers over the phone when seeking a personal loan or for a loan guarantee.
- Never give out the access code to a prepaid debit card, for any reason.
- Never conduct a wire transfer to send a fee to secure a personal loan.
- Remember that no legitimate lending agency will process a loan without conducting a credit history check.
- Never pay an advance fee to obtain a personal or any type of loan.

9.9 Debt Elimination Fraud

CASE STUDY 9.1

It is a comforting feeling knowing there are countless people who are interested in providing an average citizen excess money generated through overinvoiced government contracts in a foreign country, by entering my e-mail address in an international lottery, by paying large sums of cash to work out of my house, by working a few hours a week conducting mystery shopping visits, by allowing participation in money-making opportunities through telemarketing, and by obtaining a personal loan without conducting intrusive credit reports. It is hoped that a person or group will develop a program to allow an average citizen to eliminate personal debt and not harm their individual credit history.

I am thankful my plea has been heard, and it is possible to eliminate accumulated personal debt, all for paying an up-front fee and protecting the credit history of the applicant. The advance fee is necessary to cover the processing of information and the loan documents. The companies working to eliminate personal debt also need an advance fee to cover the past expenses of researching volumes of government regulations.

The search of the government regulations revealed constitutional provisions and statutes that allow for the elimination of personal debt. These elimination programs have also been backed by the Federal Reserve.[6]

Unfortunately, there is no government-supported program to eliminate personal debt while protecting the credit history of the individual seeking to stop making bill payments. If a person in financial trouble searches the Internet and locates a company that promises the elimination of personal debt, the benefits outlined in the case study would sound appealing. Unfortunately, the information outlined in the case study has been successful in attracting loan applicants as part of a debt elimination scam and those schemes previously discussed in this chapter. In addition, many individuals who want to reduce their debt could see a flyer posted on a bulletin board or receive an unsolicited e-mail promising debt elimination services.

With bills not being paid and demand-for-payment letters multiplying, desperation on the part of the indebted individual could become a factor. Those criminal elements defrauding money through debt elimination schemes are banking on the desperation element. The combination of uncontrollable debt and desperation equals a person that will believe almost anything is possible—enter debt elimination schemes.

With any advance fee fraud, those initiating the scheme need to be contacted by an individual who wants to benefit from the many money-making possibilities advertised. Once contact is made, the caller is told what he or she wants to hear. With the combination of debt elimination schemes and an individual actually believing financial obligations will be cleared, the introduction of requiring an up-front processing fee can seem legitimate. If the person looking to eliminate debt is acting in desperation mode, the up-front fee is a small price to pay.

As with any advance fee fraud, those initiating the scheme will maintain contact and continue the promise of delivery as long as the requested fees are paid. The reasons for the up-front fees vary, but with debt elimination schemes, the reason often given is that expenses are generated through processing and document preparation. The documents are those the indebted individual has to present to the lending agency to have the debt eliminated.

To avoid becoming a victim of debt elimination fraud, the following information has to be understood and followed:

- Never believe the Federal Reserve Bank will become a partner in the elimination of individual debt.
- The US Constitution does not have any provisions that allow the US government to tell a lending agency to eliminate individual debt.
- Legitimate debt consolidation will have a negative effect on a personal credit report.
- Never respond to personal debt management issues through information advertised on a flyer.
- Verify legitimate debt management companies through the Better Business Bureau.
- Never pay an advance or up-front fee in the belief that personal debt can be legitimately eliminated.
- Never provide personal information to any promissory company that advertises its services on a bulletin board flyer or through unsolicited e-mails.

9.10 Student Loan Fraud

Many individuals graduating from college enter the workforce with varying amounts of debt related to a student loan. A majority of these individuals work to pay back their loans without any issues. At times, some of these students get into financial trouble and will look into alternative measures to ease the burden of their monthly payments. Unfortunately, many of these former students conduct searches via the Internet or respond to unsolicited e-mails that offer debt consolidation or elimination services.

9.10.1 Student Loan Consolidation

Former students are approached via an unsolicited e-mail or conduct an Internet search for the purpose of consolidating their student loans. Unknown to many former students, the only legal venue available to consolidate student loans is through the US Department of Education/Federal Student Aid Section.[7]

People working to commit student loan fraud will convince the loan holder that their loans can be consolidated into a single monthly payment. They will produce official-looking paperwork that requests personal information and contains legal-sounding jargon. The purpose of requesting the personal information is not for the loan consolidation process but for use in identity theft.

A major warning sign of student loan consolidation fraud is the requirement for an up-front fee to cover administration, processing, or consolidation expenses.[8]

9.10.2 Student Loan Elimination

Former college students are approached via an unsolicited e-mail or through an Internet search to lower student loan payments. What begins as an innocent search for student loan reduction can result in the loan holder being convinced his or her loans can be eliminated. As with the student loan consolidation fraud, the hopeful loan holders are asked to complete official-looking documentation. This documentation is not used for student loan forgiveness but for gathering personal information that will eventually be used to commit identity theft.

A major benefit to those looking to commit loan elimination fraud is a belief in the loan recipient their debt can be forgiven. A logical person thinking through the entire student loan elimination process will notice there is no benefit to the lender. Typically, organizations that loan money want to be paid back. Lending organizations will not forgive a student loan out of their good intentions. The intent of those posing as a third-party negotiating organization is to collect up-front processing and loan elimination fees from the loan holder.[9]

9.10.3 Interest Rate Reduction

Student loan holders are approached through an unsolicited e-mail and offered the opportunity to lower their loan interest rate. As with the elimination and consolidation fraud scams, the loan holder has to complete the necessary paperwork and provide an up-front reduction or processing fee. The processing fee is the end game of the fraud, and the paperwork is used to collect personal information for identity theft.

Individuals who want to lower their student loan interest rates should contact the lender directly and not try to go through a third party. Real and up-front lenders do not require an advance fee. Also, any fees associated with the interest rate reduction are collected at closing.

In an effort to protect against student loan fraud, the following information should be understood and followed:

- Never respond to an unsolicited e-mail offering any type of service related to a student loan.
- Never pay an up-front fee to pay for any service related to a student loan.

- Understand loan-processing fees are collected at closing and never as an advance fee.
- Any student loan-related activity should take place between the loan holder and the lender, never through a third party.

9.11 Additional Advance Fee Fraud Payment Methods

There are many variations of advance fee fraud, with one major item in common: All of these frauds require an up-front or advance fee to be paid. With the increasing popularity of prepaid debit cards,[10] some people committing advance fee frauds are altering the requested payment method. Victims of advance fee frauds are requested to purchase a prepaid debit card. Based on the advance fee amount needed to receive the promise of the scheme, the victim is instructed to place a certain dollar amount on the prepaid debit card.

After the prepaid debit card is purchased and loaded with a monetary value, the victim is instructed to provide the code on the back of the card to whoever is their contact. Once the person committing the fraud has the code numbers, the monetary value of the card can be removed by the fraudster.

In addition to having the victim place money on a prepaid debit card, the victims have also been instructed to purchase a gift card for a certain dollar amount. Once purchased, the victim is instructed to provide the code numbers on the gift card to their contact individual.

9.12 Advance Fee Fraud Deposit Items

Traditionally, victims of advance fee frauds that require a check to be deposited into a personal bank account were provided with a counterfeit or bogus check. Once deposited and the advance fee is withdrawn and forwarded, the counterfeit or bogus check is returned to the bank and charged back against the victim's account. Counterfeit or bogus checks are normally quickly discovered as a fraudulent item by the bank the check was drawn on. Once discovered as a fraudulent check, it is returned to the bank where it was deposited. The return process is normally a few days.

Using a counterfeit or bogus check as a deposit item limits the window or time frame when a victim can be asked to conduct another activity or transaction. The time frame between the check being deposited and returned can be within the same week.

To delay the deposit item charge-back process, victims have been provided forged checks. The life cycle of a forged deposit item is as follows:

- A legitimate check is stolen or obtained.
- The check is from a legitimate bank account and can be from a personal or business account.

- The check is made out to the victim, and the signature of the true account holder is forged.
- The check is deposited into the victim's account.
- The bank where the forged check was deposited sends the item through normal banking channels.
- The forged check is processed as a normal transaction by the bank where the check was originally drawn.
- The forged check amount is debited, as a normal course of business, from the account of the legitimate check holder.
- The forged check amount shows up in the account where it was deposited.
- Once the legitimate account holder notices there has been a forged check processed through their bank account, they contact their bank and complete a forged check affidavit.
- The legitimate account holder is credited the amount of the forged check by their bank.
- The bank where the forged check was drawn returns the item to the bank where it was deposited. The check is returned as a forgery.
- The bank that accepted the forged check as a deposit returns the check amount to the financial institution of the legitimate check/account holder.
- The amount of the forged check is then charged back against the account in which it was deposited.
- The victim of the fraud is now out the money of the forged check that was deposited. They now know they are a victim of an advance fee fraud.

The rationale for using a forged check as part of the advance fee fraud is to delay the time between the check being deposited and eventually returned. The time frame from deposit to return can be over a month.

The benefit to those committing the fraud is to have a victim who conducts a transaction that appears legitimate. The deposited check amount shows up in their bank account, and they were able to keep the difference between the check amount and the money forwarded to the contact person. By the transaction appearing legitimate, those committing the fraud can continue to have the victim make deposits and forward the advance fees. Eventually, the victim will have several forged checks returned against their account, increasing their personal loss.

Notes

1. US Postal Inspection Service, Work-at-home scams, https://postalinspectors.uspis.gov/radDocs/consumer/ReshippingScam.html (accessed July 13, 2104).
2. It is also profitable for businesses that collect personal data for marketing purposes to sell this information to telemarketing firms.

3. It is a good idea to use caution when providing a personal check to purchase any type of product or make a payment for any service. Checks can be used to purchase groceries at a local store or when mailing a bill payment. If a check is sent to an unknown entity, especially for fraudulent purposes, these individuals now have the account number and bank routing number. This opens the door for counterfeit check activity, bank fraud, or identity theft.

4. Needleman, S. E., and Simon, R., Loan scheme belts small business. *Wall Street Journal*, May 27, 2014. http://www.wsj.com/news/articles/SB20001424052702303749904579578481820306024 (accessed May 17, 2014).

5. Ibid.

6. Federal Reserve Bank of Richmond, Debt elimination. http://www.richmondfed.org/banking/education_for_bankers/fraud_awareness/debt_elimination/#tabview=tab0 (accessed June 4, 2014).

7. Federal direct consolidation loans, http://loanconsolidation.ed.gov/ (accessed September 4, 2014).

8. Farrington, R., Beware: student loan scams victimizing students and graduates. *Forbes*, June 10, 2014. http://www.forbes.com/sites/robertfarrington/2014/06/10/beware-student-loan-scams-victimizing-students-and-graduates/ (accessed September 4, 2014).

9. Ibid.

10. Ibid.

Chapter 10

Identity Theft/ Identity Fraud

10.1 Introduction

According to the National Criminal Justice Reference Service (NCJRS), 7% of all individuals over the age of sixteen were a victim of identity theft in 2012. This is a sizable percentage of the population, and it is also a growing number. Each year, more and more people become a victim to some sort of identity theft, costing them lost time, embarrassment, a ruined credit report, and money. It takes, on average, about six months and 150 to 250 hours of personal time to recover from an attack. This is time and money spent by the individual to recover their good name and credit rating.[1]

There are many faces or aspects to the topic of identity theft; the taking of an individual's identity is the first step in the process of the criminal committing the crime and stealing money in the good name of the victim. The actual first steps begin with the criminal looking for potential targets and with the potential targets living day to day and not taking the necessary precautions to avoid becoming an identity theft victim.

From the criminal side of the equation, these individuals have spent many years learning the various methods to steal a person's identity. This can include bank account takeover, fraudulent withdrawals, check fraud, new account fraud, credit card fraud, loan fraud, and so on. The information used to assume the identity of another can include the target's Social Security number (SSN), home address, bank statement information, tax returns, personal information contained on a home computer, lax online consumer shopping habits, lost driver's license, stolen mail, and more.

On the consumer side of the identity theft process, the potential target can take steps to place a greater barrier or wall against identity theft. These steps will not stop the potential thief from committing the act of identity theft but will alter the path of least resistance and lead the criminal toward an easier target. In this chapter, many methods of identity theft are discussed along with preventive measures that can be implemented by the individual.

10.2 What Is Identity Theft?

A basic definition or understanding of *identity theft* is allowing personal information to be obtained, located, discovered, and so on by an individual who wants to use the information for criminal purposes. A criminal has the choice when committing financial fraud to use his or her own name, address, SSN, and other personal information. Or, the criminal can collect the personal information of an unsuspecting individual and use that individual's good name to open fraudulent bank accounts, obtain loans, open new credit card accounts, and more. From the aspect of not wanting to get caught stealing large amounts of money and going to prison, the assumption of the identity of another is more appealing.

When discussing identity theft, the list of victims is long and growing daily. The particular victim or victims to target is unknown until the criminal decides to commit the crime and begins looking for a target. In the world of past, current, and future identity theft perpetrators, there is no national association, local chapters, or group meetings for their special "club." These individuals do not sit around and share pictures and basic information of potential targets on a large-scale basis.[2]

Once a person or group decides to commit the crime of identity theft, one of the initial steps is to locate target individuals. This is an important step in the identity theft process, and the target identification practices of the criminal can be changed or altered by the actions of potential victims. The rationale behind the identification methods being altered during the target search process is based on the actions of each and every individual. The individual actions basically harden or weaken the target.

With the crime of identity theft, everyone is a potential target. How each individual target proceeds along the path of least resistance will direct the effort level a criminal will put forth in obtaining a person's personal information. A potential target can implement one or more of the following points in an effort to make them less of an ideal target of the identity thief. The more points implemented, the more secure their good name is protected along the path of least resistance.

- Use a post office box as your primary address for mail delivery.
- Shred all preapproved credit card applications received.
- Do not carry your Social Security card in a wallet or purse on a daily basis.

- Only travel with credit cards you plan to use on the trip.
- Do not bring your checkbook on out-of-state trips.
- Be wary of the Good Samaritan.
- Protect personal information in the family car.
- Do not leave a personal laptop unsecured in a hotel room or in a vehicle for an extended period of time.
- Utilize identity theft protection services.
- Do not willingly provide a social security number (SSN).
- Where is my social security card?

10.2.1 Use a Post Office Box as Your Primary Address for Mail Delivery and Shred All Preapproved Credit Card Applications

Credit card companies send out countless preapproved applications on a daily basis. Some mail recipients can and most likely have received more than one application in a single day. Receiving these preapproved applications in the mail lets the recipient know a credit-issuing agency is interested in their business. The recipient is only alerted of the business interest on receipt of the application. The credit-issuing agency does not send out an alert notification advising the preapproved application will be arriving in the mail on a certain date. With this uncertainty, how can a person know if a preapproved credit card application was mailed to their attention? What if an application was mailed to a certain address and prior to the intended recipient receiving the document, it was removed from the mail system?

Based on an individual's residence or community, they can receive their mail by one of many different delivery methods. A condominium/apartment complex normally has a central location where residents can pick up their mail in post office–type key-accessed cluster box settings (Figure 10.1). In rural locations, the mail is placed in a stand-alone mailbox (Figure 10.2), and the box can be accessed by anyone. Neighborhood houses can have a mailbox-like device on the exterior of the house by the front door. The neighborhood can also set up post office–type box areas, or cluster boxes (Figure 10.3), where the resident can walk or drive up and use a key to open the door to their assigned mailbox.

No matter how a person receives their mail, once the items are placed in the receptacle, the security of the items is questionable. Mailboxes without a locking device can be accessed with no extra effort. Post office–type cluster boxes are accessed by the mail delivery person with a key through the back roll-up door. Once the mail is placed in the individual slots, the back door is closed, and the intended mail recipient accesses their individual box.

Entry into these cluster boxes through the back slide-up door is not as easy as for a stand-alone mailbox. However, a person receiving mail through one of these devices should not believe a key-locking slide-up back door is a deterrent to

Figure 10.1   Condominium/apartment mail pick-up cluster box location.

criminals who want to steal mail. A cluster mailbox system is further off the path of least resistance than a stand-alone mailbox, but not by much. Master keys to these cluster box systems are easily obtained by various criminal elements. If a master key cannot be obtained by the criminal, the actual picking of the lock is an alternative and easy process.

Based on the low-security features of the devices discussed for a person to receive daily mail, an ideal alternative is a post office box located at the local post office. Although no mail delivery receptacle is 100% secure from unauthorized access, using an official post office box is the best alternative.

Using an official US Post Office mailbox provides the greatest level of security against delivered mail being stolen before the intended recipient accesses the mailbox. By not knowing how many preapproved credit card applications have been mailed to a particular address, obtaining the highest level of protection against delivered mail theft works to raise the resistance barrier against becoming a victim of identity theft.

Figure 10.2   Stand alone unsecured mailbox.

Preapproved credit card applications that fall into the wrong hands can lead to unauthorized individuals obtaining and using credit cards in the name of the intended recipient. Other items a normal individual receives through their mailbox on a daily basis can contain personal information that can be used for identity theft. These items can include credit card statements, bank statements, loan information, and so on. All of these items contain sensitive personal information that can be used to assume the identity of another.

The ideal method to protect against identity theft through stolen but delivered mail is by using the most secure device possible. Once an individual has moved further off the path of least resistance to protect against identity theft by using an official US Post Office box, they can be more assured they are receiving all of the mail intended for them.

Prior to placing unwanted mail containing personal information or pre-approved credit card applications in the trash or recycling bin, the paper items have to be shredded. Every home or office location should have a high-quality shredder

Figure 10.3 Neighborhood mail pick-up cluster box location.

on site to ensure personal information on any document no longer desired cannot be read by unauthorized individuals.

CASE STUDY 10.1

When discussing the topic of identity theft or identity fraud, people are curious regarding how they can protect their good name and credit rating. Many experts on the topic will provide popular prevention tools, such as the following:

- Make sure to shred all documents containing personal information.
- Destroy all preapproved credit card applications.
- Never provide your SSN to an unsolicited caller.
- Maintain control of credit/debit cards and checkbooks.
- Make sure to password protect personal computers and e-mail accounts.
- Review individual credit reports at least once a year.

These prevention topics are good and effective and should be followed. This includes strict adherence while at home and out of town for vacation or on a business trip. Individuals not adhering to the security practices outlined will operate on the path of least resistance and become more vulnerable based on select personal items taken unwittingly on a business trip, for example.

I have provided fraud awareness and prevention training seminar sessions across the country to a number of attendees. A large majority of those in attendance are from out of town and stay in a hotel near the event. A favorite topic of mine to discuss or ask of those in attendance concerns the personal checkbook. I have all those who have their personal checkbook in their possession stand up. The first question I ask is where they plan to write or cash an out-of-state check.

The next question concerns the number of the last check they wrote or whether they know the number series of the checks currently in the checkbook. Most do not know the check number information and bring the checkbook out of habit.

- If lost, what check numbers does the person place a stop payment on, or do you cancel an entire series of checks, even though some were issued as a normal course of business?
- If lost, how much time will go by until the checkbook is noticed missing? Normally, this is not until the monthly bills are paid.

I follow up this line of questioning with the question of how many in attendance have more than one credit card in their possession. Normally, if this is a conference attended as a business trip, usually the business credit card is the only one that will be used at the conference. It is surprising the number of people who always travel with all the credit cards/debit cards they have in their name. I then ask why they travel out of state with a credit card if they do not plan to use it. Also, I wonder if they have a list somewhere of the credit cards owned and the card numbers. I hope they are retained in a home safe and not in a Word document with the title, "Credit Card/Debit Card Numbers," on a personal computer. If there is no list of credit cards/debit cards that the individual carries in a wallet or purse, how does the consumer know what cards to report as lost or stolen?

10.2.2 Be Wary of the Good Samaritan

To protect the account holder information on a checking account or ensure the security of a credit/debit card number, prevention steps also need to be taken when a checkbook, credit/card, or wallet is lost or stolen. Many times, a person will find someone's lost checkbook and return the item to the rightful owner. Once returned, the checkbook owner is thankful he or she does not have to change account numbers and wait for new checks to be issued. What they do not consider is that the person who found the checkbook copied down the account number or made a copy of the check face containing the bank routing number, check number, and account number. The consumer believes a bullet has been dodged, and the identity thief has a new victim with minimal effort. Even if a checkbook is lost and returned, go through the steps and close the account, open a new account, and wait for a new series of checks.

This also holds true for a lost wallet or purse. To show good faith, a fraudster finding a wallet or purse will return the item exactly as lost/found, even if cash was present. By returning the item with the cash, the person who lost the wallet/purse feels satisfied about the Good Samaritan, and they go about their business as if nothing happened. What they do not realize is that, prior to returning the lost wallet/purse, the so-called Good Samaritan copied all of the credit/debit card information. As with the information previously stated about a lost checkbook, when a wallet or purse is returned that contained credit/debit cards, close the credit/debit accounts and have new cards issued.

10.2.3 Protect Personal Information in the Family Car

Most people spend a lot of time in their vehicles on a daily basis, traveling to and from work, shopping, visiting friends or relatives, making sales calls, and so on. For some, the car is a second office. Although convenient, many people maintain a large amount of personal information in their vehicle. If their car is broken into and items stolen, the owner can make an immediate police report and provide basic information on what was taken.

A popular item many people have in their car today is some type of navigational system by which they can program in a destination and receive instant directions—a good and time-saving tool. If a person has their car broken into and this device is stolen along with other items, the owner will most likely list the navigational device missing on the insurance claim and eventually purchase another one. A key item that is overlooked by the consumer is having their address programmed under the Go Home function.

An identity thief with this information and knowledge that the vehicle's owner is not home at the time can also break into the residence to look for personal information about the automobile's owner. The personal information from checking accounts, bank statements, credit card statements, and so on can then be used to assume the identity of the vehicle's owner for the purpose of committing financial fraud.

In addition to protecting the navigational device, there are other items in most cars that contain personal information. Most drivers have their insurance card and vehicle registration in the glove box. Both items contain personal information. As a process of record keeping, a glove box can also contain work documents from the local garage with a credit card receipt stapled to the customer copy. Most, if not all, documents received by the vehicle owner for service conducted on their car contain personal information: Proof of recommended vehicle service work completed by the dealership, invoice for new tires, oil change completion document, vehicle inspection report, and so on.

In order to take their identity off the path of least resistance, the vehicle owner can adhere to the following steps when it comes to keeping personal information out of the family car:

- Keep the proof of insurance card in the wallet or purse of the driver.
- Keep the vehicle registration on your person and not in the car's glove box.
- Keep all vehicle work receipts in a file at home and not in the car.
- Do not visit the mailbox and pick up the mail when leaving for the day; wait until you come home for the evening (family mail could have bank statements, credit card statements, and the like and be left in the car until the driver returns home).
- Program your navigational device with your Go Home address as an address of a location close to home because all you need is the device to get you in the general location of your house.
- Never leave your laptop in the car when you are not operating the vehicle.

10.2.4 Unsecured Personal Laptop Computer or Computer Tablet

The laptop computer and the computer tablet are popular items for many individuals to play games, shop on the Internet, and store data. If these technological items are lost, stolen, or accessed by an unauthorized person, the owner can easily become a victim of identity theft and other incidents of fraud.

Large amounts of personal data are contained on these individual computing devices, such as individual identification information, downloaded bank and credit card statements, Word document listings of credit card account numbers, and more. A laptop that is not password protected and left alone in a hotel room can be easily compromised by a maid or hotel maintenance worker. The same holds true for a laptop or tablet left in a vehicle while its owner is at work, the gym, or shopping.

If the laptop or tablet is accessed by hotel personnel, the owner will most likely be unaware of the intrusion. If the laptop or tablet is stolen from a vehicle the owner will take notice, but their action steps after the theft will determine the threat level for identity theft or additional incidents of fraud.

To protect against the unauthorized access of personal information on a laptop or tablet, the owner has to maintain control of these items at all times:

- If the hotel room has an in-room safe, a personal access code can be entered into the safe, and the safe can then be used to secure personal items.
- If there is no in-room safe, the computer owner should take the item with them to protect against unauthorized access of personal information.
- If the computer owner is leaving the hotel room for a beach visit or some other activity for which taking the laptop is cumbersome, at a minimum the battery and charger should be removed from the room.

If the computer is removed from a hotel room, the owner needs to make sure it is not left in a vehicle for an extended period of time. This is especially true during out-of-town visits and with the use of a rental car. Thieves like to target rental cars, especially in popular tourist locations, knowing the vehicle most likely contains valuable electronic items (laptop/tablet).[3]

Prior to taking a personal or business laptop on a trip, it is necessary to ensure documents or files containing personal or important business information are transferred to a thumb drive and left at home. Many laptop computers have several documents saved that contain personal information that can be used to commit identity theft:

- Résumés
- Job applications saved and submitted online
- Saved online credit applications
- Downloaded bank and credit card statements

As will be discussed in Chapter 11, computer owners need to ensure they have not allowed their Internet browser to remember log-in passwords to frequently visited websites.

As discussed in Chapter 4, small businesses are also targeted for small business account takeover and small business identity theft. All of the prevention measures applied to protect the individual against identity theft also have to be followed by small business owners.

If a personal or small business laptop computer is stolen, the owner has to go beyond reporting the theft to the police. It is hoped the computer owner has detailed knowledge of the personal and financial information contained on the laptop. Based on the personal and financial information contained on the laptop, if it is stolen the owner might be forced to close bank and credit card accounts. It should never be safe to assume password-protected laptops and documents are safe from access if the computer is stolen.

10.2.5 Identity Theft Protection Services

There are several companies operating in the United States that provide individual protection against identity theft, new bank account fraud, unauthorized purchases, and so on. These identity theft protection service companies collect personal information (name, address, date of birth, SSN, etc.) from their customers. Once an account is established, customers are notified any time attempts are made to open bank/credit card accounts in their name. If the consumer actually opened the financial account, no further action takes place. If the customer did not open the account, steps are taken to shut down the process, basically protecting the customer from identity theft.

Legitimate identity theft protection companies provide the aforementioned services and generate new customer accounts once contacted by individuals requesting assistance. In an effort to protect against unsolicited phishing e-mails (Chapter 11), consumers who want to obtain identity theft protection services need to conduct the proper research concerning any organization offering these services. With the growing popularity of website hijacking (Chapter 11), consumers who receive solicitation e-mails from these organizations could be directed to an unauthorized website. It is up to the consumer to make the effort to locate a reputable identity theft protection company and not respond to solicitation attempts made via electronic communication methods.

Any individual or small business owner has to ensure they are not operating on the path of least resistance. It is necessary to ensure barriers are erected by the individual or small business owner prior to the loss of a laptop or other event by which personal and financial information falls into the wrong hands. The services of one of the many identity theft protection companies can erect another barrier against identity theft.

10.2.6 Providing a Social Security Number

Protecting an individual SSN is the number one prevention tool that can be used to combat identity theft. An individual SSN can be used to assume the identity of an unsuspecting person. Having obtained the name and SSN of an individual, the person committing identity theft can

- Open bank accounts in the name of the victim
- Obtain credit cards in the name of the victim
- Establish lines of credit in the name of the victim
- Purchase large-dollar items in the name of the victim

To ensure the integrity of an individual's name, address, date of birth, and SSN, caution has to be used in willingly providing the requested information. Typical locations where this personal information is requested are medical offices. New patients at a dentist's or doctor's office are provided with medical questionnaires and forms requesting personal information. The basic information requested includes name, address, contact information, and so on. Many of these information collection forms also ask for the new patient's SSN.

Individuals completing personal information request forms have to be concerned about who has access to the documents and how the data will be used:

- Is the personal information simply placed into a database?
- If so, is the database of information easily accessed?
- Before the information is entered into the database, how are the forms secured?
- After the information is entered into the database, how are the forms discarded?
- Are the forms placed into the office recycling bin?
- Are the forms placed into a secure device and later destroyed?

Doctor's offices and other customer-based locations have their rationale for requesting detailed personal information. It is up to the individual to inquire about the purpose behind the need to provide a date of birth and SSN. More important, it is up to the individual to obtain answers to the questions listed.

Placing personal information on an information request form can lead to the data being used for the purpose of identity theft. Good intentions can be behind the information requested by the doctor's office or other agency, but is the integrity of the data guaranteed?

10.2.7 Where Is My Social Security Card?

Many individuals go throughout their day making sure to protect against identity theft by protecting their personal information. Following the procedures outlined, an individual can erect numerous barriers to take them off the path of least resistance. These protection measures can include protecting bank and credit account information, securing the information on a personal computer, keeping personal information outside the car glove box, and so on. The major item each and every person needs to know a location for is their individual Social Security card. For some, the Social Security card was obtained around their sixteenth birthday; younger individuals received the card right after their birth. Typically, the only time a person locates their Social Security card is to provide verification when they begin a new job or change positions with a new organization. Unless a career change is in order, the Social Security card is out of sight and out of mind.

To prevent use of a lost Social Security card for identity theft, it is vital the card holder adhere to the following:

■ Locate the Social Security card and maintain the card in a secure location.
■ Take the Social Security card out of a wallet or purse and place in a secure location.
■ Only remove the Social Security card from the residence if it is needed as verification as part of a career change move.

10.3 Preventing Identity Theft

In this book, the chapters on frauds that target the individual discuss numerous fraud schemes that focus on victimizing individuals. Of all the fraud schemes listed in Chapter 7, Chapter 8, and Chapter 9, individual victimization requires an overt act on the part of the target. For these fraud attempts to be successful, the victim has to

■ Respond to an advertisement that lists an offer that is too good to be true
■ Respond to an amazing mystery shopping job offer
■ Fail to conduct due diligence prior to participating in a charitable cause
■ Failure to conduct proper due diligence before hiring in-home care (the fault could also reside with other family members)
■ Develop a belief they were singled out to receive a large lump sum of money
■ Respond to an amazing work-at-home job offer
■ Develop a belief they were selected at random as a lottery winner
■ Develop a belief they were selected at random to receive an amazing loan offer

Individuals who want to commit the numerous types of frauds listed in Chapters 7 through 9 make an overt act. These overt acts involve creating an offer or opportunity that attracts the attention of the eventual victim.

For the crime of identity theft to be successful, targeted victims need to go through their daily activities on the path of least resistance. Individuals who want to commit the crime of identity theft look for easy targets. These targets go about their day-to-day business, placing few prevention barriers in place in an effort to prevent identity theft. Differing from the fraud schemes detailed in these chapters, the eventual identity theft victim commits one or more overt acts. These overt acts include the following:

- Not using a post office box as your primary address for mail delivery
- Not shredding all preapproved credit card applications received
- Carrying an individual Social Security card in a wallet or purse on a daily basis
- Keeping all credit/debit cards on their person (including for out-of-state trips)
- Taking a checkbook on out-of-state trips
- Placing good faith in all Good Samaritan actions
- Keeping documents containing personal information in the family car
- Leaving a personal laptop unsecured in a hotel room or in a vehicle for an extended period of time
- Not signing up for identity theft protection services
- Willingly providing an SSN on all personal information request forms
- Carrying their Social Security card on their person on a daily basis or not knowing the location of the actual card

When an individual or business becomes a fraud victim, the opportunity created can be identified. For a business, many fraud losses can be traced to an employee. Through an investigative effort, it is possible to locate the opportunity or weakness in the daily operating systems. For an individual, the opportunity could have been created in a response to a phishing e-mail or participation as the result of receiving an advance fee letter. If either the business or the individual suffers a fraud-related loss, many times the cause can be identified.

With the crime of identity theft, victims become aware of the fraudulent activity after their identity (individual or small business) was assumed by another. With a majority of identity theft victims, the opportunity used by the criminal cannot be identified. Identity theft victims have to ask the following questions:

- Was it the utility bill I put in my mailbox at the end of the driveway?
- Did I not receive a preapproved credit card application?
- Did I not cancel my credit cards after my lost wallet/purse was returned with these items intact?
- Was my Social Security card in that returned wallet/purse?
- Did someone access my laptop that I left in a hotel room all day?
- Did that doctor's office properly discard my personal information form?
- Could my identity have been protected by signing up for an identity theft protection service?
- Where is my Social Security card?

With most frauds, businesses and individuals can recognize the threat and close the window of opportunity. With identity theft, it is up to the individual and small business to move their threat level as far off the path of least resistance as possible.

10.4 Keeping Credit/Debit Cards in Sight

The ability to use a credit/debit card to make product purchases eliminates the need to carry a checkbook or large amounts of cash. At most retail locations, the items purchased are paid for at the register. The consumer simply hands the clerk a credit/debit card and the transaction is complete. Many retail locations also allow the consumer to use self-checkout locations. No matter the process used by the consumer, the credit/debit card never leaves the eyesight of the consumer.

The only retail outlets that require the credit/debit card to leave the eyesight of the consumer is restaurants. Once a meal is completed, the server issues the check to the table. On most occasions, the server is provided with a credit/debit card as payment. The server takes the credit/debit card provided, removes the card from the sight of the cardholder, and rings through the transaction. Once the transaction process is complete, the credit/debit card and receipt are returned to the table.

As mentioned, many victims of identity theft have no knowledge of where the opportunity was created. Another question an identity theft victim can ask is, "Was my credit/debit card information compromised when I paid for a meal at a restaurant?"

Sticking with the path of least resistance theory, a consumer can remain further off the path by paying for meals at a restaurant with cash, using a prepaid debit card, or paying the check at the bar. If the restaurant does not have a walk-up bar, consumers can use the option of walking their check and credit/debit card to the cashier's station.

A major prevention measure in the fight against identity theft is protecting the integrity of the credit/debit card account number, account holder name, card expiration date, and the card security code (CSC) located on the back of the credit/debit card. This information, in the wrong hands, can be used to make unauthorized purchases and to create a duplicate credit/debit card. Protecting the integrity of the credit/debit card information, as outlined, could be perceived as paranoia. Paranoia does take the consumer further off the path of least resistance.

10.5 Credit Card Impressions

For various reasons, merchants and other business operations require maintaining an impression of a customer's credit card. Remembering what millennials[4] refer to as the olden times, merchants actually took an impression of the face of the credit card on a sales slip as part of their operating procedures. The actual credit card was placed into what is called a manual credit card imprinter (Figure 10.4), and an impression of the card's face was transferred to a sales slip. The credit card information on the sales slip[5] (Figure 10.5) was later used to complete the transaction, with the purchase amount transferred to the business account of the retail operator.

Now, a majority of credit card/debit card transactions take place with the customer running the card through a swiping machine (Figure 10.6). Merchants no

Figure 10.4   The manual credit card imprinter.

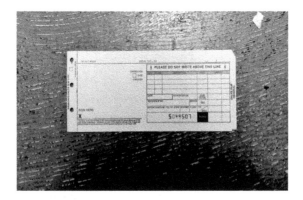

Figure 10.5   The sales slip.

longer have to use the credit card information on the sales slip to complete transactions. Credit/debit cards processed through a swiping machine do not require the card account number and account holder name to be recorded on a sales slip. Swiping machine transactions take place electronically, and sale amounts are automatically transferred to the merchant account of the business.

In the technology-based world of today, merchants and other business operations can have a need to take a manual impression of a credit/debit card:

- The swiping machine could not be operating correctly, which means real-time transactions cannot take place. Merchants take an impression of the credit/debit card, record the sale amount, and have the customer sign the sales slip. Once the swiping machine is operating correctly, the credit/debit card information (card number, expiration date, and CSC) is manually entered into the swiping machine.

Figure 10.6   The card swiping machine.

- Hardware and home improvement stores normally rent various kinds of equipment to their customers. Many of these locations take what is referred to as an open deposit and run the credit card through a manual credit card imprinter. The purpose of taking an impression of the customer's credit card is to cover the amount of the item rented. With rented tools, the price can vary based on the time frame the customer retains the item outside the rental location. Once the rented item is returned, the transaction is completed, and a receipt is provided to the customer.
- Customers checking into a hotel/motel may be required to provide a credit/debit card to cover what is referred to as incidental expenses. These expenses are typically for in-room movie rentals, minibar items, WiFi services, and so on. These expenses are above the amount paid for the room rental and are normally added to the bill on checkout.

Merchants and other retail locations can have other justifications for requiring customers to have their credit/debit card processed through a manual credit card imprinter. To protect the integrity of the credit/debit card account information and to protect against identity theft, the following information can take the consumer off the path of least resistance:

- Consumers need to ask the merchant where the sales slip will be maintained during their absence and who will have access to the information.
- Once the transaction is completed, consumers need to ensure they receive all copies of the sales slip.
- Consumers need to inquire if it is possible to leave a cash deposit rather than leaving an impression of the credit/debit card.
- If possible, locate a merchant operating in the selected service industry that does not require an impression of the credit/debit card.

10.6 Mailbox Fishing

Chapter 11 discusses frauds related to phishing that take place over the Internet. Although pronounced the same, mailbox fishing takes place at the actual receptacle where letters are deposited by postal customers. Items deposited in mail drop boxes (Figure 10.7) by consumers range from letters, holiday cards, bill payment envelopes, and so on. In an effort to obtain personal information from items placed into mail drop boxes, criminals will attempt to remove previously deposited items through mailbox fishing.

Figure 10.7   Mail drop box.

Figure 10.8   Mailbox fishing simply requires coating a heavy object with a sticky substance and attaching a string.

Mailbox fishing is simply attaching a string to a heavy object covered in some type of sticky substance (Figure 10.8)[6]:

- The item covered with the sticky substance is lowered into the slot on the mail drop box.
- Once lowered far enough into the mail drop box, previously deposited envelopes stick to the heavy object.
- The heavy object is slowly pulled out of the slot on the mail drop box with previously deposited envelopes attached.

The goal of individuals participating in mailbox fishing is to obtain mailed items containing individual financial information:

- Credit card payments: These items have the account holder's personal information, as well as their checking account number and bank routing number.
- Bill payments: As with a credit card payment, the criminals have access to personal and bank account information.
- Utility payments: These envelopes provide the criminal with personal and bank account information.

Many items deposited into mail drop boxes contain personal information that provides a gold mine for identity thieves. To prevent personal and bank information from falling into the hands of identity thieves, all mail has to be deposited into receptacles at the local US Post Office.

10.7 Stop the Preapproved Credit Card Applications

Many individuals believe they cannot get through a week without receiving a preapproved credit card application in the mail. It is hoped those receiving these applications take the proper precautions and shred the documents. It is also hoped that those receiving these preapproved applications receive their daily mail through their official US Post Office mailbox.

To eliminate a threat surrounding the crime of identity theft, consumers need to opt out of receiving preapproved credit card applications. The process requires a visit to the website of the Federal Trade Commission, where consumers can opt out of receiving these applications on a permanent basis or for five years.[7]

10.8 Obtaining a Credit Report

A credit report can provide an individual with their credit score and a summary of all open credit accounts. In addition, the consumer can review all credit-related accounts associated with their name and SSN. A review of an individual credit report is also a vital tool in the fight against identity theft. Information contained on the credit report can alert the consumer of unauthorized activity and credit-related accounts opened under their name and SSN. Basically, a credit report can be used by the consumer as an alert that their identity has been compromised.

It is vital that individuals obtain a copy of their credit report at least once a year to ensure the integrity of their name, identity, and credit history. To ensure consumers can access their individual credit report, the Federal Trade Commission has established the following:

> The Fair Credit Reporting Act (FCRA) requires each of the nationwide credit reporting companies—Equifax, Experian, and TransUnion—to provide you with a free copy of your credit report, at your request, once every 12 months. The FCRA promotes the accuracy and privacy of information in the files of the nation's credit reporting companies. The Federal Trade Commission (FTC), the nation's consumer protection agency, enforces the FCRA with respect to credit reporting companies.[8]

10.9 Advance Fee Fraud Letter Solicitations

Chapter 9 provides detailed information on the many tactics used so recipients provide some type of an up-front fee for a promise that is never kept. With many of the advance fee fraud schemes, the individuals committing the activity have a secondary goal of using the personal information obtained for identity theft purposes.

Newer versions of the advance fee fraud letters are surfacing that inform the recipients they are due a large sum of money and provide information on the process the country of Nigeria is taking to clear their good name. Recipients are informed the Nigerian Ministry of Finance is aware of the use of bogus advance fee letters in the past, and any letter not endorsed by the ministry should be discarded.

Some recipients of these newer-version letters, as in the example detailed at the end of this section, are asked to provide a greater amount of up-front personal information. Recipients are asked to provide the name of their bank, their personal bank account number, bank routing number, SSN, and driver's license number.

These letters are delivered with the initial purpose of committing identity theft, with no requests made for up-front fees. It is possible recipients of these letters believe the letter was sent on behalf of the Nigerian government and that they will actually receive the monetary amount promised. Once this level of belief is generated, recipients will provide all of the personal information requested.

After the personal information is provided, the letter's recipient will sit back and wait for the large monetary payout. The individuals sending the letter, via an unsolicited e-mail, will use the personal information to commit identity theft. With the name, address, banking account information, SSN, and driver's license number of the recipient, those committing this type of fraud can quickly work to attack the future victim's financial accounts.

Individuals who commit this type of fraud, via an advance fee letter, can quickly obtain a fraudulent driver's license (one that contains the actual license number) in the name of the future victim. With the necessary bank account information, counterfeit checks can also be produced in the name of the intended victim. These counterfeit checks will have the actual account holder name, address, bank information, and account number.

By obtaining the large amount of personal information from the letter's recipients, the following crimes can take place:

■ The counterfeit checks can be used to purchase merchandise at retail locations. The cashier is presented with a check containing the legitimate account number and a driver's license in the name of the intended victim. Once these checks are used to purchase unauthorized merchandise, the dollar amounts are deducted from the legitimate bank account of the victim. These unauthorized transactions can lead to the account being overdrawn and cause checks actually written by the victim to bounce.

■ Stolen and forged or other types of counterfeit checks can be deposited into the bank account of the victim in an effort to increase the available balance. Before the deposit items are returned as a forgery or counterfeit, unauthorized withdrawals are made against the bank account of the victim. Checks can also be written at retail locations to purchase merchandise as a result of the increased account balance.

After the deposit items are returned, the victim is left with an overdrawn bank account. If the overdrawn bank account causes the checks written to the various retailers to be returned because the account has insufficient funds, the intended victim will be targeted by the businesses for restitution.

■ Individuals committing this type of fraud can also open fraudulent bank accounts at other financial institutions. The person opening these accounts has the necessary personal information of the intended victim, as well as a driver's license containing a valid number. Once the accounts are opened, forged or counterfeit checks are deposited and the money withdrawn prior to the checks being returned.

Once the financial institution suffers a loss as a result of an overdrawn account, the letter's recipient will be the initial focus of the financial loss. This person now has to prove he or she did not open the account or make any of the transactions.

■ With the SSN and other personal information of the intended victim, unauthorized credit cards can be applied for and received. Once the credit cards are obtained in the name of the victim, they can be used to make all types of purchases.

Once the unauthorized credit cards are maxed out and no payments are received by the issuing company, the victim becomes the initial target for restitution.

Criminals will use varying tactics to commit identity theft. No matter the method used, the results are typically as mentioned. The identity theft victim becomes the focus for restitution. Because the victim did not actually commit the financial crimes, they do have to spend a large amount of time and money to clear their good name.

In an effort to prevent identity theft, individuals need to take whatever steps are necessary to protect their personal and financial information and make others a more attractive target on the path of least resistance.

From: Federal Ministry OF Finance <test@kcs.net>

To:

Subject: The Federal Executive Council(F.E.C), Code of Conduct Bureau

FEDERAL MINISTRY OF FINANCE.
Office of the Minister of Finance
12 LEKKI PENNINSULA, LAGOS-NIGERIA.
TEL: (01-1)+234-808-515-9809 (Hot-Line)
Ref: FMF/SGH/101/231

Date:22nd September 2014.
ATTN: Beneficiary.
PAYMENT FILE NUMBER: A
Release/TransferNoticeforyourdueFunds(US$3,500,000:00).
Payment File No: A.
24Hrs Service

It is very important that the recipient of this Letter should call this office in order to confirm it to us that this very Letter was received by you, the true beneficiary. You are advised to read this Letter very carefully because every paragraph explains what you need to know about the Release and Transfer of your due Funds.

You are advised to read this Letter very carefully because every paragraph explains what you need to know about the Release and Transfer of your due Funds.

At this point, we wish to remind you to stop all further contact with any person or person(s) whom is not recommended by this Ministry. Our Intelligence Monitoring Unit (I.M.U), Code of Conduct Bureau, Legal Unit and The Nigerian Police Force (N.P.F) have already apprehended some of those suspects whom attempted to divert your Funds.

You are advised to stop all further contact with some scammers you have been dealing with, that have defrauded you of huge sums because they are WANTED criminal suspects.

As the honorable Minister of Nigeria, I work on behalf of the Paying Bank of Nigeria Keystone Bank (formerly Bank PHB)under the supervision of the honorable President of The Federal Republic of Nigeria.

We are glad to announce it to you today that the honorable President of The Federal Republic of Nigeria and the Accountant General of the Federation have collectively Approved and signed the Order to Release and Transfer being the certified documentation authorizing us (The Federal Ministry of Finance) to credit your nominated Bank Account..

A copy of the Order to Release and Transfer have been forwarded to our international remittance department for the onward crediting of your Funds.

In other words, we put it to you that we are ready to remit your said Funds into your nominated Bank Account because we have a 3-4 working days time constrain to Pay-off each beneficiary short-listed to be Paid by this Ministry. Our Legal Unit have already reviewed your Payment Files and they have passed it on to my desk for me to Pay you accordingly, so be rest assured that you will receive your due Funds as soon as possible. Officially, you will receive your due Funds via an "Electronic Wire Transfer" which will enable your Funds reflect in your Nominated Bank Account within 48hrs after effect. This mode of Payment is defined as one of the best and safest mode to remit huge Funds internationally as it is absolutely different from the usual swift transfer which takes longer time. Most Banks within the United States of America, Europe and other developed countries operate with the "Electronic Wire Transfer" for international transfers because it is a recent innovation in the Banking industry.

Certainly we shall transfer your valued US$3,500,000:00 from the Sundry/Suspense Account of the Federal Government of Nigeria being the official Account for international/foreign Payments/debts. A Sundry/Suspense Account can be defined as a secret Account owned by a government and operated by certain assigned government officials being the authorized signatories whom must sign before Funds can be remitted from such account. For this very account no form of direct withdrawals can be made from it except a Bank to Bank wire transfer which must be Approved by the honorable President being the principal signatory to the account.

Consequent to the fact that I am responsible to Pay you, it is still my duty to enlighten you on the accurate steps to take in order for you to gain full possession of this said Funds being Approved in your name.

In the combat against fraud, Funds diversion and Funds delay, we have re-lengthily ensured that several foreign beneficiaries have been Paid accordingly in order to retain and rekindle our country's reputation on the global map because this recent government dispensation is focused and targeted to relieve all foreign debts as mandated by The Senate, The National House of Assembly, The Federal Executive Council (F.E.C), Code of Conduct Bureau and The Federal Ministry of Finance (F.M.F). Already, a lot of foreign beneficiaries have been Paid by this Ministry so yours will not be an exception considering the fact that the honorable President have Approved your due Funds today dated 22nd September 2014..

In accordance to section (1) paragraph 9 of the Settlement Edict Law of The Federal Republic of Nigeria of 1992, it is imperative that you provide us with the below listed information so that we can Pay you.

1. Full Name:
2. House Address:

3. Mobile Phone:
4. Home Phone:
5. Country:
6. Occupation:
7. Date Of Birth:
8. Bank Name:
9. Bank Address:
10. Bank Account Number:
11. Bank Routine/Swift Code:
12. A form of identification (Social Security Card or Driver's License) required for official references.

To this effect, kindly call this office immediately after you read this official Letter. TEL: (01-1)+234-808-515-9809This Official Letter is being issued to you (THE BENEFICIARY) by "The Federal Ministry of Finance" in collaboration with The Presidency.

Copied to:
The Accountant General of The Federation.
Keystone Bank (formerly BankPHB).
The President's office.
Yours Sincerely,
Dr.Ngozi Okonjo Iweala
Minister Of Finance
Federal Republic Of Nigeria.

10.10 Keeping the Crime Intent Silent

As previously discussed, many types of fraudulent activity take place in an overt manner once the opportunity has been identified. With the crime of identity theft, individuals will not know they are a target until it is too late. If a targeted individual believes a person is working to assume their identity, prevention measures will take place.

For the crime of identity theft to be successful, steps will take place on the part of the criminal to keep the activity out of the spotlight:

■ If the targeted individual uses an unsecure device to receive personal mail, unauthorized access can take place. Most would believe the unauthorized individual accessing their mail receptacle will take items that can be used for identity theft.

To keep their intended activity under wraps and not alert their target, sensitive mail items will be removed and opened and the necessary information copied. Once the desired personal information is obtained, the mail items are resealed and placed back in the mail receptacle.

As far as the victim knows, all mailed financial statements were received on time.

■ Individuals involved in mailbox fishing have also been known to remove mailed items from the receptacle and copy the sensitive information from mailed bill payments, including check data, before placing the items back in the mailbox. Because the targeted individual's bills are received in a timely manner, this works to keep the intended crime in the dark.

■ Sensitive items containing personal information that was left in the family car can be accessed during a vehicle break-in or by the hotel valet. Identity thieves will copy the sensitive personal information and place the documents back in the vehicle, leaving the owner to believe everything is normal.

The same holds true for sensitive information left in a hotel room and on a personal computer left unsecured. The intent of the identity thief is to have the targeted individual believe nothing was tampered with so they will not begin the process of diverting off the path of least resistance.

■ Remembering the discussion of the Good Samaritan, identity thieves want the intended target to believe "all is right with the world."

By following the awareness and prevention measures mentioned throughout this chapter, an individual or small business owner can work to ensure they are operating off the path of least resistance.

Notes

1. National Criminal Justice Reference Service, In the spotlight: Identity theft—facts and figures. https://www.ncjrs.gov/spotlight/identity_theft/facts.html (accessed on May 12, 2014).
2. This is not to state that criminals do not talk or share information. Some criminals might choose to work together, and information is most likely shared among this element. It is also known that a majority of criminal information, tactics, outside contacts, and so on is shared within the walls of local, state, and federal prisons.
3. Travel Insurance Review, Avoiding rental car break-ins and thefts. http://www.travelinsurancereview.net/tips-and-advice/travel-safety-tips/avoiding-rental-car-breakins-and-theft/ (accessed July 24, 2014).
4. Millennials, also referred to as Generation Y, are technology savvy individuals born between 1980 and 1995.

5. Information recorded on a sales slip includes the customer's name, card account number, card expiration date, and CSC.

6. Kang, E., Police advise identity theft precautions after a string of mailbox thefts in Manhattan Beach. http://www.easyreadernews.com/60971/police-advise-identity-theft-precautions/ (accessed July 26, 2014).

7. Federal Trade Commission, Consumer Information, Stopping unsolicited mail, phone calls, and email. http://www.consumer.ftc.gov/articles/0262-stopping-unsolicited-mail-phone-calls-and-email (accessed July 28, 2014).

8. Federal Trade Commission, Consumer Information, Free credit reports. https://www.consumer.ftc.gov/articles/0155-free-credit-reports (accessed July 30, 2104).

Chapter 11

Internet Fraud

11.1 Introduction

The cyberworld has evolved into various avenues that can be used to connect people, purchase merchandise, communicate, advertise a business, participate in worldwide auctions, and more. No longer do people send detailed letters through the US Postal Service or have to get in their car to make a purchase from a store. Traditionally, people wishing to sell unwanted items had to advertise and take a weekend morning to have a yard or garage sale. Thanks to the cyberworld, unwanted personal items can be sold online through a variety of Internet auction websites. In addition to making purchases through online auction websites, consumers can purchase almost any item via the Internet, including clothes, books, household staples, electronics, rare coins, vintage cars, and so on.

11.2 Internet Auction Fraud

Individuals have the ability to purchase items through Internet websites on a daily basis. Consumers have a choice to make a purchase through the website of a retailer or locate and bid on an item via an Internet auction website. As mentioned, people make Internet purchases on a daily basis, and a majority of the transactions are legitimate. The consumers are shipped the merchandise promised, and the retailer or auction site receives the proper payment.

With almost every legitimate business operation, there are those who see an opportunity to make some sort of financial gain through fraud or deception. As the popularity of the Internet increases in the world of consumer transactions, so do the avenues for fraud. People conducting commerce through the Internet rely on the growing simplicity, whereas the criminal element relies on individual complacency.

The more transactions the average person conducts through the Internet, the greater their internal level of trust for the entire online shopping process.

Consumers conducting online purchases through well-known Internet shopping websites can easily gain a level of confidence in the system. When the online shopper strays from the trusted and well-established online shopping venues, they can become a victim of potential fraudulent activity. One of the main reasons for deviating their online shopping attention away from the traditional retailers is the cost factor. When making a purchase online through a traditional retailer, the consumer is offered to make a purchase of an item at a set price. In an effort to purchase the same item at a lower price, consumers look toward Internet auction websites.

11.2.1 Internet Auction Websites

- Internet auction websites create an opportunity for a person (seller) to list an item they wish to sell.
- The seller creates a personal account with the Internet auction website.
- Sellers can list items they wish to sell on the Internet auction website.
- Sellers provide a picture of the item for sale, along with a description.
- Once the item for sale is listed, a starting bid price is generated along with a time frame during which bids can be placed.
- Buyers place bids on items they wish to purchase. The buyer can make multiple bids on an item as the price increases through the bidding process.
- Once the bidding window closes, the person who made the highest price bid is awarded the opportunity to complete the transaction.
- Based on the policies of the Internet auction website, the payment transaction can be made directly to the seller or through the website. Fees for processing and listing an item vary based on the Internet auction website.

In the cyberworld, a buyer can choose between numerous Internet auction websites. Sellers also have a choice when it comes to selecting a venue to place their item up for bid. Based on the overall integrity of the Internet auction website, the buyer has to be aware of the potential for fraud.

Internet auction frauds are developed to cause the buyer a financial hardship through nondelivery, product deception, and bid rigging. The various methods of Internet auction fraud are discussed next.

11.2.2 Nondelivery of Product

When wanting to purchase an item online through an Internet auction website, the buyer has an option of many sites. Fortunately for the consumer, there are reputable and well-known auction websites. Unfortunately, there are consumers who look for the ultimate bargain and will work with sellers offering the best deal on any Internet auction website.

The most popular method of fraud for buyers purchasing items through auction websites is nondelivery. Once the bidding process is completed, the buyer makes the payment to the seller. Unfortunately, the seller never delivers the purchased item to the buyer. For many Internet auction frauds involving nondelivery, the individual listing the item for sale had no intention of ever making delivery.

To make the bidding process appear legitimate to the buyer, pictures of the item are posted on the auction website. The individual listing the product for auction can post pictures of items that were taken pretty much anywhere. This can include on a retail store shelf or in other display settings. The seller can also have physical possession of the item and post a picture on the auction website with no intent of making delivery.

Another negative outcome associated with the nondelivery of merchandise purchased through an Internet auction website is the unauthorized use of buyer account information. Individuals who provide credit card information to a seller practicing Internet auction fraud through nondelivery can face the potential for further victimization. The credit card information of the buyer can be used by the seller to conduct unauthorized transactions.

11.2.3 Posting Counterfeit Merchandise

Individuals selling counterfeit merchandise through Internet auction websites are spurred on by easy access to a great number of buyers looking for collectibles as well as other goods and services. A good mix for fraud through Internet sales is a buyer looking to purchase that rare item and a seller offering the collectible at an attractive price.

Many consumers search the Internet looking for that

- Rare signed baseball card
- Autographed sporting equipment signed by a premier athlete
- Rare piece of art
- Great deal on a designer watch
- Ideal engagement ring at an unbelievable price

These are just a few of the items buyers search for on the Internet to find the ultimate bargain. Working to the benefit of the seller of counterfeit merchandise through Internet auction websites is having the buyer making the initial contact. Just as in a normal retail establishment, a product is advertised for sale and the consumer makes a purchase. The difference with Internet auction websites is that the asking price for the item sought by the buyer is dramatically lower than what the normal retail purchase price would be.

An added benefit for the seller of counterfeit merchandise is having several bargain-seeking buyers caught up in a bidding war. Having a perfect mix of offering a discounted price for a collectible coupled with the satisfaction of buyers hoping to win a bidding contest places the seller in an ideal position to sell counterfeit merchandise. As with many frauds, the hope is to create a situation that diverts the target onto the path of least resistance.

11.2.4 Product Deception

Product deception differs from the selling of counterfeit merchandise through Internet auction websites because the seller has the actual product to deliver to the buyer. Unfortunately for the buyer, the item auctioned is not up to the quality level advertised by the seller.

Technology that allows consumers to make purchases over the Internet also provides the opportunity for Photoshopping.[1] Buyers take a digital picture of the item for sale, Photoshop the picture, and post the altered image on the Internet auction website. The seller who is technology savvy posts a picture of the item for sale that is not the actual product intended for delivery.

Internet auction sellers will post an item they wish to sell that does not meet the quality standards advertised. The description provided may detail the item as

- Almost brand new
- Barely used
- Never taken out of the box
- Recently overhauled

Based on the item being sold, the description details higher quality than the actual product in the possession of the seller. To add credibility to the item described on the Internet auction website, the seller will post a picture of what is being sold. Unfortunately, the item pictured is not the one the seller intends to ship to the buyer. Individuals using product deception as part of Internet auction fraud will post pictures of the item being sold that portray higher quality; for instance, they post a picture of a bicycle that is being sold in a retail store but are in possession of an older and more used mountain bike.

After the bidding process is complete and the buyer provides payment for the item sold, the seller ships a product of lower quality.

11.2.5 Triangulation

Triangulation used as part of Internet auction fraud involves the participation of three parties. One of the three parties is the individual committing the Internet auction fraud. The other two parties unwittingly involved in the scam are the consumer/bidder (buyer) and a legitimate online merchant. Internet auction fraud triangulation works as follows:

- The individual committing the fraud makes online purchases from a legitimate online merchant.
- The items purchased through the legitimate online merchant are paid for by the individual committing the fraud with stolen identities and credit card information.

- Once the transactions are complete through the legitimate online merchant, the products paid for with stolen credit cards are shipped to the person committing the Internet auction fraud.
- Once the purchased items are received by the individual committing the fraud (seller), they are resold on an Internet auction website.
- The information and pictures of the items being resold are of the actual products.
- Buyers make bids on the items being resold.
- The resold items eventually wind up in the hands of various buyers.
- The individual committing the Internet auction fraud receives payment for the items being resold. These same resold items were initially purchased online with stolen identities and credit card information.[2]

11.2.6 Bid Rigging

When a seller places an item for sale through an Internet auction website, they post a beginning bid price. Once the opening item amount is established, a bidding window time frame is set. Individuals interested in placing a bid on an item for sale can participate in the bidding process until the closing date and time. Once the auction window closes, the person placing the highest bid can purchase the item being sold.

To make the purchase of a desired item for sale on an Internet auction website, a buyer will make multiple bids. The bids on the desired item are made by one buyer using various aliases. The buyer will place low and high bids using different names, with the hope the high bids will cause the price of the item for sale to increase. As the price increases, the person making the multiple bids hopes the increasing item price will cause other buyers to drop out of the auction process. Right before the auction window closes, the multiple bidder withdraws the high bids and eventually has the ability to make the purchase at a much lower price.

The practice of making phony bids for an item on Internet auction websites can also take place by the individual seller. To drive up the sale price of their item, the seller will make continuously higher bids. These increasingly higher bids made by the seller are also placed using different names. The hope of the seller is to increase the item's purchase amount through the phony bidding process and make the sale at the highest price possible. With this type of Internet auction price increase scam (also referred to as shill bidding), the seller will also employ the assistance of friends and relatives to participate in the phony bidding process.[3]

11.2.7 International Auction Fraud

Individuals operating out of foreign countries are active in Internet auction fraud. These criminal elements are known to search Internet auction websites and locate popular items that are continually purchased by various buyers. After identifying attractive items for purchase by various buyers in the United States, these exact items are put up for auction. To attract a wide range and number of potential buyers, numerous Internet auction websites are used to advertise the popular items for sale.

Once the bidding process has been completed and a buyer has been offered the opportunity to complete the purchase, warning signs arise during the payment completion process. The buyer is asked to wire transfer half the purchase amount to an individual located in a foreign country (typically an eastern European country). The buyer is advised that the purchased item will be shipped on the receipt of the initial payment. The buyer is also advised of the need to make the final payment to the seller once the item sold has been received. Once the up-front payment has been sent via wire transfer and received by the seller, the item purchased is not delivered.

To avoid becoming a victim of the various aspects of Internet auction fraud, the following avoidance information is provided:

- Prior to entering the bidding process through an Internet auction website, conduct due diligence on the website. Understand the website's customer protection policies, time frame of operation, and customer reviews.
- Check with the Better Business Bureau about the specific Internet auction website.
- Once a decision is made to enter the bidding process, develop a detailed understanding of the entire auction process. What are the obligations of both the buyer and the seller throughout the bidding, payment, and shipping process? What actions, if any, will the website take if any problems or issues arise during the entire auction process?
- Does the seller provide any type of warranty on the item being sold, and what is the return policy of the seller and the Internet auction website?
- Use extreme caution if the seller requests payments to be made via wire transfers or prepaid debit cards.
- Exhibit the same amount of caution for completing transactions with companies or individuals located outside the United States.
- If possible, payment should be made with a credit card and not a debit card. Credit card transactions provide greater protection measures for the account holder.
- Make sure the selling price is the actual amount to be paid. Many times, sellers will tack extra costs on the transaction, such as additional shipping costs, handling costs, and the like.
- Determine if the Internet auction website offers a buyer the ability to insure the transaction and product shipment.
- Use caution for sellers providing a post office box as their only address and those not willing to provide a telephone contact number. If a telephone number is provided by the seller, call the number to determine the legitimacy. It is also a good idea to conduct a reverse 411 check through one of the many

Internet search engines. By placing the phone number in the search tab, results will be returned regarding the holder of the particular number.

- Never conduct purchasing business over the Internet with a seller providing an e-mail address as the only method of contact.
- Never provide unknown sellers with a personal driver's license number or Social Security number.
- Remember that anyone can create a professional-looking website.[4]
- Also discussed further in the chapter is the increasing popularity of website hijacking. Phony websites can be created to look like that of a legitimate operation.

11.3 Internet Mass Marketing Fraud

Internet fraud is not limited to the purchase and transfer of physical property, but it can also include a promise of financial gain through a wide variety of tactics. Internet frauds are successful because they are mainly based on providing an unbelievable opportunity to an unsuspecting victim. Many of the victims have a belief that they have been individually provided an opportunity for some type of financial gain. These unbelievable opportunities are offered to the unsuspecting victims through unsolicited e-mails or by people looking to avoid the traditional path of normal business operations, basically using an Internet search to steer them directly onto the path of least resistance.

When discussing Internet fraud as it relates to mass marketing fraud, many of the schemes and delivery methods interact with more defined topics detailed throughout the previous ten chapters. These various schemes are discussed briefly in this category of mass marketing fraud to portray how the growing popularity of the Internet is providing the primary victim contact venue.

In the general sense, mass marketing fraud covers delivery or target victim initial contact methods ranging from e-mails, Internet social media websites, telephone calls, and letters delivered through the traditional US mail delivery system. For the purpose of Internet mass market fraud, the focus of the various schemes will revolve around the use of e-mails and social media websites.[5]

Internet mass marketing fraud is broken down into two categories.

1. The mass marketing of various schemes to numerous individuals with the intent of defrauding them out of small-dollar losses. Small-dollar losses typically range from $300 to $500.
2. The mass marketing of various schemes to numerous individuals with the intent of defrauding them out of large-dollar losses, typically ranging from thousands to hundreds of thousands of dollars.[6]

A majority of Internet mass marketing frauds revolve around the use of a wide variety of advance fee frauds (see Chapter 9). The most popular and successful of the advance fee frauds are as follows:

- **Credit Card Account Interest Reduction Schemes:** Potential victims are solicited via e-mail about an amazing opportunity to lower the credit card interest rate percentage. To lower the credit card interest rate percentage, the account holder has to provide an up-front fee to cover paperwork processing and other administrative expenses.
- **High-Dollar Item Internet Retail Fraud:** This differs from the Internet auction fraud discussed previously in this chapter, by which the buyer seeks an item for purchase through various auction websites. With Internet mass marketing fraud, the contact method is made via an unsolicited e-mail. The e-mail recipient is alerted through the message about a rare opportunity to purchase high-dollar items (computers, jewelry, collectables, etc.) at a greatly discounted price. To hold the item and secure the sale, an up-front fee is requested.

  Victims have also been requested to wire transfer the seller a percentage of the total item cost, with the remaining balance due on delivery.
- **Work-at-Home Schemes:** The potential victim is contacted via an unsolicited e-mail and is informed of the potential to earn thousands of dollars from the comfort of their own home. Typically, victims are asked to provide up-front fees to pay for items needed to operate the in-home business or to obtain needed certification.
- **Lotteries, International Lotteries, Sweepstakes Schemes:** The victim receives an unsolicited e-mail informing them they are the winner of some type of lottery or contest. To pay for international taxes or processing fees, the victim is asked to pay an up-front fee.
- **Inheritance Fraud:** The victim is informed through an unsolicited e-mail about the death of a distant relative or a wealthy individual who passed away without heirs. To pay legal fees, unpaid taxes owed by the deceased, or processing fees, the inheritance recipient is asked to provide an up-front fee.[7]

To avoid becoming a victim of Internet mass marketing fraud, individuals contacted through an unsolicited e-mail that eventually leads to the requirement of an up-front fee need to break off all contact. Recipients of the unsolicited e-mails offering a money-saving or money-making opportunity or touting their unbelievable luck need to understand they are not the only person receiving the notification. These mass marketing e-mails are forwarded to thousands of accounts with the hope some recipients actually believe they can take advantage of an "it's too good to be true" opportunity.

11.4 Classified Advertising Websites

Growing in popularity are websites where consumers can obtain a wide variety of services. These services include selling items, posting jobs and résumés, personal ads, the ability to look for items to purchase, housing opportunities, and so on. Instead of looking through the classified ads in the local newspaper, all a consumer has to do is access one of the many classified advertising websites.

The activity taking place on many of the classified advertising websites is beneficial to all parties involved. Convenience is offered to both the person posting the advertisement and those responding. Also, with the Internet advertising websites, the person posting the classified ad has the ability to provide detailed descriptions and photographs. No longer is a person charged by the word to create an ad in the classified section of a traditional newspaper.

Along with the great benefits provided by classified advertising websites is a growing level of fraud. The scams presented are many and are based on the imagination of the person committing the fraud. As with the many who are victims of other types of fraud, warning signs are overlooked, clouded by the offer of an unbelievable opportunity. Instead of conducting due diligence on the opportunity presented through a classified advertising website, the consumer chooses to forget the adage that "if it sounds too good to be true, it is."

Criminals understand the popularity of classified advertising websites and the ability to deceive victims through the offer of an unbelievable opportunity, which combine to create the fraudulent activity discussed next.

11.4.1 Apartment/Home Rental Fraud

An individual who wants to find an apartment to rent can locate many opportunities via a simple Internet search. Apartments for rent can be located through a realtor, rental agency, or the individual complex. Based on the size of the unit a renter seeks, the monthly rental prices are pretty much set throughout community areas. Because of leasing agreements with current renters, move-in availability dates vary per complex.

A person who wants to rent an apartment quickly and at a rate lower than the market average monthly rate can attempt to find the ideal opportunity through a classified advertisement website. Individuals committing apartment rental fraud through classified advertisement websites will post pictures of an apartment for rent at an attractive monthly rate and an immediate move-in date. The advertisement will also claim the apartment listed is the last one available, and it is available on a first come, first served basis. The desire of the person posting the advertisement is to attract as many potential renters as possible. Those potential renters, believing this is their lucky day, are unfortunately among many.

Because of the hot rental opportunity and to secure the last unit available, the potential renter is advised to immediately send the deposit amount and the first and last month's rent. If the money is not received by the future landlord within a set time frame, the apartment will be rented to someone else. Not wanting to miss out on a great opportunity, the potential tenant makes the requested payments and is provided with a lease agreement and a move-in date.

When the move-in date arrives, more than one apartment rental fraud victim realizes the lease agreement is part of the overall scam. The person posting the rental advertisement is not the actual landlord of the apartment, but collected money and completed lease agreements with more than one individual.

The same type of rental fraud is used with people who want to rent a house. They want the ability to rent an actual house at a great monthly rental rate with a quick move-in date. To add credibility to the scam, the potential renter is invited to the actual rental location and can physically walk through the house. As with the apartment rental scam, the person posting the advertisement is not the actual owner of the house.

Individuals committing the house rental scam will locate foreclosed and bank-owned properties that are vacant. Illegal access is used to enter the house, and once inside, the person committing the fraud will change the door locks. Once the locks are changed and the location cleaned, it is posted for rent on a classified advertisement website. As with the apartment rental scam, promises are made, rent money is collected, bogus leases are signed, and the new tenants are given a move-in date. On numerous occasions, several home rental victims have arrived on the same date and time to move in to their new rental home. Unfortunately for all potential renters, they are the victims of home rental fraud.

11.4.2 Reverse Apartment/Home Rental Fraud

Individuals who want to rent an apartment or house are not the only people in the rental process who can become a victim of rental fraud. Landlords and home owners are also targeted by individuals who want to commit rental fraud.

A person who is legally authorized to rent an apartment or house will post an ad on an Internet advertisement website. This individual is contacted by a prospective renter, who agrees to rent the property. The prospective tenant also informs the landlord or home owner that they are relocating from out of town and will have to complete most of the paperwork through the mail or via e-mailed documents. After the leasing paperwork is completed, the prospective renter mails a check to the landlord or home owner.

Unknown to the landlord/home owner beforehand, the check is intentionally written for an amount greater than requested to cover deposits and rent. Directly after the check is received by the landlord/home owner, they are contacted by their new tenant, who apologizes for making an error and sending in too much money.

Claiming to be in a financial bind that could hinder their relocation, a request is made to have the overpayment amount wire transferred back to the future renter. If the landlord/home owner falls for the scam, they will soon be in possession of a counterfeit check and out the monetary amount wired back to who they thought was their new tenant.

Warning signs and prevention measures to avoid becoming a victim of tenant and landlord rental frauds are as follows:

- Prior to signing an apartment lease, verify with the management office that the unit is for rent and who is authorized to represent the complex.
- Use caution when renting an apartment and there is no requirement for a background check.
- When looking to rent a house, conduct an Internet search to ensure the location is not in the foreclosure process.
- Internet searches of the house address and home owner's name have revealed prior information on home rental scams. It is also a good idea to conduct the same verification process on the house address and home owner's name through the Better Business Bureau.
- To avoid apartment or home rental fraud, the services of a real estate agent can work to prevent rental fraud.
- Legitimate landlords and home owners should never accept any form of overpayment from the prospective tenant.

11.5 Nanny/Housekeeper Fraud

Internet classified websites are used by individuals who want to find a job as a nanny or housekeeper. Many of these domestic household-related job seekers will locate the perfect match for them and the hiring family. These websites allow the job seeker to post pictures and qualifying job history information. People who want to hire domestic help can search the various Internet classified websites to find someone to help with child care and house cleaning.

With almost any transaction conducted through the Internet, fraudsters have found a way to scam job seekers out of money. A popular scam that initiates through classified Internet websites is often referred to as the *nanny scam*.

Individuals who post their information on classified Internet websites in a desire to be hired as a nanny are contacted by a person who almost immediately makes an offer of employment. Most of the contact between the job seeker and potential employer is conducted through e-mail. The job seeker (nanny) is normally offered the position with an immediate start date and without going through a formal interview. The reason provided by the individual who wants to hire a nanny and cannot have a face-to-face meeting is that their family is currently moving from overseas.

Once the offer of employment is accepted by the job-seeking nanny, the new employer requests assistance in obtaining necessary items for their house. The reasons for an immediate start date and assistance are as follows:

- They are in the process of relocating to the town where the job-seeking nanny resides.
- The move is imminent, and the family wants to have a few basic items available the moment they arrive at their new house.

Once the newly hired nanny agrees to provide the new employer with relocation assistance, the wheels of the fraud are placed in motion:

- To further entice the newly hired nanny, the nanny is provided a generous first week's salary and additional bonus money for working to help the family as they move into their new home.
- The nanny is sent a check or money order via overnight mail and is requested to deposit the item into his or her personal bank account.
- After the check or money order is deposited, the newly hired nanny is requested to withdraw a portion of the money for the first week's salary and their assistance bonus and to purchase items requested by the new employer. The nanny is asked to purchase items that would be consistent with a family relocating to a new town. These are typically baby food items, household staples, a stroller, and the like.
- The amount of the check or money order is always greater than the cost of the salary and bonus money and for purchasing the material requested.
- The newly hired nanny is requested to immediately wire transfer the leftover check amount back to their new employer.

Falling in line with an advance fee fraud, the deposited item is counterfeit and eventually charged back against the bank account of the nanny/victim. The individual victimized by nanny fraud is responsible for the amount of money wire transferred to the individual they believed was a new employer.

11.6 Reverse Nanny Fraud

People also post information on classified advertising websites under the seeking employment section. Individuals who want to commit reverse nanny fraud will post a picture and qualifications on a classified advertising website. Typically, their current position is given as working as a nanny overseas, but they want to work in the United States.

Eventually, the person committing the fraud will be contacted by prospective employers and go through the interview and hiring process. Posing to be working at an overseas location, the interview process takes place over the telephone or via e-mail and Skype.[8] Prospective employers are provided with contact information for prior work history verification of the nanny job applicant. Unfortunately, the individuals posing as previous employers of the job applicant are part of the scam and provide glowing work history information about the job seeker.

Once a person makes an offer of employment to the job-seeking nanny, an immediate request is made for money to be forwarded to the newly hired nanny. The purpose of sending the money is to assist with the cost of applying for an entry visa and other relocation expenses. If the employers send their newly hired nanny money to help the nanny get to the United States, they have become the victim of reverse nanny fraud.

To prevent becoming a victim of nanny fraud and reverse nanny fraud committed through classified advertising websites, the warning signs and prevention measures are as follows:

- The offer is too good to be true. The beginning salary offered is above the market average.
- Individuals are hired without going through an interview and background verification.
- The new nanny is asked to purchase family items prior to beginning work or meeting the family.
- The nanny/victim is asked to conduct financial transactions that require sending money via a wire transfer.
- The nanny is hired by an individual from a family currently living out of the country.
- The nanny is hired by a person without a face-to-face meeting because the person lives outside the country.
- The new nanny is asked to provide financial assistance to help with relocation expenses.
- Use caution and extreme due diligence when making any hiring decisions with a person claiming to currently live outside the country.

11.7 Internet Job Scam Warning Signs

Classified advertising websites offer many consumers a wide variety of legitimate services and have the ability to provide marketing pictures and information that go way beyond what can be found in a traditional newspaper classified section. With the nanny scam information previously discussed, many individuals become fraud victims on these websites as part of employment schemes. Job scams also take place outside classified advertising websites, but do take place in the cyberworld. With the job scams changing on a daily basis, the various warning signs and verification methods are as follows:

- Watch for offers that are too good to be true. Many fraud victims enter into the scheme believing they were afforded an opportunity that no one else was.
- The job notification was delivered via an unsolicited e-mail. The beginning portion of the e-mail informs the recipient that his or her résumé information was found online and that they are the perfect fit for the open position.
- The information and job description are not clear, but there are simple employment qualifications, typically a minimum age of eighteen, current citizenship, and Internet access. There is no reference to years of experience and required work history.
- Fraudulent job scams typically offer the applicant a salary or hourly wage that is above the market average.
- During the application and hiring process, there is no formal face-to-face interview. A majority of the contact is through e-mail. Many times, the reasoning for the lack of a formal meeting is that the employer is currently out of the country but needs to fill the position immediately.[9]
- The job offer is made soon after the initial contact.
- With many Internet scams, a large majority of the contact is made via e-mail. A clear warning sign for a potential job scam is the lack of professionalism of the e-mail. Many times, the introductory e-mail contains poor grammar and spelling errors. (See Appendixes B and C and Figure 11.1 for examples of unprofessional e-mails that were generated for the purpose of fraud.)
- Use caution when asked to make check deposits for a new employer. A legitimate professional organization will not ask newly hired employees to deposit nonpayroll checks to their individual account. With the request to have a check deposited into an individual account, an accompanying request is made to have a portion of the check amount sent back to the employer via a wire transfer.

Due diligence needs to take place on the part of the applicant, especially for those contacted via an unsolicited e-mail.

- Never click on links provided in unsolicited e-mails for open job positions. An Internet search needs to take place to locate the website of the organization outlined as having an open position.
- Many unsolicited job notification e-mails will list a contact person and phone number. Never call the phone provided in the e-mail. Locate the organization's contact information through its legitimate website. Contact the organization to verify that the person listed in the e-mail actually works for the company.
- A search needs to take place through the legitimate organization's website to determine if the position offered is actually an open position. Numerous organizations provide a link through their website for job seekers and list open positions, job titles, and job descriptions.

From: Rjs <amacorpiezyf@europe.com>

To: Postmaster <rjs33@cox.net>

Subject: Part Time Business

manager that is currently open.
Please find the job description below:
Role: Quality Control inspector
Employment: Part-time
Requirements are as follows:

- Previous experience with Adobe Acrobat Reader and Microsoft Office
- Basic computer skills
- Access to printer and scanner
- Previous experience with household and kitchen appliances.

The position involves doing quality control and writing inspection reviews for new models of household and kitchen appliances.

If you believe you meet these requirements and wish to apply for this part-time job opportunity, please contact us by email at:

Joseffdlsf@gmx.com

Our Human Resources Manager will contact you to schedule an interview soon.

- - -

Este email está limpo de vírus e malwares porque a proteção do avast!

Antivírus

está ativa.

http://www.avast.com

Figure 11.1   Actual unsolicited e-mail sent with the intent of initiating work-at-home fraud scams.

■ Understand that company websites can be hijacked and used for fraud purposes. This information is detailed further in this chapter.
■ Personal information (résumés) should never be provided as part of a job search that generates from an unsolicited e-mail.

11.8 Phishing, Vishing, Smishing, Spoofing, and Cramming

11.8.1 Phishing

Phishing takes place through the opening of unsolicited e-mails. The unsolicited e-mails will have a Subject line used to attract the attention of the recipient. The e-mail can be formulated to appear to be from a trustworthy organization, financial institution, cell phone carrier, and others (refer to Figures 11.2 and 11.3). The goal of the phishing e-mail is to have recipients believe they are being contacted by a

---

From: Apple Support <dsoger@howellco.com>

To:

Subject: Account Limited Till We Hear From You

Hello!

We could not validate your last purchase cause your credit card/billing address did not correspond with your account information. For your security we need you to validate this change/update to avoid suspension of your account.
   <a id="yui_3_7_2_1_1374307542888_3001" rel="nofollow" target="_blank" class="yiv2113917415aapl-link" style="color:#0088cc;class=" yiv2113917415aapl-link" href="http://www.jonathanglassner.com/wp-content/uploads/2011/10/10/">Click here to complete validation
   Failure to complete our validation process will result in a suspension of YOUR Apple ID. We take every step needed to automatically validate our users, unfortunately in your case we were unable to. The process only takes a couple of minutes and will make sure there is no interruption to your account.
   This is an automated message; do not reply to this letter. If you need additional assistance, please go to the site Apple Support.

Thank you!

Apple Support.

Figure 11.2   Phishing e-mail.

From: PayPal Security Team <noreply9@ppsec.com>

To:

Subject: Account Reviewed

Attachments: FileAttached.html (35.5 KB)

PayPal Account System Upgrade Verification.

Technical services of the PayPal Inc. are carrying out a planned system upgrade. We earnestly ask you to start with the procedure of confirmation on customers data.

This email has been sent to all PayPal members, and we ask a few minutes of your online experience. We have sent you an attachment form through this email. Please download and open it in your web browser.

Your personal information is protected by state-of-the-art technology. After you have filled in all the required fields in the form, our verification system will automatically update your account records.

We apologize for any inconvenience.

Thank you for using PayPal.

Please do not reply to this email. This mailbox is not monitored and you will not receive a response. For assistance, log in to your PayPal account and click Help in the top right corner of any PayPal page.

Copyright © 1999–2014 PayPal. All rights reserved.
Open Attachment FileAttached.html

Figure 11.3 Another example of a phishing e-mail.

legitimate organization. These can be companies with which they have conducted prior business transactions or a current financial institution.

Once the target opens the phishing e-mail, they are informed of a pressing issue with their account or service. They are informed of a need for immediate action and provided with a link to the organization's website. If the targeted individual clicks on the link provided, they are directed to a bogus website. The bogus website presents the appearance of being the true organization's website.

The overall goal of a phishing e-mail is to have the recipient click on the link provided and to comply with the requests made through the bogus organization's website. Typical requests ask for verification of personal information to proceed. Respondents are asked to provide name, address information, and Social Security numbers. After providing the desired personal information, a credit card number is requested to avoid the interruption of service.

The variations of phishing attempts are numerous and are unlimited and based on the imaginations of individuals committing the scam. Phishing e-mails could contain, but are not limited to, the following:

- "We have noticed several fraudulent transaction attempts on your credit or bank debit card. To avoid an unauthorized transaction against your account, please click on the link provided and you will be directed to the official company website."
- "We recently updated our in-house account-processing software and need all customers to verify their account holder information. This verification can be conducted quickly through our company website. A link has been provided to our website where you can verify your account information and avoid an interruption in service."
- "Our customer service department noticed your account was recently overcharged. Please click on the link provided in this e-mail and you will be directed to the company website so the overcharged amount can be placed back in your account."
- Requests can come ostensibly from a college alumni association or to students of a university they are currently attending.
- Requests can be made through representations as the various public utility companies. These can include those for gas, electricity, water, waste, and so on.
- Requests can be made to clear up issues with a gym membership, season ticket account, wine-of-the-month club, and so on.

The greatest prevention measure against phishing attempts is the unsolicited e-mail. Any time an unsolicited e-mail is received from any organization that an individual currently conducts or has ever conducted business with should be ignored. When organizations contact a current customer through an unsolicited e-mail about account services, this is not the routinely accepted manner of conducting business. A business or service providing unsolicited e-mails to customers normally sends a do not reply e-mail thanking a customer for making a payment.

On receipt of an unsolicited e-mail from a current service-providing organization, adhere to the following prevention measures:

- Never click on the link provided.
- Never provide any personal financial or account information as a result of the e-mail.
- If there is concern about the status of a service account, contact should be made with the customer service department.
- Locate the organization's website through a search from a trusted Internet search engine.
- Use directory assistance to locate the customer service phone number for any organization you want to call.

11.8.2 Vishing

Vishing is the equivalent of phishing but involves the use of a phone. Individuals committing vishing fraud will contact unsuspecting individuals via phone call. Once the call is answered by the targeted individual, the caller pretends to be a representative for the target's bank. The goal of the caller is to have the targeted individual believe there is an issue with their bank account. Once convinced of the caller's legitimacy and a pending financial issue, the targeted individual is asked to provide financial information. Based on the focus of the call, attempts are made with vishing scams to request

- Bank debit card numbers
- Debit card personal identification numbers (PINs)
- Checking/savings account information

Callers participating in vishing fraud typically favor claiming to represent the targeted individual's financial institution. As with phishing, the caller can also claim to represent a service-providing organization. The goal of the caller is to convince the targeted individual they need to make a payment against the account to avoid a disruption in service. If the caller is successful, the targeted individual will provide the requested credit/debit card information.

Vishing calls are also made for the purpose of identity theft. Callers will contact a target individual claiming to represent an organization that issues credit cards. The caller informs the targeted individual that the individual is prequalified to receive a credit card with an attractive credit limit. The goal is to have the targeted individual provide personal information to the caller: name, address, e-mail address, Social Security number, date of birth, and the like.

The greatest protection against vishing attempts is not to answer calls from unknown individuals or unrecognized phone numbers. Let the call go to voice mail. If the caller leaves a message claiming to represent the financial institution or service provider of the individual called and provides a callback number to resolve account-related issues, do not call the phone number provided.

Some credit card/lending agencies will make telephonic notifications of an overdue payment. The same holds true for other service-providing organizations. Any attempt to contact the organization represented in the voice mail has to be initiated by the person receiving the call.

The customer service number should be located through the organization's official website or through directory assistance.

11.8.3 Smishing

Smishing is a combination of phishing and Short Messaging Service (SMS) or texting. With a smishing scam, an unsuspecting individual receives a text message.

The text message appears to be legitimate and informs the recipient of an issue that requires their immediate attention. Typically, the text message informs the recipient his credit card has been suspended or there were fraudulent attempts against his checking account.

The recipient of the text message is informed to call the phone number provided or click on the link provided. The purpose of the callback number is to have the e-mail recipient call the number provided and ultimately provide personal and account information that can be used to commit identity theft. The individual answering the phone at the callback number provided will work to convince the targeted individual of a legitimate issue with the target's bank account.

CASE STUDY 11.1

480797002@verizon.net
(contact-WLSFRG) Call (609) 8001044

This message is an actual text message sent to my cell phone. After calling the number provided, my call was answered by an automated answering machine. I was informed by the robotic voice that there was a technical issue with my account, and my debit card has been deactivated. To reactivate my debit card, I needed to proceed through the verification process. Through a series of prompts, the goal was to have me enter my name, address, Social Security number, and the debit card number, expiration date, and card security code.

The goal of individuals who initiate this type of smishing fraud is to have the text message recipient enter the requested personal and account information. After entering the requested personal and account information, callers are informed that their debit card has been reactivated.

An unsuspecting debit card holder would believe their debit card issue has been corrected and will go on as normal and conduct transactions. Unfortunately, the individuals who received the debit card information will have created counterfeit debit cards to be used for fraudulent purposes. In addition, the personal information provided will be used to commit other types of identity fraud.

The purpose of providing a link in a smishing scam is to have the text message recipient click on the link. Thinking they will be directed to the website of the organization represented in the text message, they are actually providing unauthorized individuals access to their device. By clicking on an unknown link, unauthorized individuals can access the device and install spyware, malware, or viruses (spyware, malware, and viruses are detailed in Chapter 12).

To protect a mobile device from fraud and internal security issues, text message recipients should never click on a link provided from an unknown individual. If the text message recipient/targeted individual is concerned about issues with their financial accounts, they need to locate phone numbers of their bank and contact the bank directly. Never provide personal or financial account information as the result of receiving a smishing text message.

11.8.4 Spoofing

E-mail spoofing is used to trick the recipient into believing they received an e-mail from a trusted source. With a spoofed e-mail, the name of the sender in the From line is a person the recipient has corresponded with previously. The perceived sender could also have a name associated with the recipient's friends on social media websites.

To add validity that the e-mail was sent from a trusted source, the recipient's actual e-mail address is correct on the To line. Typical Subject line information uses the recipient's first name and recommends a website to visit.

The next example is an actual e-mail I received from a person I know. We have exchanged e-mails in the past, and this individual is a trusted source.

From: Bobbie XXXXX <nickowen.latent@btconnect.com>

To: jyoungblood5@cox.net

Subject: Perfect site for James

With most spoofed e-mails the only information in the e-mail body is a website link.

Bobbie XXXXX is an actual friend of mine, but she did not send me this e-mail or recommend the link provided in the message. I have also received similar spoofing attempts that contained the names of my kids and other friends. A telling sign that is present on a majority of e-mail spoofing attempts is the address associated with the sender name on the From line. The e-mail address linked to Bobbie's name was nickowen.latent@btconnect.com. This is *not* the actual e-mail address of Bobbie.

The intent of the individuals who send out countless spoofing e-mails is to gain the confidence of recipients and hope the recipients believe the link provided is trustworthy. A recipient of a spoofed e-mail can click on the link provided, and the destinations vary. The link destinations are based on the intent of the spoofing e-mail sender, and their goals are as follows:

- Marketing e-mails and the link take the recipient to a website where a product is being offered for sale.
- The intent could be based on taking the recipient to a website where they are offered an opportunity to participate in every fraud detailed in this chapter. Popular spoofing links take the recipient to websites advertising work-at-home and mystery shopping opportunities.
- The purpose of the link could allow for unauthorized software to be downloaded onto the targets computer (Malware/Spyware).

The purpose of a spoofing attempt is to develop an added level of trust concerning the solicitation. Past victims of this type of activity continued with the process based on a trust level associated with the perceived sender. Many victims believed a friend or family member would not send them a link and an opportunity that resulted in fraud.

Individuals who receive e-mails sent from friends or family members that contain a simple and brief message need to

■ Make sure the e-mail address following the sender name in the From line is the actual e-mail address.
■ Think back and remember if this individual normally provides this type of information on a random basis.
■ Contact the friend or family member *prior to* clicking on any link provided. The recipient needs to ensure the person listed on the From line actually sent the e-mail, and the link provided is legitimate.

11.8.5 Cramming

In the past, cramming involved a very late night in an attempt to learn an entire semester's worth of information. Technology has changed the manner in which students communicate and receive information, but many probably spend many late nights cramming for information. With the change of technology, the term *cramming* also relates to fraudulent activity that targets an individual's cell phone.

Most cell phone users cannot go through a day without receiving at least one text message. Many of these text messages are from friends, relatives, and coworkers. As mentioned, some text messages are sent with the intent of committing some type of fraudulent activity. Cramming can be added to that list.

> **CASE STUDY 11.2**
> A typical cramming scam begins with a text message informing the recipient they are a winner of a $1,000 gift card. Along with the text message that informs the recipient of their good fortune, a link is provided. An individual who believes they are the winner of a contest that they never entered clicks on the link. After clicking on the link, the individual is routed to what appears to be a website from a legitimate organization (see website hijacking later in this chapter). Believing their good fortune and the legitimacy of the website, the recipient follows the prompt to claim their prize.
> After clicking on the prompt, the recipient is asked to enter their name and address and confirm their cell phone number. After confirming their phone number, they receive a follow-up text that contains their secret PIN. Once the PIN is received, the recipient is directed to enter the number on the form provided and submit it. The lucky winner is informed the prize is on the way.
> Unfortunately, the lucky prize winner never receives the $1,000 gift card. What the lucky winner later realizes is that their cell phone account was charged with unauthorized purchases. With a cramming scam, the cell phone holder's

phone bill is treated like a credit card. Their account is charged for services they never authorized or approved for purchase.[10]

The goal of a cramming scam is to have the text message recipient follow the link provided and eventually enter the requested information. Believing they are going to receive a prize or service, their cell phone bill is charged for small-dollar services. These services can range from trivia, daily horoscope, ringtones, premium text messaging services, and so on. Many of the services provided are billed for $9.99, which is an amount that can be overlooked with a quick review of a monthly bill.

To avoid becoming a victim of cramming, cell phone users should

■ Never believe they were selected at random to win a prize.
■ Delete any unsolicited text messages.
■ Make a detailed review of the monthly cell phone bill to locate any unauthorized charges. Keep an eye out for generic-sounding fees with names such as subscription, use fee, member fee, activation, and so on.
■ Ask the cell phone carrier about blocking third-party charges. Some carriers might charge a fee for this service.[11]

11.9 Social Security Administration Fraud

Individuals who want to commit various types of fraud will use the names of government agencies and individuals in an effort to add validity to the scam-related introduction. Numerous advance fee letters (see Appendix B) use the name of the Federal Reserve Bank, World Bank, Federal Bureau of Investigation, and so on in an effort to convince the recipient the offer is legitimate. Various scare tactic frauds (see Chapter 7 for additional discussion) will claim to come from a local police department or government office to add to the fear aspect of the fraud.

A popular phishing e-mail is sent to the recipient as generated from the Social Security Administration (SSA). Recipients of this unsolicited e-mail are informed they have become eligible to receive additional government benefits. To qualify for the additional benefits, the recipient is asked to click on the link provided and complete the form provided. The recipients are asked to provide their name, address, Social Security number, driver's license number, and so on.

Unsolicited e-mails of this type are generated in an effort to obtain personal information. This personal information is later used to commit identity theft (see Chapter 10 for detailed information on identity theft). E-mails of this nature have also been sent to individuals in Canada and claim to be from Service Canada.[12]

Recipients of these types of unsolicited e-mails need to develop detailed understanding of the following:

- Government agencies correspond through the US mail and not through text messages and e-mails.
- The SSA already has the personal information of individuals receiving benefits.
- Never click on any link provided that is part of an unsolicited e-mail.

11.10 Company Website Hijacking

To attract the attention of potential fraud victims through unsolicited e-mail notifications, the individuals generating the correspondence will use like-sounding names of government programs and legitimate organizations. In the home mortgage fraud arena, variations of the official acronym of HARP (Home Affordable Refinance Program) will be used. In an attempt to add legitimacy to the bogus notification about home refinance opportunities through the US Government, acronyms such as HEMP, HAMP, and so on are used.

In addition to using like-sounding names of official programs, individuals who want to commit fraud through the Internet will also create bogus websites in the name of a legitimate organization. To trick the recipient of an unsolicited e-mail, like-sounding variations of the legitimate company name are used.

Another popular variation of using bogus websites to conduct varying types of fraud is to use the actual name of a legitimate business, basically hijacking the good name of the organization in an attempt to deceive the target audience into believing they are doing business with a legitimate company. When it comes to hijacking a legitimate company website, the actual organization's name is used along with official website pages.

> **CASE STUDY 11.3**
>
> HS Brands International is a legitimate business that specializes in loss prevention consulting and mystery shopping. HS Brands International is an industry leader in providing mystery shopping services for a wide variety of retail locations. HS Brands International typically recruits, through its website, individuals to apply to become mystery shoppers. Applicants applying to become a mystery shopper go through an actual interview and background verification. With fraudulent mystery shopping phishing scams, all discussion takes place through e-mails.
>
> Mike Mershimer, president of HS Brands International, and his organization have become unparticipating and unwitting victims in mystery shopping phishing scams and website hijacking. Individuals committing this fraud have created a phony website in the name of HS Brands. This illegitimate website was created using web pages from the official HS Brands website. HS Brand International logos were also copied and used in the phony website. To add further legitimacy to the unauthorized HS Brands website and correspondence sent to fraud victims, the name and actual signature of Mike Mershimer were copied and used.
>
> After the unauthorized HS Brands website was completed, countless phishing e-mails were sent to targeted individuals. The following is one of the actual

introductory e-mails (the company logos of Sam's Club, Victoria's Secret, and Walmart were also copied without permission and added to the e-mail to add legitimacy, but none of the three company names used were actual clients of HS Brands International):

From: hsbrands@walmart.com
To:
Subject: Walmart Product Evaluation
Date: Sun, 13 Jul 2014 09:13:50 −0700

  VICTORIA'S SECRET

You are invited to participate in our Evaluation. Compensation: 200/300 US Dollars on every survey you conduct.

HS BRANDS INTERNATIONAL assigns over 100,000 in-store surveys each year and has provided evaluation services for over 15 years.

Participating in our surveys is always free of charge, and we are always looking for enthusiastic new evaluators.

Through our business evaluation surveys, HS BRANDS INTERNATIONAL deliver an accurate picture of the consumer experience and services using on-profile people in real situations to report on their interaction.

Details on Survey:
1) How long it took you to get services.
2) Efficiency of the attendant.
3) Customer service professionalism.

To participate in assignments http://hsbrands.walmart.com/?povid=P1171-C1093.2766-L8

Locations of Survey (Wal-Mart, Victoria's Secret, Western Union and Money Gram) It keeps changing, survey might take place at banks or Wal-Mart.

P:S: This survey can be handled in your spare time.

You would be given full details of every activity you have to carry out and your payment would be included in your acceptance mail.

Best Regards,

Robin Nelson.

Individuals receiving the unsolicited mystery shopping phishing e-mail can conduct an Internet search of HS Brands International. The Internet search will reveal HS Brands International is a legitimate loss prevention/mystery shopping organization. After conducting their due diligence, individuals interested in conducting mystery shopping services can click on the link provided. The link takes the mystery shopping applicants to a web page that asks for further information:

http://hsbrands.com-user.us/register/

Apply to join our panel and get paid to shop, enjoy leisure activities and directly influence which products gets developed to meet consumers demands.

To participate in assignments, please fill the requested application below:

Full Name

Street Address

Apt/Suite (optional)

City

State

Zip Code

Home Phone #

Mobile Phone #

Date of Birth

19

Email Address

SUBMIT

The information mentioned is a copy of the actual web page the applicants are directed to by clicking on the link provided. Legitimacy is added to the scam with the use of the HS Brands International logo and the unauthorized use of the logos of Sam's Club, Victoria's Secret, and Walmart. (The address listed at the bottom of the web page is the actual address of HS Brands International.)

Individuals convinced they are applying to work as a mystery shopper for a legitimate organization can fill in the information requested and click on the Submit tab.

After providing the requested information, applicants are hired without going through a formal interview process. Not having to participate in an actual face-to-face interview might seem odd to some. But, fears are put aside because HS Brands International is a legitimate mystery shopping organization and the applicants did visit what they deemed to be an official company website.

Once hired as a mystery shopper, individuals are sent the following e-mail:

HS BRANDS INTERNATIONAL
251 East 5th St. 9th Floor | Cincinnati, OH 45202 | Copyright © 2014.

Date: Tue, 15 Jul 2014 19:40:55 +0000

From: rnelson@hsbrandsintl.com

To: XXXXXXXXXXXXXXXXXX.com

Subject: Important - First Assignment (MT Service Evaluation)

Dear XXXXXX,

This is the first of what we hope are many exciting shopping experiences. We are happy you received your starter pack which contains your check and ask that you take it to your bank as soon as possible and have it deposited into your account.

Please note, you are to keep $300.00 from the total amount as payment for your work. The balance after you have taken your statutory compensation for the first assignment will be used for your product evaluation assignment.

Your assignment this time is to try out a Money Transfer service, Western Union. Western Union is a globally known Money Transfer provider serving both local and international concerns, helping people send and receive funds as fast as possible. Western Union is concerned that many locations where it's services are offered adhere to company policies.

Your job will be to locate a Western Union outlet closest to your home or work location. Take with you the remaining funds as you will be required to conclude a transaction. This is simple and all you need to do is locate a "SEND" form and fill it out with the following Receiver's Information stated below.

RECEIVER'S NAME: Promise ########## (Edited by Author)
ADDRESS: ### ###### street (Edited by Author)
Applecreek Ohio 44606

Once your form is complete take it to the clerk and they will prepare to send it. There is a charge for sending funds, so take that amount out of the funds you have left and not out of your $300.00. It is important that you remember that you are doing all of this as a Secret Shopper. You will need to pay attention to the things that you will report on after your visit. We do not want you to take notes or bring attention to the fact that you are there to report on them.

Please do not take this letter in with you. If you cannot remember the information you need to send the funds then write it on a notepad which you would take along with you to the outlet. As soon as you finish your transaction we want you to email us with the following information:

1. Full name and address of the Western Union location that you visited.
2. Was the location clean and well organized? Could you find forms?
3. How many people were there to wait on people?
4. Was there a security system?
5. How long did it take for you to complete your transaction?
6. How would you rate your experience? 10 being the very best - 1 being very poor service.

ALSO SEND THE FOLLOWING INFORMATION ABOUT THE TRANSFER FROM TRANSCRIPT YOU RECEIVE UPON COMPLETION OF THE TRANSACTION.

1. Senders Name and Address as provided on the duplicate copy in your possession.
2. The 10 digit MTCN (Money Transfer Control Number)
3. The Amount Sent, exclusive of charges incurred.

Email the requested details as soon as possible so as to enable up profile the outlet and process your next service testing assignment.

Regards,

Robin Nelson
Research & Evaluations.

In addition to the first assignment e-mail mentioned, the mystery shopping victim was mailed a counterfeit cashier's check in the amount of $2,390.00. As requested, the check was deposited into the victim's account and $2,090.00 was sent via wire transfer.

With this company website hijacking fraud, there are two victims. The first victim is the individual who was tricked into believing they were applying for a mystery shopping job for a legitimate mystery shopping organization. The second victim is the good name of HS Brands International. Although HS Brands International did not suffer any monetary loss, it has been in a continuous process of repairing the company reputation.

Victims of the website hijacking mystery shopping phishing fraud contact HS Brands International believing HS Brands committed the fraud and provided them with a counterfeit check. Company President Mike Mershimer and his employees have to inform the fraud victims HS Brands International was not involved in hiring mystery shoppers through unsolicited phishing e-mails. The fraud victims who suffered a monetary loss are also informed HS Brands International was victimized through company website hijacking.

11.11 Business E-mail Hacking/Payment Redirect

Company websites are not the only aspect of legitimate business operations that are targeted for hacking purposes. Criminals are hacking into the e-mail accounts of legitimate business operations and obtaining information on company managers and associates working for the Accounts Payable Department. In addition to obtaining the names and e-mail information of company employees, they are locating data for vendors that work with the targeted organization. Once the desired e-mail and vendor information is obtained, the fraudulent activity is focused on the Accounts Payable Department.

With payment redirect fraud, the initial focus is directed toward a member or members of the organization's Accounts Payable Department. The fraud works as follows:

- A member of the Accounts Payable Department receives an e-mail from his or her boss or an individual high up in the organization structure.
- The e-mail appears on its face value to come directly from a person working within the organization (e-mail sender address and manager's name).
- The recipient is directed in the e-mail to change the process of payment to a specific vendor.
- The recipient is informed to make the current payment to the vendor via a wire transfer and not through the traditional process.
- Unfortunately, the money is not wired to the vendor's account but to an account of an individual involved in the scam.
- With this scam, several company Accounts Payable employees and vendors can be identified and targeted.

Organizations need to develop an understanding that hackers can develop access to company information and create frauds that are outside the organization's current protective posture. In an effort to avoid becoming a victim to payment redirect fraud, the following prevention procedures need to be implemented:

- As discussed in Chapter 3, no payments should be forwarded until reviewed by a disinterested third party working in the organization.
- Any changes to vendor payment policies sent via e-mail need to be verified in person with the person making the request.
- Employees need to make sure all company e-mails received were sent from an actual account. Individuals who want to commit this type of fraud will create similar e-mail sender addresses.
- Accounts Payable associates need to be educated on hacking scams that can take place in relation to their place of employment.[13]

Another variation of payment redirect fraud involves hackers accessing the e-mail accounts of vendors. The intent of the hacker is to gain access to the contact information of the vendor. Once the contact information is obtained for the various organizations the vendor works with, the actual business is targeted with payment redirect e-mails:

- The Accounts Payable Department of the targeted organization is informed, via e-mail, of a request from a specific vendor for a change in payment procedures.
- The unauthorized e-mail sent representing the vendor directs the organization to provide payment through a wire transfer.
- The money sent via wire transfer actually goes to the account of an individual involved in the scam and not to the actual vendor.

In an effort to prevent this type of payment redirect fraud, the following procedures need to take place:

- Any requests for a change in payment policies need to be physically verified by the receiving organization and the specific vendor.
- No matter the delivery method, the payment information needs to be verified by a disinterested third party.
- Associates need to be on the lookout for sender e-mail addresses that appear similar to an actual address. Scammers will attempt to fool individuals working in an Accounts Payable Department that the e-mail came from a well-known vendor. The actual e-mail address and the one used will be similar in nature.[14]

11.12 Brand Name Coupon/Discount Fraud

Individuals who want to commit fraud will steal the good name and brand information from legitimate business operations, as discussed for website hijacking. Not wanting to go as far as creating a bogus business operation based on the name of a legitimate operation, criminals are also using company names for mischievous purposes.

Consumers are sent e-mails and text messages that contain the name of well-known local and national business operations. A large majority of the business names used are fast food restaurants.

Using e-mails, individuals are sent legitimate-looking discount coupons for the recipient to use on their next visit. People are also receiving text messages with the offer to receive a free restaurant product by simply texting back the requested response ("If you would like a free slice of pizza from XXXXXXX Pizza, text back yes"). Once the requested response is sent, the recipient is sent another text message that notifies them to visit the restaurant to receive their free item.

With these types of fraud, business operations are presented with coupons they did not authorize or shown a text message that was not approved for a free offer. Many business locations inform the coupon holder and text message recipient the information received is invalid. Other locations have to go through the process of posting a notice on the door of their store to inform customers that certain coupons will not be honored.

The purpose of these types of fraud can be twofold:

- The coupons and text messages can be simple harassment techniques targeted toward the business operation.
- The coupons and text messages can also be created by someone associated with the business operation with the hope of having people come to their location. The thought is that because the individuals who received the fraudulent information are at the business, they might make a purchase.

With this type of fraud, neither the business operation nor the consumer is a victim of a financial loss. If generated for harassment purposes, the creators have achieved their goal.

One caveat consumers need to be made aware of is the possibility of receiving an e-mail discount coupon offer and being requested to click on a link provided to download the coupon. By clicking on the provided link, the recipient can potentially expose their computer to malware and spyware. The same holds true if the recipient of a free offer text message is requested to click on a provided link.

Notes

1. Photoshopping is basically altering a digital photograph. Image-editing techniques are used to change the appearance of an item photographed, creating a better-looking end product.
2. Lookstogoodtobetrue.com, Action items. http://www.lookstoogoodtobetrue.com/fraudtypes/auctionfraud.aspx (accessed July 1, 2014).
3. Ibid.
4. Federal Bureau of Investigation, Internet fraud. http://www.fbi.gov/scams-safety/fraud/internet_fraud (accessed July 2, 2104).
5. The initial contact method for both categories of Internet mass marketing fraud is via the cyberworld. Based on the scheme used, the US mail system will be used to deliver counterfeit checks to the potential victim.
6. US Department of Justice, Mass marketing fraud. http://www.justice.gov/criminal/fraud/internet/ (accessed July 2, 2104).
7. Ibid.
8. Skype is an Internet program that allows people to communicate through their computer. Once logged in to the program, each person on the call can see the other individual on their computer screen and talk as if conducting a normal telephone conversation.
9. Doyle, A., Top ten Internet job scam warning signs. http://jobsearch.about.com/od/jobsearchscams/a/top-10-internet-job-scams.htm (accessed July 5, 2104).
10. Better Business Bureau. Fake gift card leads to monthly charges. http://www.bbb.org/council/bbb-scam-stopper/top-scams/phishing-scams/ (accessed July 6, 2104).
11. Federal Trade Commission, Consumer information, mystery phone charges. http://www.consumer.ftc.gov/articles/0183-mystery-phone-charges (accessed August 2, 2014).
12. Better Business Bureau. Scammers hijack business email, redirect payments, http://www.bbb.org/council/bbb-scam-stopper/top-scams/phishing-scams/ (accessed August 4, 2014).
13. Ibid.
14. Ibid.

Chapter 12

Internet, Computer, and E-mail Fraud

12.1 Introduction

The personal computer and the office intranet system are the main targets for a wide variety of frauds, many of which were discussed in the previous eleven chapters. The actual individual computers and office computer systems are targeted in an effort to access both personal and business information. In an effort to protect the personal and business information housed in the various computer systems, protection measures can be put into place to prevent unauthorized access.

Firewalls can be established to prevent outside access to an internal business computer system. Employees can be educated on the necessity to practice computer security measures and the importance of protecting and changing individual log-in information. Individuals can also practice personal computer protection by installing antivirus and antimalware[1] software. For both personal and company computers, the tools are available to prevent a majority of fraudulent activity that initiates with unauthorized computer access.

No matter the prevention measures employed by a business operation or the software installed on a personal computer, the overall computer protection process still comes down to the actions of the individual.

For those individuals who target computer systems in an effort to commit various types of computer-related fraud, their goal is to create opportunities in the mind of the individual that place the person or business on the path of least resistance. No matter the prevention measures in place to prevent unauthorized access to personal and business computer systems, it all comes down to altering the thought process of the individual operator.

12.2 Spamming

Gone are the good old days when spam was a harmless can of processed meat. An Internet search using the keyword "spam" will reveal discussion of the canned meat product as well as a reference to unwanted e-mail. In the world of technology, spam is basically unsolicited and mostly unwanted e-mail. A majority of the spam generated is harmless advertising and will most likely wind up in the spam folder of an individual's e-mail account. Based on the company an individual uses for their e-mail service, there are varying levels of spam filter settings.

Many users can manually set the spam filter settings provided by the e-mail service provider. Spam filter settings usually range from "do not use a spam filter" to an "extremely high spam filter." E-mail recipients can choose to have all e-mails posted in their inbox or select varying settings for spam filtering. The higher the spam filter setting selected, the user runs the risk of having desired e-mails sent to the spam folder.

E-mail users who have selected a high level or any level of spam filter setting can still access their spam folder and see the sender information and the e-mail subject line. The more e-mails in the spam folder that remain unopened, the greater the deviation the user has taken off the path of least resistance.

The goal of an individual sending spam e-mail for malicious purposes is to have the recipient open the e-mail message and click on the link provided. To have the recipient open the unsolicited e-mail and follow the instructions provided, there has to be an attraction. Typically, the attraction described in the unsolicited e-mail is an offer to the recipient that falls in line with the adage that it is "too good to be true."

Contained in the malicious links are varying forms of unwanted software that can be used to access personal and business information contained within the computer system. The malicious software could also be used for outright vicious intents, with the focus on causing damage to the computer's operating systems.

No matter the intent of the malicious software attached to various forms of unsolicited spam-type e-mails, the goal of the computer user is to avoid the temptation level generated in the subject line of the e-mail.

12.3 Unsubscribing from Spam E-mails

E-mails sent from legitimate operations offer the recipient the option of clicking on the unsubscribe link at the bottom of the message. By clicking on the unsubscribe link, the computer user is taken to a separate screen that asks the user to enter their e-mail address. After the e-mail address is entered, the user is asked to click on the submit tab to stop the receipt of future messages. By going through this process, the user will typically stop receiving future spam-type e-mails.

Unfortunately, recipients can also receive spam-type e-mails that are sent as part of a phishing attempt but also offer the option of opting out of receiving future messages. With these types of spam e-mails, the intent could be based on collecting legitimate addresses.

By clicking on the unsubscribe tab in this type of e-mail, the user is taken to a separate screen that asks for them to enter their e-mail address. So far, the unsubscribe process follows the normal steps, leaving the computer user with a level of confidence the amount of future spam received will decrease.

With phishing-type spam e-mails, one of the intents is to have the user select the unsubscribe option. By going through the unsubscribe process, the senders are actually collecting legitimate e-mail addresses. These legitimate e-mail addresses are later sold to other spammers.

By selecting the unsubscribe option for spam e-mails, the users are hoping to decrease the number of unwanted messages. What they could be doing is completing a step that actually increases the number of spam messages received.

Figure 12.1 shows an actual spam message that is part of a phishing attempt but has the dual purpose of collecting legitimate e-mail addresses.

12.4 Spoofing (E-mail)

From a malware/spyware aspect, spoofing is used to gain access to a computer through deception. The deception or trick is to have the e-mail recipient believe the message received is from a trusted source. Typically, the trusted source could be a family member, a person the target interacts with through e-mail, or an organization or service provider. The goal of e-mail spoofing is to trick the recipient into opening the message and clicking on any links.

To have the e-mail recipient open the message, the attraction resides in the From line, which indicates who sent the e-mail. An individual named John Smith might interact through e-mail with his son, Bill Smith. John could receive an e-mail with a From line that lists Bill Smith as the sender. In a normal e-mail sent to John by his son, the From line will be

From: Bill Smith billsmith@XXX.com

With spoofing e-mails, the intent is to have the recipient believe the sender is someone the sender knows. John Smith has a son named Bill Smith, and Bill normally sends e-mail messages to his father. If John Smith were to open the e-mail

From: New Credit Cards <eey97QB@ntE1qUi.malendistico.com>

To:

Subject: New Visa or MasterCard Available For You 1331

To Unsubscribe From our Email List Click Here

Figure 12.1   Spam message as part of a phishing attempt.

sent by Bill Smith and click on the Reply option, the actual e-mail address of Bill Smith will not appear in the To line.

When many individuals receive an e-mail, they typically read the information on the From line to determine the sender of the message. If John Smith notices the From line has the name of Bill Smith, the normal belief is that his son sent the e-mail. What John Smith fails to do is to look at the actual e-mail address that accompanies the sender name in the From line. As referenced, Bill Smith's actual e-mail address is billsmith@XXX.com. In the spoofed e-mail received by John Smith, the From line reads:

billsmith@Imagonasteal@fraud.com

In addition to using the name of a trusted individual to attract the attention of a spoofing e-mail recipient, legitimate company names are used. The information used pertaining to the sender could indicate it is from an organization with which the recipient actually conducts business. In the following spoofing e-mail, the recipient is led to believe it was sent from a national organization:

From: Amazon.com <delivers@grepciti.com>

To: jyoung5416@cox.net, jyoung67@cox.net, jyoung70@cox. net, jyoung79@cox.net, jyoung81@cox.net, jyoung87@cox.net, jyoung96@cox.net, jyoung994@cox.net, jyoung9@cox.net, jyoungblood5@cox.net, jyounger@cox.net

Subject: Transactions Report by users from 2014-08-12 to 2014-08-12

Attachments: order_report.zip (54.1 KB)

National

Good morning,
Thank you for your order. We'll let you know once your item(s) have dispatched.You can check the status of your order or make changes to it by visiting Your Orders on Amazon.co.uk.

Order Details
Order LX6108225 Placed on June 16, 2014
Order details and invoice in attached file.

Need to make changes to your order? Visit our Help page for more information and video guides.
We hope to see you again soon. Amazon.com

Many individuals conduct business with Amazon at least once a year, if not more. By using the name of a trusted and widely used Internet retail company, the attention of the recipient can be gained quickly. In addition, if the recipient has used Amazon services in the past, they could fall for the deception intended by the sender, the intent being to have the recipient click on a link provided.

With the example provided, there are several warning signs:

- The e-mail address listed after Amazon.com on the sender line is not a legitimate e-mail address from Amazon.
- The names listed on the To line contain several variations of the same type e-mail address.
- The Subject line lists a transaction report for the date August 12, 2014. Within the e-mail body, the order date is June 16, 2014.

With spoofed e-mail, the initial fraud resides in the information contained in the From line:

- The actual e-mail account holder has no knowledge their name is being used for spoofing purposes.
- The e-mail recipient is led to believe the message has been sent from a trusted source.
- The e-mail recipient only looks at the sender name in the From line and not the address accompanying the sender name.
- As long as the deception remains intact, the intent of the fraudulent e-mail can move forward.

The intent of the individual generating the spoofed e-mail can vary but usually falls in line with the following:

- To install unauthorized malicious software that can cause damage to the computer or overall system.
- To install spyware/malware software in an effort to access personal information in the computer system.

For fraudulent activity to take place via unsolicited e-mails, the recipient has to believe in the integrity of the sender. This is true for both spoofing and phishing attempts.

With phishing, which was discussed in Chapter 11, a main goal is to have the e-mail recipient provide personal account or credit card information to a third party. The goal of the third party is to use the information for fraudulent purposes, causing financial harm to the recipient of the phishing e-mail. Also following along with spoofing, the goal could be to install unauthorized malware or spyware on the recipient's computer.

From a fraud perspective, phishing and spoofing are developed with the same goal in mind. Spoofing differs from phishing, in the computer e-mail environment, based on the method of attraction. Both use e-mail to attract the initial attention of the recipient. Spoofing is used to trick the e-mail recipient into believing the message was sent from a trusted source by using recognizable names in the From line.

The phishing attraction is developed from the information contained in the Subject line of the e-mail.

12.5 Malware/Spyware

Malware is described as malicious software; it is introduced to a computer system when a user unknowingly clicks on a link contained in an unsolicited e-mail. These links are typically located in unsolicited e-mails sent via spamming, spoofing, and phishing. Malware can contain computer viruses that are developed and delivered with the intent of disrupting the computer operating system. From a fraud perspective, malware is used to deliver spyware. By clicking on a link in an unsolicited e-mail, the spyware can be loaded into the computer operating system.

The intent of spyware resides in the name. The software is unknowingly installed on computer systems; its purpose is spying. Spyware can track the activity of the individual operating the computer and collect varying amounts of information:

■ Internet surfing habits of the computer user
■ Log-in information of the computer user
■ Personal information of the computer user
■ Bank account information of the computer user
■ Credit/debit card information of the computer user
■ Online user passwords, gained by monitoring keystrokes through keylogging

The methods used to have the targeted individual click on a link that contains malicious software vary. As mentioned, many attempts come through spamming, spoofing, and phishing e-mails. One of the many versions used is shown in the following example, which was delivered as part of an unsolicited phishing e-mail:

From: Delta Air reply@execuair.com

To: jyoungblood5@cox.net

Subject: Your ticket is ready

Attachments: ET-48645298.zip (118.6 KB)

Order Notification,

TICKET/ET-56692363
SEAT/67F/ZONE 1
DATE/TIME 7 OCTOBER, 2014, 11:45 AM
ARRIVING/Las Vegas
FORM OF PAYMENT/CC

TOTAL PRICE/222.31 USD
REF/LE.8267 ST/OK
BAG/6PC

Your bought ticket is attached.
To use your ticket you should print it.

Thank you for your attention.

Delta Air Lines.
Open Attachment ET-48645298.zip

It is hoped that any individual receiving an unsolicited e-mail such as this will quickly hit the delete button and take the matter no further. The intent of the sender is to have the recipient believe his or her credit card was used to make an unauthorized airline ticket purchase. In an effort to correct the situation, the e-mail recipient will most likely click on the link provided to obtain the information necessary to dispute the believed unauthorized purchase.

Unsolicited phishing and other type e-mails contain warning signs of attempted fraud. Prior to accessing a link provided in any e-mail received, the recipient should look over the information and wording of the e-mail:

- A legitimate e-mail sent from any airline will have a company-related sender address in the From line.
- An e-mail sent from a legitimate organization will be addressed by name to the recipient.
- This particular e-mail informs the recipient their seat is 67F. It would be a really long plane to have a row 67.
- No information is provided for a departure location.
- "Your bought ticket is attached" is not the type of sentence structure used by a legitimate airline.

12.6 Protecting the Computer

The goal of the individual sending unsolicited e-mails through spamming, spoofing, and phishing is to deceive the recipient into providing personal information or financial data. An additional purpose is to have the recipient click on the link provided via an unsolicited e-mail in an effort to have malware/spyware installed on the computer's hard drive. No matter the initial intent of the spamming, spoofing, or phishing, the goal is to commit fraud.

To protect a personal computer or computers used in a small business operation, employees and users need to practice spamming, spoofing, and phishing prevention measures:

■ Individuals and small business owners and their employees routinely purchase items through the Internet. As discussed in Chapter 7, the computer user needs to ensure the URL for a purchase has the letters HTTPS included in the web address. In addition, the individual making a personal or business purchase through the Internet needs to look for a prechecked box. When shopping online, many order confirmation pages will preselect a check box. The information for the check box states the user agrees to allow the company to sell their e-mail information to responsible parties. Users need to uncheck the box to ensure the e-mail address does not wind up in the hands of individuals who want to commit fraud through spamming and phishing.

■ Not responding to an unsolicited e-mail is the best protection against becoming a victim of spamming, spoofing, and phishing. Computer users need to use caution prior to clicking on any attachment/link contained in an e-mail. Users need to watch for files the have the extensions .exe, .bat, .vbs, .reg, .msi, .pif, .pl, or .php. These indicate executable files that can perform unauthorized functions and operations on the computer.[2]

■ Make sure the system's firewall is turned on and updated regularly. Firewalls can protect a personal computer or private network from receiving malicious software or malware. From a business perspective, a firewall can be used to block employees from accessing certain websites from a company computer, such as social media sites. Firewalls can also be used to prevent employees from sending select types of e-mails or data that are deemed sensitive by the business owner. Any time a new system is purchased, the owner has to ensure the firewall is turned on. At times, some manufacturers will ship the system with the built-in firewall in the off mode.

■ It is never a good idea for a consumer or business operator to respond to an unsolicited e-mail alert that informs the individual of pending action on a service-provided account. Typically, a return phone number will be provided for the recipient to call to clear up the issue. If calling, a warning sign will be if the customer service call is answered immediately. Normally, calls to a customer service phone number are not answered directly by a service representative. A typical customer service call is answered by an automated system that requires the caller to enter certain account-related information and informs them of the expected wait time.

■ A frontline defense is always necessary in an effort to protect individual or small business[3] computer systems. Antivirus/spyware software is necessary as a frontline defensive measure. This software can protect the system against computer viruses that can be unknowingly uploaded to the computer via clicking on links in unsolicited e-mails. Spamming and phishing attempts to the system of an individual or small business computer are a constant threat to data security and provide the potential for compromised financial information.

- Chapter 2 discussed the need for all employers to conduct detailed background checks on applicants prior to making an offer of employment. Individuals who want to commit various frauds against a business operation will work to be hired in an effort to commit criminal activities. Once hired, the fraudster can access the organization's computer system as a matter of conducting their daily job functions. A prearrangement can be made to have phishing-related e-mails sent to the employee at their company's work e-mail address. If the business has weak computer protection measures in place, this individual can click on the links provided and allow malicious software to be installed.

In addition to the prevention measures previously discussed, many questions are raised from the security professional to the layperson regarding why a person or employee would fall victim to the related frauds initiated in the delivery of unsolicited e-mails. A possible explanation could be provided by understanding the impatience factor.

12.6.1 Impatience

It was not so many years ago that communication took place over the family telephone or landline. The telephone was attached to the wall, and if no one was home to answer the call, it was missed. There were no answering machines to record a message left by the caller. Eventually, the telephone answering machine was invented, and it became a household item—no more missed telephone calls.

As the telephone went through a process of evolution, a person could have one installed in their car, accompanied by a huge vehicle-mounted antenna. The telephone evolution also created the bulky bag phone that allowed a person to remain in contact with friends and the office. Eventually, the mobile phone was streamlined to fit in a small purse or pocket, allowing instant communication.

Along with the evolution of the cell phone came the streamlining of the personal computer. Laptops are now commonplace, along with the tablet, increasing an individual's level of instant access. In today's society, a person has instant access to the Internet. The Internet can be accessed from a computer, tablet, or cell phone from any location, allowing answers to almost any question to be obtained, purchases made, social media chatting, and college attendance.

Personal communication can also take place in a flash with instant messaging, text messaging, and cell phones. Individual communication to a business entity deviates from the accepted instant standard. Many people who call the customer service phone number for any service-providing organization are typically placed on hold and can spend a long time waiting for the next-available service representative. If this same individual uses the technology avenue to contact a customer service department via the organization's website, the response or answers are also not immediate.

The impatience factor favors those individuals committing fraud through sending unsolicited e-mails. With a society built on instant contact, instant access, and instant results, the last thing a person wants to waste time on is waiting on the phone for the next-available service representative. When asking why a person would click on a link provided in an unsolicited e-mail or text message, the answer could be one of the following:

- There is a belief or understanding that business entities have evolved into the technological world and could possibility alert a customer of an account issue.
- The e-mail or text message alert provides an avenue to address the issue (click on the link provided).
- A call to the customer service department will take time just to speak with the next-available service representative.
- Using the online contact feature available through many organizational websites will not provide quick or instant results.

Many individuals are used to the technology of today and spend their days multitasking and receiving information almost instantly. Basically, technology has created a society that has no patience for waiting. The cell phone and computer allow for instant contact and information; they can also be used to resolve problem issues and to receive instant results.

If curiosity killed the cat, impatience killed fraud awareness and prevention.

12.7 Password Protection

When it comes to establishing a policy for changing computer log-in passwords, two arguments are presented. Some will argue it is necessary to have a policy that requires passwords to be changed every ninety days. Others will argue it is not the frequency of changing log-in passwords but the strength of the password. No matter what side of the password change issue a person or small business follows, the following is important information to consider:

- Computer password security provides greater protection based on the strength of the characters used. Individuals or employees using short single name or other easily remembered computer passwords make access to the system easier for unauthorized users. If an individual or business chooses to change the computer password on a routine basis, efforts need to be made to develop a strong access code. Characteristics of a strong password are as follows:
  1. The password must be at least eight characters in length and not contain names, such as user's name, street name, company name, and so on.
  2. The newly created password has to be vastly different from any previous password used.

3. The password should not contain complete names.

4. A password should have at least one lowercase letter, one uppercase letter, and one number. In addition, the password should have at least one symbol: ~ ! @ # $% ^ & * () _ - + = {} [] \ | : ; " ' < >,. ?/. Symbols are located on the computer keyboard.[4]

■ It is possible that requiring employees to change log-in passwords on a frequent basis places computer integrity at risk. Not wanting to risk forgetting a newly implemented log-in password, an employee could write the new password on a Post-it® note or other piece of paper around their workstation. This brings up the question: Is it more secure to keep a log-in password for a long period of time versus having the password written on a piece of paper within hand's reach of the computer?

■ If the password is compromised on day 10, will computer security remain strong if a change is made eighty days later? When a log-in password is compromised, the person looking to commit fraud will immediately obtain the desired information, such as financial account information, retained on the computer. Once the necessary financial information is located, the person committing the fraud will not wait a period of time before removing assets from the individual or company bank accounts.

■ A computer password can also become irrelevant if unauthorized access to a computer system takes place via the installation of malicious software. Individuals or employees not adhering to system security protections by clicking on unsolicited links sent via phishing e-mails render password change policies irrelevant. With the unauthorized installation of malicious software, computer hackers can create a backdoor access code. Once established, the hacker can access computer information without providing the computer user's entry password.

To ensure the integrity of the personal, business, and financial information housed on a personal computer or system, more than one protection/prevention measure has to be in place. These measures are the following:

■ An individual or business computer user has to develop a detailed understanding of computer spamming, spoofing, and phishing. For a small business, a computer security protection and information policy has to be implemented.

■ All computer users need to develop an understanding of fraud attempts that are initiated through the Internet and computer e-mail.

■ It is necessary to install and constantly update antivirus/spyware software.

■ The integrity of all computer passwords must be maintained. In addition, there is a need to develop and keep secret strong access passwords.

12.8 Do Not Remember Me

All computer users need to avoid the habit of falling into complacency when it comes to logging on to websites. Many web browsers give the user the option of remembering log-in passwords to websites and e-mail accounts. A computer user can decide to visit an Internet payment system website. Once the individual enters a user name and password, some web browsers will provide a pop-up box asking for permission to remember log-in information. Within the pop-up box, a question asks the user if they would like the browser to remember the log-in password for the e-mail address used at the website visited. For example, "Would you like (Web Browser Name) to remember the password for xxxxxxxxx@xxx.com for www.xxxxxxxx.com?"

The options available for the user are typically "Yes, remember me," "Not at this time," or "Never." All computer users need to select the "Never" option. If the legitimate computer user allows the web browser to remember website log-in password information, their sensitive account information can be compromised. Anyone using a computer where a previous user has selected the "Yes, remember me" option to save time logging on to a website or e-mail account is basically allowing access to another person using the same computer. All the web browser remembers is the website name entered on the URL and that this particular computer allows password log-in memory. The web browser has no method of recognizing the individual using the actual computer.

Also, users of computers, whether personal or business, need to make sure to sign out from a website or e-mail account. With some websites and e-mail providers, access remains open until the log out/sign out option is taken. Simply closing the session will not log the authorized user out of the website or e-mail account. A follow-up computer user can type in the e-mail server or website address and have access to the account if the authorized user did not physically log out/sign out.

12.9 Protecting Social Media Accounts

As the ever-evolving world of technology changes the way we communicate and stay in touch with friends, the simplicity has to come with a word of caution. In today's world of instant communication, users of the various social media services need to develop an understanding of fraud trends. In an effort to protect an individual or business from becoming victim to the numerous types of fraud, a proactive posture has to be developed. This proactive posture has to revolve around detailed knowledge of the methods used to gain the attention of targeted individuals or business operations. The same posture also has to be based on the evolution of access to the intended targets.

Looking at fraud trends and methods of delivery to the targeted individuals, an evolution has taken place. Gone are the days of the handwritten chain letters, typewriter-composed advance fee letters, fraud attempts delivered through the mail,[5] and so on. As technology grew, the individuals lurking in the fraud world made sure to evolve with the times. With the increasing popularity and simplicity of the Internet and e-mail, a new delivery method for fraud attempts was capitalized on. Many types of fraud attempts now take place through the Internet and unsolicited e-mails.

As the growth of technology continues, individuals who want to find new methods of gaining the attention of potential victims are also evolving. The Internet and unsolicited e-mails are still popular arenas used to target potential fraud victims. To put the necessary barriers in place to stay off the path of least resistance, individuals and business owners need to look toward the next delivery arena. This new arena is the various social media websites.

Many of the successful fraud schemes generated through the sending of unsolicited e-mails are now being delivered to the targeted individuals on social media websites. Instead of receiving an unsolicited phishing e-mail, targeted individuals are now provided with the same information through their various social media accounts.

To develop a strong fraud prevention posture, individuals and business owners need to adhere to the same rules of prevention with social media fraud attempts:

- If it sounds too good to be true, it is.
- Never respond to an unsolicited phishing e-mail or social media phishing attempts.
- Never provide an advance fee to any get-rich-quick request provided through social media.
- Work-at-home opportunities offered through unsolicited e-mails are also fraud attempts if delivered through social media.

No matter the previous frauds discussed, the fact that initial contact takes place through social media does not change the intended outcome.

Individuals and business owners not only have to adapt their fraud prevention posture regarding social media but also have to create an understanding of the threats presented to all associates and family members. This is especially true for younger associates and children using business or family computers to access their social media accounts.

These younger individuals need to be educated on the many aspects of fraud attempts and the various delivery methods used on social media. Many of these younger computer users might not have a credit card to provide to the person initiating the fraud attempt, but they are able to click on links provided. By clicking on these links, dangerous malware and spyware can be unknowingly installed on a business or family computer. Once installed, this unauthorized software can spy on or cripple the family or business computer.

In addition to protecting the integrity of family and business computers, younger social media users need to be educated on what exactly to post on social media accounts. With many individuals active on social media websites, conversation flows freely with little regard for operational security. A popular area of discussion could be related to an upcoming family vacation and a reminder to friends of where the family is going and the dates they will be out of town.

Burglars and individuals working in the identity theft arena look for the opportunities presented by a vacant residence. From the burglar's perspective, the goal is to identify an unoccupied residence to remove as many valuables as possible. For those in the identity theft arena, the goal is to operate in the shadows so their targets do not know they have become a victim until the crime is complete.

If they know a residence is unoccupied, identity thieves have several target areas to gain access to sensitive information: the actual family home, any vehicles left behind at the house, and the hope that a stop was not placed on mail delivery during the family's absence. As discussed previously, individuals who want to commit identity theft do not want their target to know sensitive information has been sought or compromised.

If a burglar enters an unoccupied residence or vehicle, the owner will know of the crime on their return. When collecting sensitive personal information, unauthorized access could be made to the house or vehicle. On return, the home or vehicle owner will not notice signs of unauthorized entry. With unsecured mail, items (bank statements, credit card bills/statements, preapproved credit card applications, etc.) can simply be opened and the personal information compromised. Once the desired personal information is obtained, the envelopes are placed back in the mailbox. Again, the goal of the identity thief is not to raise suspicion.

To erect barriers to protect against additional fraud attempts, it is vital younger associates and family members are educated on what to post and not post[6] on social media accounts. What might seem like simple daily conversations to the younger individual is gold in the eyes of those who want to commit fraud.

In addition, all family members and associates need to be provided an understanding of fraud attempts through e-mail. Phishing attempts are made to countless e-mail accounts with the hope the recipient clicks on a link provided. In understanding the impatience and trust levels of many younger individuals, know that a second thought will not be given to a spoofing e-mail. When recognizing the sender's name as a friend with whom they normally communicate via e-mail, the recipient will most likely click on the link provided. Unless these younger individuals are educated on what constitutes phishing and spoofing e-mails, threats remain against the family and business computer.

Younger individuals active in social media are also avid users of cell phone text messaging. The same education has to be provided on the threats delivered through the cell phone. These threats include vishing, smishing, and cramming. These messages are sent with malicious intent: the hope of obtaining sensitive personal or business financial information.

The youth of today have embraced technology, but are they educated on the related fraud threats?

12.9.1 Social Media Phishing

Social media provide popular venues for users to post videos of themselves or others doing a variety of activities. Posted videos can also include family pets doing a unique trick or there can be other animal recordings. Users of social media websites post videos with good intent, and it has become a way to share interests with friends and other connections.

Unfortunately, individuals who want to commit malicious activity have also become active on social media websites. Users are being sent teasers that contain a headline written to attract the attention of the recipient. Enticed by the headline, the user clicks on the link provided and is greeted with a pop-up. The pop-up information informs the user that their video player requires updating. Instead of providing the user with a newer version of a video player, the link is actually downloading malware/spyware.

Other variations of this scam ask the user to complete a brief survey before the exciting video can be viewed. The intent of the survey is to have the recipient provide personal information that can be used to commit identity theft.

To avoid becoming a victim of social media phishing,

- Users need to use caution with videos containing teaser headlines that contain words such as *exclusive*, *shocking*, *sensational*, and the like.
- Place the mouse over any link provided to see the destination website. Do not click on website links that go to an unknown destination.
- Understand that a friend's page can be hijacked, and the friend is not the one who actually recommended the video link.[7]
- Never complete a pop-up survey associated with a video link.

Notes

1. *Malware* is a term used to refer to malicious software. This malicious software is used by hackers to gain access to computers and computer systems. The purpose of the software is to disrupt computer operations or obtain personal/business information.
2. Intuit, Phishing, pharming, vishing and smishing. https://security.intuit.com/phishing.html (accessed July 9, 2014).

3. Many small business operations do not have elaborate firewall-protected computer systems such as are common in large organizations. Some small businesses might have a small computer network or a few company computers for the employees to access. The fraud potential for a large corporation is not being ignored in this chapter's discussion. It is understood that large corporate organizations have separate information technology departments to protect their networks.

4. Microsoft, Tips for creating strong passwords and passphrases. http://windows. microsoft.com/en-us/windows7/tips-for-creating-strong-passwords-and-passphrases (accessed July 12, 2014).

5. A popular fraud attempt used through the US mail service was sending the target a postcard offering protection for their credit card accounts. Space was provided on the postcard for the recipient to list all of their credit card numbers and the postcard was to be mailed back to the sender. The intent of the person initiating the fraud was to obtain the legitimate credit card numbers of the individual targeted. It may sound silly, but this method was a successful fraud.

6. At no time should a person post their physical address or phone number on social media accounts. With a phone number, there are numerous websites available to obtain an address linked to it.

7. Better Business Bureau. Don't take the bait, shocking videos lead to malware, http:// www.bbb.org/council/bbb-scam-stopper/top-scams/phishing-scams/ (accessed August 29, 2014).

Appendix A: Social Security Number Prefixes

New Hampshire	001–003	Louisiana	433–439 and 659–665
Maine	004–007	Oklahoma	440–448
Vermont	008, 009	Texas	449–467 and 627–647
Massachusetts	010–034	Minnesota	468–477
Rhode Island	035–039	Iowa	478–485
Connecticut	040–049	Missouri	486–500
New York	050–134	North Dakota	501, 502
New Jersey	135–158	South Dakota	503, 504
Pennsylvania	159–211	Nebraska	505–508
Maryland	212–220	Kansas	508–515
Delaware	221, 222	Montana	516, 517
Virginia	223–231 and 691–699	Idaho	518, 519
West Virginia–North Carolina	232	Wyoming	520
West Virginia	233–236	Colorado	521–524 and 650–653
North Carolina	237–246 and 681–690	New Mexico	525, 585, 648, 649
South Carolina	247–251 and 654–658	Arizona	526, 527, 600, 601, 764, 765

Georgia	252–260 and 667–675	Utah	528, 529
Florida	261–267, 589–595, and 765–772	Nevada	530 and 680
Ohio	268–302	Washington	531–539
Indiana	303–317	Oregon	540–544
Illinois	318–361	California	545–573 and 602–626
Michigan	362–386	Alaska	574
Wisconsin	387–399	Hawaii	575, 576, 750, 751
Kentucky	400–407	District of Columbia	577–579
Tennessee	408–415 and 756–763	Virgin Islands	580
Alabama	416–424	Guam, American Samoa, and Philippines	586
Mississippi	425–428, 587–588, and 752–755	Puerto Rico	596–599
Arkansas	429–432 and 676–679		
Railroad	700–728		
Enumeration of entry[a]	729–733		

Source: Social Security Administration. http://www.mrfa.org/ssn.htm (accessed June 7, 2104)

[a] Pertains to immigrants admitted as lawful permanent residents.

Appendix B: Advance Fee Fraud Scheme Letters

This appendix provides actual unsolicited e-mails sent in an attempt to generate an advance fee fraud scheme. No changes were made to the e-mails as far as the From, To, and Subject lines. This information is posted exactly as received. No changes were made to the actual e-mails on the part of the wording. Poor spelling and grammar issues are common in many advance fee fraud letters and are a warning sign of potential fraud. All of the examples provided were received in 2014.

EXAMPLE B.1
This is a sympathy letter hoping to tug at the heart strings of the recipient. The sender is posing as a widow of a wealthy gentleman who is looking to bring prosperity to a random individual. This introductory letter reveals the promise of a large sum of money, asking the recipient to send a small up-front fee. Once the recipient becomes involved in the process by sending the initial advance fee, the person is strung along with promises of a large monetary payout that keeps being interrupted by the need to send additional payments to cover unexpected expenses.

> **From:** Mother.Mrs Edith Albertsen Torkild <whz@zegers-inc.com>
> **Subject:** claim notification of your funds below. contact dhl below

Good day to you and your family today

I am sure this mail would be coming to you as a surprise since we have never met before and you would also be asking why I have decided to chose you amongst the numerous internet users in the world, precisely I cannot say why I have chosen you but do not be worried for I come in peace and something very positive is about to happen to your life right now and to the lives of others through you if only you can carefully read and digest the message below.

The internet has made the world a global village where you can reach anybody you have not met before. Before I move further, permit me to give you a little of my biography, I am Mother.Mrs Edith Albertsen Torkild, 87 Years old woman and the wife of Late Sir Albertsen, Torkild who died in a Plane crash on Monday the

7th of September 1998 GMT 14:22 UK while they were flying from New York to Geneva. Please see website below for more information.

http://www.cnn.com/WORLD/9809/swissair.victims.list/index.html

After the death of my husband I became the Head of his investment and now that I am old and weak I have decided to spend the rest of my life with my family and loved ones whom I never had time for during the course of my business life, but before the death of my husband we had a plan to use the last days of our lives to donate half of what we have worked for to the less privilege and charity homes and the other half for ourselves, family members and close friends, and it is so unfortunate that my husband is not alive today to do this with me and I am very weak and old now, hence I have decided to do this philanthropic work on behalf of my late husband and I.

Presently, I have willed out almost half of our assets to several charity homes and to some of the less privilege in different countries. Despite the agreement between my late husband and I to give aid to the deprived, we also agreed to render support to an individual we have not meet before in life due to the fact when we were still young in life we receive an anonymous help from an individual we did not know and which we have not being able to know or met again till date, the impact we got from such gestsure made us wabt to do same.

I am sorry to inform you that you will never have the chance to know me because I have just concluded the assignment which my husband and I have agreed upon before his sudden death and you happened to be the beneficiary of our last WILL, irrespective of your previous financial status, hence I need you to do me a favor by accepting our offer

I have presently deposited a bank draft in the sum of $3.5million with DHL express to deliver to you when i visited west Africa to conclude some unfinished transaction and investment on behalf of my late husband,So i have contacted the ATTORNEY in charge of the deposited bank draft which i left there so that he can go to the DHL delivery company there to know when they will deliver the bank draft package to you because of the expiring date.

For your information, I have paid for the delivery Charges, Insurance Premium and Clearance Certificate Fee of the bank draft showing that it is not a Drug Money or meant to sponsor Terrorist attack in your Country You have to contact the DHL COURIER SERVICE now for the delivery of your bank draft with this information bellow;

DHL address: DHL International Nigeria Ltd
DHL House Isolo Expressway Abuja Nigeria
Contact Person: DR DONALD IKE
Email DR DONALD IKE: dhlexpressofficer9@gmail.com

Again, you are not to pay for the delivering Charge, the Insurance premium and the Clearance Certificate Fee of the bank draft because I have already paid for them, the only money you are expected to pay is $185 for the security keeping & intuity fee of the bank draft so far.

I would have paid the fee but the company insisted that I should not because they don't know when you will be contacting them and to avoid demurrage or further cost.

You are to reconfirm the below information to them to avoid any mistake on the Delivery.

Your Full Names:
Direct telephone number;
Your Postal/delivery address;
Age/sex/status
Nationality:

Below is the security keeping code: (DHL/0433/SKC) of you draft, you are to also present it to them for verification before delivery.

Try to contact them as soon as you receive this mail to avoid any further delay and remember to ask them to provide you with the method they wish to use in receiving their security keeping fee of $185 for from you for their immediate action.

Note: Please I do not want you to thank me or my husband all I need you to do is to invest wisely with it and do the same good to someone's life someday as this is the only way this world would be a better community if we render selfless services to one another.

Be also notified that I will no longer be reading my emails or surfing the internet as I have retired completely from the outside world to my ranch, at this moment I have nothing to do with cars, emails and other luxuries, all further correspondence should be forwarded to the courier company for the delivery of your bank draft to you.

Yours Faithfully,
Mother.Mrs Edith Albertsen Torkildez

EXAMPLE B.2
Next is an introductory letter sent in the hope of attracting the attention of the recipient by including a discussion of a transfer of a large monetary amount. The hope is to get individuals to respond with the requested personal information. If the recipient provides the requested personal information but fails to provide any future up-front fee as requested, the information collected can be used for identity theft fraud.

From: Mr Ema Iyabo <davidmoore1010@outlook.com>
Subject: FROM UNION BANK OF NIGERIA PLC.

This Union Bank of Nigeria the Foreign Remittance Department Called me that they have transferred the sum of $8 Million Usd into your nominated bank account but it has not yet be credited into your account,that the funds wouldn't reflect into your account until you obtain the required Certificate that is needed to complete your funds transfer.

Please re-confirm to me if this is online with what you have in your record and also re-confirm to me the followings.

1) Your full name.
2) Phone, fax and mobile

3) Age and marital status.
4) profession,
5) Copy of int'l passport,drivers linsense,or any valid ID card.

Mr Ema Iyabo
Management Union Bank Of Nigeria.

EXAMPLE B.3

This is an example of a letter claiming to be sent from the sitting secretary of the treasury. Again, the recipient is tempted by the promise of a large monetary payment, coupled with a request for a minimal up-front fee. Once the initial up-front payment is received, additional issues arise that require the victim to provide future payments. As long as the victim continues to pay the requested up-front fees, the individual committing the fraud will inform them their large monetary reward is just around the corner.

From: U.S. Department <infotreasury@gmail.com>
Subject: U.S. Department of the Treasury
1500 Pennsylvania Avenue, NW
Washington, D.C.
Website: http://www.treasury.gov
Date: 06/20/2014

Attn: Sir

Please consider this letter highly urgency to avoid cancellation of your United Nations Compensation payment. I am Jacob "Jack" Lew the Secretary of the Treasury under the U.S Department of the Treasury. The executive agency responsible for promoting economic prosperity and ensuring the financial security of the United States. I was confirmed by the United States Senate on February 27, 2013, to serve as the 76th Secretary of the Treasury. I was the Director of the Office of Management and Budget (OMB), a position I also held in President Clinton's Cabinet from 1998 to 2001.

By virtue of my position as the Secretary of the Treasury, I have irrevocably instructed Bank of America, which is the authorized paying bank to release your $500,000.00 United Nations Compensation payment via SWIFT telegraphic bank transfer into your provided bank account.

However, I wish to state categorically that your fund transfer valued at sum of $500,000.00 will be transferred into your provided account within 24 hours.

Every and all cost associated with the fund transfer has been pre-paid by the United Nations. The only cost associated with your fund release is the cost of processing a "Fund Clearance Certificate", which is estimated to the value of $150. The "Fund Clearance Certificate" is required in accordance with the U.S Monetary Policy; and it is the ONLY expenses you will incur before the fund will be reflected into your account.

For your information, the "Fund Clearance Certificate" is a valid document required to certify that the $500,000.00 in question has been cleared and certified by the U.S. Federal authorities as a legitimate compensation payment approved by the United Nations.

You can get more facts about the U.S. Department of the Treasury on this link

http://www.treasury.gov/about/Pages/Secretary.aspx

You can mail me directly via: infotreasury@terra.com

Yours Sincerely,
Jacob "Jack" Lew
Secretary of the Treasury

EXAMPLE B.4

A basic introductory letter that is hoped will initiate a response from the recipient is presented next. If contact is made by the recipient to the sender, future e-mails will discuss the need for up-front payments and a requirement to provide personal information to complete the money transfer process.

> **From:** David Akati <mydeskoffi2014@globomail.com>
> **To:** me <mydeskoffi2014@globomail.com>
> **Subject:** THE MESSAGE IS A DEAL.

Dear Friend,

How are you doing today and your family? Hope this mail meets you in fine health. My name is Mr. David Akati a Ghanaian citizen with all good intention I bring to you this transaction worth Us$17,500,000.00 (Seventeen Million, Five Hundred Thousand Us Dollars) if you think you have the heart to handle it with me I will present you with more details on how we can work it out for our mutual benefit.

Best regards,
Mr. David Akat

EXAMPLE B.5

The unsolicited e-mail in Example B.5 attracts the attention of the recipient by informing them they were the sole random beneficiary to receive a large amount of money. Once the intended victim contacts the sender, requests for personal information about the recipient are made. In addition, the issues of unforeseen fees and international taxes arise, and the eventual cash award recipient needs to provide the various up-front fees.

> **From:** Chuck Feeney <feeney.f.chuck@rogers.com>
> **To:** You@Grant-Recipient
> **Subject:** Grant Donation To You

Hi,

My name is Charles Francis Feeney (Chuck Feeney), a philanthropist and the founder of one of the largest private foundations in the world. My motto is ?giving while living.? I had one idea that never changed in my mind ? that you should use your wealth to help people and I have decided to give USD 1.924 Million to an individual. On receipt of this email, you should count yourself as the individual.

Your email address was selected online randomly while searching.

Kindly get back to me at your earliest convenience, so I know I have reached a valid email address before I can disclose more information.

Visit the web page to know more about me: http://www.nytimes.com/2012/08/08/nyregion/a-billionaire-philanthropist-struggles-to-go-broke.html or you can search an article of me on wikipedia (Chuck Feeney).

Regards,
Charles F. Feeney.

EXAMPLE B.6

The unsolicited e-mail in this example is intended as a follow-up invitation to collect a large amount of money. The purpose is to entice the recipient into believing the legitimacy of the endeavor. The e-mail also references previous assistance on the part of the past recipient. As the recipient of this particular e-mail, no prior contact was made on my part with any previous contacts.

From: UDO <sudo001@outlook.com>
To:
Subject: GOVERNOR CENTRAL BANK

Bank check of $1.2 million dollars

Dear Friend

How are you today? Hope all is well with you and your family? I hope this mail meets you in a perfect condition. You may not understand why this mail came to you. But if you do not remember me, you might have receive an email from me in the past regarding a business proposal which we never concluded.

I am happy to inform you about my success in getting those funds transferred under cooperation of a new partner from Dominican Republic. Presently I'm in Dominican Republic for investment projects with my own share of the total sum meanwhile,I didn't forget your past efforts and attempts to assist me in transferring those funds despite that it failed us some how. Now contact my REV FATHER in Benin rep Africa, his name is REV FATHER JOHN EZE

EMAIL: revjohn200@outlook.com TELEPHONE :+2347030614433 OR +22998199281

Ask him to send you the total cash check of $1.2 million dollars which I kept for your compensation for all the past efforts and attempt to assist me in this matter. I appreciated your collective efforts at that time so feel free and get in touch with my Rev Father john and instruct him where to send the amount to you. Do it fast before the CASH CHECK EXPIRED.

Please do let me know immediately you receive it so that we can share the joy after all the sufferings at that time. In the moment, I am very busy here in Dominican Republic because of the investment projects which I and the new partner are having at hand without confrontations,Finally, remember that I had forwarded instruction to the secretary on your behalf to receive that CASH CHECK, so feel free to get in touch with REV JOHN EZE my secretary he will send the CHECK to you without any delay

CHARLES UDO
FORMER GOVERNOR CENTRAL BANK OF AFRICA

EXAMPLE B.7

The letter in Example B.7 informs the recipient of their great fortune of being selected to receive a large sum of money. The method of delivery is through an ATM card that is initially loaded with $500,000. The recipient is informed that only $5,000 can be withdrawn through the ATM card on a daily basis. To receive the ATM card, the recipient has to begin the process by providing personal information. After contact is initiated, the request for advance fees follows.

From: Ban Ki-moon <scanner@caperatliff.com>
To: Undisclosed recipients:
Subject: CLAIM OF $2.5M FUNDS COMPENSATION

UBA COMPENSATION UNIT, IN AFFILIATION WITH THE UNITED NATIONS.

Attention: Sir/Madam,

Due to the petitions received by the UN, I Secretary-General Ban ki-moon from all over the continent in regards to the fraudulent activities going on in the West Africa sub-region with security's agent and diplomats who has been delaying people's funds, consignment and valuables in their custody and demand outrageous fees to get their consignment released to them.

We have been having a meeting for the passed months which ended 2 days ago with the former Secretary-General (Hon. Kofi Annan) to the UNITED NATIONS. However, We went to the African head quarters in NIGERIA on the 15TH SEPTEMBER 2013 and set up this committee with sole aim of settling all these anomalies and due to that we are contacting you today in that regards.

This email is to all people that have been scammed in any part of the world, the UNITED NATIONS have agreed to compensate them with the sum of USD 2 500,000,00 This includes every foriegn contractors that may have not received their contract sum, and people that have had an unfinished transaction or international businesses that failed due to Government problems etc.

We found your name in our list and that is why we are contacting you, these have been agreed upon and have been duly signed.

Therefore, we are happy to inform you that an arrangement has perfectly been concluded to effect your payment as soon as possible in our bid to be very transparent. However, it is our pleasure to inform you that your ATM Card Number; 2354-3456-0952-4204 has been approved and upgraded in your favor.

Meanwhile, your Secret Pin Number will be available as soon as you confirm to us the receipt of your ATM CARD. The ATM Card Value is USD2 500,000 USD Only. You are advised that a maximum withdrawal value of USD5,000.00 is permitted daily. And its is duly inter-switched and you can make withdrawal in any location of the ATM Center of your choice/nearest to you any where in the world. We have also concluded delivery arrangement with our accredited courier service Companies to oversee the delivery of the ATM Card to you without any further delay. Your payment would be sent to you via Federal Express Diplomatic and Sky link fast delivery, ARAMEX, DHL AND FedEx, and UPS EXPRESS DELIVER. Because we have signed a contract with the courier companies above.

Below is an example of tracking numbers you can track from UPS and ARAMEX Courier website to confirm people like you who have received their ATM CARD successfully:

(1).Name: Mr. DAVID EMERSON
http://www.fedex.com/Tracking
Tracking Number: 876323725112
(2)Name : Steve Bond:
Website:www.aramex.com
Tracking Number: 7846966960

Be informed that your response would be by telephone or through email Only. Any further delay will be the pleasure of the UNRC to use your fund to help the people who have been displaced in Darfur, Sudan Africa which you can see it in this site www.savedarfur.org and the Tsunami's victims in Asia. So you are hereby advice to forward to this office Director ATM SWIFT CARD Department Therefore, you should send him your full Name and telephone number/your correct mailing address where you want him to send the ATM to you.

Conatct Mr. Person to Contact MR. GEORGE EZE immediately for your ATM CARD:

Person to Contact: MR. GEORGE EZE
Email: georgeeze211@gmail.com
Tel:+234-813-884-1071

We are working according to the constitution binding this committee as well as helping the less privilege through this means. You will be required to contact the above mentioned institution via telephone or email. Hoping to hear from you as soon as you receive your ATM.

Please call MR. GEORGE EZE for your claim.

Making the world a better place
Regards,
Mr. Ban Ki-moon
Secretary-General UNITED NATIONS).
http://www.un.org/sg/biography.shtml

EXAMPLE B.8

The letter for Example B.8 is an initial solicitation to attract the attention of the receiver. The sender is advised of the opportunity to receive 40% of a $20 million money transfer that will originate in Iraq. A link is provided to add validity to the request, coupled with the need for the process to be completed with a low profile. The low-profile request is made to keep the targeted individual from discussing the process with another. If the targeted individual discusses their good fortune with another, they might be advised the whole process is an advance fee fraud.

From: Mr.William Bill <bongbal@postech.ac.kr>
Subject: Business Proposer

Dear Friend.

I hope my E-mail meets you well, I am in need of your assistance My Name is Mr.William Bill of the engineering Unit here in Baghdad in Iraq; we have about $20 Million US dollars that we want to move out of the country in two digital boxes. My partners and I need a good partner out there, someone we can trust to receive the funds on our behalf.

It is oil money and legal we have made arrangements with a United Nation Courier service that will move the funds out of Iraq as a Family Treasures, The most important thing is; Can We Trust you once the funds get to you?, simply take out 40% as your share and keep the remaining 60% for us.

Your own part of this deal is to find a safe place where the funds can be sent to, ours is sending it to you safely also you can view the Link

http://news.bbc.co.uk/2/hi/middle_east/2988455.stm

If you are interested I will furnish you with more details upon receipt of your response and contact details But I can assure you the whole process is simple and we must keep a low profile at all times.

I look forward to your reply and co-operation.

My Personal email: williambill@365trade.net
Warm Regards.

EXAMPLE B.9

The purpose of the letter in this example is to gain the attention of the recipient by using the name of the Federal Bureau of Investigation (FBI) and mentioning their work with the government of Nigeria. According to the letter, based on the agreement made between the FBI and the Nigerian government, the recipient is due a large sum of money. To obtain an ATM smart card that is loaded with the large payout, the recipient has to provide a small up-front payment of $150. In a further effort to add credibility to the letter, the name of the sitting director of the FBI is used.

From: FBI <coonai@coonai.com.br>
To:
Subject: SCAM REIMBURSEMENT PAYMENT

ATTN: ATM CARD PAYMENT BENEFICIARY,
(FBI) PAYMENT MEMO TO PAYMENT BENEFICIARIES.

THIS IS GOOD NEWS FOR YOU FROM THE FBI. WE HAD A MEETING WITH INTERNATIONAL MONETARY FUND (IMF) AND THE FEDERAL GOVERNMENT OF NIGERIA OVER YOUR LONG

OVERDUE CONTRACT PAYMENT AND WE AGREED WITH THEM THAT YOUR FUND SHOULD NOT COST YOU ANYTHING BECAUSE IS YOUR MONEY, SO WE FINALLY REACHED AN AGREEMENT THAT ALL THE PAYMENT WILL BE PAID VIA ATM SMART CARD WHICH IS THE SIMPLEST WAY TO TRANSFER HUGE AMOUNT OF MONEY TO AVOID COST OF TRANSFER AND OTHER STATUTORY DOCUMENTS, WHICH WE STRETCHED TO HAVE A STRONG AGREEMENT OVER THE PAYMENT THAT WILL COST YOU ONLY $150 USD FOR DELIVERY OF YOUR ATM SMART CARD VIA TNT DELIVERY COMPANY DEPENDING ON YOUR CHOICE.

HOWEVER, YOU HAVE ONLY TWO WORKING DAYS TO SEND THIS REQUIRED DELIVERY FEE OF $150 USD TO TNT COURIER COMPANY FOR DELIVERING OF YOUR CARD BECAUSE YOUR CARD WILL BE DISPATCH TO THEM IMMEDIATELY. AND IF WE DON'T HEAR FROM YOU WITH THE PAYMENT INFORMATION; THE FEDERAL BUREAU OF INVESTIGATION WILL NOT HESITATE BY GIVEN INSTRUCTION TO FEDERAL GOVERNMENT OF NIGERIA AND THE INTERNATIONAL REMITTANCE DEPARTMENT TO CANCEL YOUR PAYMENT THAT HAS BEEN ALREADY APPROVED AND PROGRAMMED IN AN ATM SMART CARD.

I WANT YOU TO READ BELOW CAREFULLY, THE NOTICE BELOW STAND AS CAUTION BEFORE IT IS LATE. FOR YOUR CONSIDERATION, YOU MUST BE CONSCIOUS OF THIS PROJECT, AS I WILL SOON CONCLUDE THIS TRANSACTION WITH YOU, LET THIS STAND AS A WARNING BEFORE YOU INCASE YOU RECEIVED ANY E-MAILS OR CALLS REGARDING TO THIS FROM ANY INDIVIDUAL, OFFICE, ORGANIZATION AND BANKS CLAIMING TO BE ME.

BE INFORMED THAT YOU MAY ALSO RECEIVE SEVERAL E-MAILS AND TELEPHONE CALLS FROM ANY ORGANIZATION, SUCH MUST BE FORWARDED TO US IMMEDIATELY FOR VERIFICATION. IT MIGHT COME TO YOU WITH DIFFERENT PROPOSALS WITH DIFFERENT NAMES INCLUDING MY NAME ASKING YOU TO COME AND PUT CLAIM ON YOUR ESTATE OR EVEN FUNDS BELONGING TO YOU OR TO SOMEBODY YOU DO NOT KNOW, I URGE YOU TO IGNORE SUCH E-MAILS OR CALLS, WHILE YOU FORWARD IT TO US. I WANT YOU TO UNDERSTAND THAT THE MOST IMPORTANT THING FOR ME IS YOUR UNDERSTANDING AND CO-OPERATION. WHILE RESPONDING TO THE ATM CARD PAYMENT OFFICER YOU MUST CONFIRM THIS CODE (WUP/MGP/PMT) FOR IDENTIFICATION.

HOWEVER, BE INFORMED THAT THE PAYMENT, WHICH IS 1,000.000.00 MILLION U.S. DOLLARS HAS BEEN LOADED IN YOUR ATM SMART CARD THIS PAYMENT WOULD BE SENT TO YOU VIA TNT, BECAUSE WE HAVE SIGNED A CONTRACT WITH THEM WHICH SHOULD EXPIRED BY NOVEMBER 25 2014.

MEANWHILE,BE ADVISED BASED ON OUR RECOMMENDATION/ INSTRUCTIONS THAT YOUR UN-COMPLETE CONTRACT/ INHERITANCE OVER-DUE FUNDS WILL BE RELEASED IMMEDIATELY UPON YOUR CONTACT TO THE NEWLY APPOINTED PAYMENT

OFFICER THAT WILL CARRY OUT THE DISPATCH OF YOUR ATM SMART CARD TO TNT COURIER COMPANY WITH THE PAYMENT FOR DELIVERY OF YOUR PACKAGED. YOU ARE THEREFORE ADVISED TO CONTACT AGENT STEPHEN GREEN IMMEDIATELY WITH THIS CODE (WUP/MGP/PMT) WITH THE CONTACT BELOW AS HE IS THE APPOINTED DIRECTOR OF ATM SMART CARD/FOREIGN OPERATION DEPT AND ASK HIM ON HOW AND WHERE TO SEND THE PAYMENT OF $150.00 ONLY TO TNT COURIER COMPANY.

CONTACT PERSON: AGENT STEPHEN GREEN
PRIVATE EMAIL ADDRESS :(infostephengreen@yeah.net)

YOU'RE ADVISED TO CONTACT HIM IMMEDIATELY TO ENABLE HIM FACILITATE A SPEEDY PROCESSING AND RELEASE OF YOUR DELIVERY SINCE IT IS THE $150.00 USD THAT IS KEEPING YOUR ATM SMART CARD. CONTACT HIM WITH THE FOLLOWING INFORMATION AS LISTED BELOW:

1. YOUR FULL NAME...........................
2. CONTACT ADDRESS..
3. YOUR AGE...
4. OCCUPATION...
5. PHONES AND FAX NUMBER..................

NOTE: YOU'RE ADVISED TO FURNISH YOUR INFORMATION TO INTERNATIONAL REMITTANCE DEPARTMENT DIRECTOR AGENT STEPHEN GREEN WITH YOUR CORRECT AND VALID DETAILS TO ENABLE HIM EXPEDITE SPEEDY ACTION ON THE PROCESSING OF YOUR PAYMENT. WE EXPECT YOUR SWIFT RESPONSE TO THIS EMAIL TO ENABLE US MONITOR THIS PAYMENT AND THE DELIVERY OF YOUR ATM SMART CARD EFFECTIVELY THEREBY MAKING CONTACT WITH THE INTERNATIONAL REMITTANCE DEPARTMENT AS DIRECTED TO AVOID FURTHER DELAY.
YOU'RE ALSO EXPECTED TO FOLLOW HIS ADVICE AND DIRECTIVES TO AVOID DELAY IN RELEASING YOUR PAYMENT BECAUSE YOUR PAYMENT FILE HAS ALREADY BEEN MOVED TO IMF OFFICE FOR PROCESSING AND VERIFICATION.

CONGRATULATIONS.
YOURS IN SERVICE,
CC: PAMELA JOHNSON
CC: DIRECTOR ROBERT MUELLER,
FEDERAL BUREAU OF INVESTIGATION
UNITED STATES DEPARTMENT OF JUSTICE
WASHINGTON, D.C. 20535

Note: Disregard any email you get from any impostors or offices claiming to be in possession of your ATM card, you are hereby advice only to be in contact with Agent Stephe Green who is the rightful person to deal with in regards to your payment and forward any emails you get from impostors to this office so we could act upon it immediately. Help stop cyber crime.

EXAMPLE B.10

Example B.10 is a slightly different variation on an advance fee letter that actually asks for the advance fee in the introductory e-mail. In an effort to add credibility to this correspondence, the writer dismisses all other types of advance fee letters as frauds. An added attraction is the promise of cost saving to the recipient if the advance fee is paid for in a timely manner. Using the Department of Justice and the Federal Bureau of Investigation as participants in the process might actually catch the attention of the recipient and add credibility to the overall monetary promise.

> **From:** Mrs. Stella Evans <kevin@andainvest.com>
> **Date:** Thursday, July 31, 2014 9:52 PM
> **To:**
> **Subject:** Federal Bureau of Investigation (Good News).
>
> Federal Bureau of Investigation
> Anti-Terrorist and Monitory Crime Division
> Edger Hoover Building Washington Dc
> Customers Service Hours/Monday to Saturday
> Office Hours Monday to Saturday:

Attention!

Series of meetings have been held over the past 2 months with the secretary general of the United Nations Organization. This ended 3 days ago. It is obvious that you have not received your fund which is to the tune of $1, 500, 000.00 due to past corrupt Governmental Officials who almost held the fund to themselves for their selfish reason and some individuals who have taken advantage of your fund all in an attempt to swindle your funds which has led to so many losses from your end and unnecessary delay in the receipt.

The National Central Bureau of Interpol enhanced by the United Nations and Federal Bureau of Investigation have successfully passed a mandate to the current president of Nigeria his Excellency President Good luck Jonathan to boost the exercise of clearing all foreign debts owed to you and other individuals and organizations who have been found not to have receive their Contract Sum, Lottery/Gambling, Inheritance and the likes. Now how would you like to receive your payment? Because we have two method of payment which is by Check or by ATM card?

ATM Card: We will be issuing you a custom pin based ATM card which you will use to withdraw up to $10,000 per day from any ATM machine that has the Master Card Logo on it and the card have to be renewed in 4 years time which is 2016. Also with the ATM card you will be able to transfer your funds to your local bank account. The ATM card comes with a handbook or manual to enlighten you about how to use it, Even if you do not have a bank account.

Check: To be deposited in your bank for it to be cleared within three working days. Your payment would be sent to you via any of your preferred option and would be mailed to you via DHL. Because we have signed a contract with FedEx which should expire by August 6th 2014 you will only need to pay $175 instead of $420 saving you $245 So if you pay before August 6th 2014 you save $245 Take note that anyone asking you for some kind of money above the usual fee is definitely a fraudsters and you will have to stop communication with every other person if you have been in contact with any. Also remember that all you will ever have to spend is $175.00 nothing more! Nothing less! And we guarantee the receipt of your fund to be successfully delivered to you within the next 24hrs after the receipt of payment has been confirmed.

Note: Everything has been taken care of by the Federal Government of Nigeria, The United Nation and also the FBI and including taxes, custom paper and clearance duty so all you will ever need to pay is $175.

DO NOT SEND MONEY TO ANYONE UNTIL YOU READ THIS: The actual fees for shipping your ATM card is $420 but because DHL have temporarily discontinued the C.O.D which gives you the chance to pay when package is delivered for international shipping We had to sign contract with them for bulk shipping which makes the fees reduce from the actual fee of $420 to $175 nothing more and no hidden fees of any sort!

To affect the release of your fund valued at $1,500,000. 00 you are advised to contact our correspondent in Africa the delivery officer Mr. Joseph Ibe with the information below.

Email: mr.josephi@yahoo.com.hr
Tel: +234-8182-6899-77

You are advised to contact him with the information's as stated below:

Your full Name:
Your Country:
Your Address:
Home/Cell Phone:
Preferred Payment Method (ATM/Cashier Check)

Upon receipt of payment the delivery officer will ensure that your package is sent within 24 working hours. Because we are so sure of everything we are giving you a 100% money back guarantee if you do not receive payment/package within the next 24hrs after you have made the payment for shipping.

Yours sincerely,
Mrs. Stella Evans
FEDERAL BUREAU OF INVESTIGATION
UNITED STATES DEPARTMENT OF JUSTICE
WASHINGTON, D.C. 20535

Note: Do disregard any email you get from any impostors or offices claiming to be in possession of your ATM CARD/Cashier Check, you are hereby advice only to be in contact with Mr. Joseph Ibe of the ATM CARD/Cashier Check CENTRE who is the rightful person to deal with in regards to your ATM CARD/Cashier Check PAYMENT and forward any emails you get from impostors to this office so we could act upon and commence investigation.

EXAMPLE B.11
This example provides a new twist that is used in the hope that it will add credibility to the recipient. At the end of the message body, there is a note informing the recipient that their Internet provider is responsible if the message arrives in the

spam folder. The message also advises the recipient that a large amount of money has been successfully removed from the sender's country and is currently in a European country. All that is required is the assistance of an honest person to help smuggle the money to the United States.

From: MARC.E... <000.000@56788.com>
To:
Subject: Can you be trusted? Acknowledge

GOOD DAY

I KNOW THIS WILL COME TO YOU AS A SURPRISE BECAUSE YOU DO NOT KNOW ME. I AM. MR MARC.E.OVERTONE, I WORK IN THE RICH OIL REGION, NIGER DELTA DEVELOPMENT COMMISSION (NDDC); I GOT YOUR CONTACT IN MY SEARCH FOR A HONEST PERSON AND SOME ONE I COULD TRUST.

I WANT YOU TO HELP ME CLEAR THIS PACKAGE THAT IS ALREADY IN EUROPE WHICH I SHIPPED THROUGH N.D.D.C/C.B.N, ACCREDITED COURIER AGENT BUT THE CONTENTS OF THE PACKAGE IS $20,000,000.00 ALL IN $100.00 BILLS, BUT THE FIDUCIARY COMPANY DOES NOT KNOW THAT IT IS MONEY THAT I HAVE IN THE PACKAGE.

ALL I WANT YOU TO DO FOR ME NOW IS TO GIVE ME YOUR MAILING ADDRESS, YOUR PRIVATE PHONE AND FAX SO THAT I CAN GIVE YOU MORE DETAILS.YOU CAN CALL OR E-MAIL ME FOR SECURITY REASONS OTHER MODALITIES WILL BE DISCUSSED AS SOON AS YOU GET BACK TO ME, INCLUDING SENDING YOU THE PIN NUMBERS TO THE PACKAGE WITHIN THE STIPULATED TIME. CAN I TRUST YOU??

MR. MARC.E.OVERTON
PHONE: +2348080434430

NOTE : If You Receive This Message In Your Junk Or Spam Its Due To Your Internet Provider.

EXAMPLE B.12

This letter example begins with the hope of attracting the attention of the recipient with the offer of a million-dollar-plus certified bank draft. The uniqueness of this advance fee letter is the up-front request for $385 to cover the security keeping fee. The sender attempts to add legitimacy by stating that no other fees should be paid by the recipient except the security keeping fee. In addition to asking for a small up-front fee, personal information is requested.

From: HILDA MARTINS <tjoe@mbay.net>
To:
Subject: CERTIFIED BANK DRAFT

Monday to Saturday
Office Hours Monday to Saturday:

Greetings!!!

I have been waiting for you to contact me for your International Certified Bank Draft worth 1,650,000.00 (One Million, Six Hundred and Fifty Thousand United States Dollars), being compensation fund for 150 scammed victims, but I did not hear from you all this while. I have deposited the International Certified Bank Draft with Royal Chase Courier Company, West Africa, as I traveled out of the country for a 3 Months Course and I will not be back until completion of my 3 months course. What you have to do now is to contact the Royal Chase Courier Company immediately to know when they will deliver your parcel to you because of the demurrage date from the day of deposit.

For your information, I have paid for the delivery Charge, and Clearance Certificate Fee of the parcel showing that it is not a Drug Money or meant to sponsor Terrorism attack in your Country. All you are to send to the Royal Chase Courier Company to deliver your International Certified Bank Draft direct to your postal Address in your country is just the sum of $385.00 United state dollars being Security Keeping Fee of the Courier Company so far. Again, don't be deceived by anybody to pay any other money except $385.00 United state dollars.

I would have paid that but they refused, All because they don't know when you will contact them and in case of demurrage.

You have to contact the Royal Chase Courier Company immediately for the delivery of your International Certified Bank Draft with this information below:

Company's name: Royal Chase Courier Company
Contact Agent: Mr James Douglas
Email Address: jamesdoug220@gmail.com

Your full information will be required from you
Request for the tracking number of the parcel to enable you track and know when it will get to your address. Let me repeat again, try to contact them immediately you receive this mail to avoid any further delay and remember to pay the Security Keeping fee of $385.00 united state dollars for their immediate action. You should also let me know through email as soon as you receive your parcel.

Yours Faithfully,
Mrs. Hilda Martins

EXAMPLE B.13
The advance fee fraud letter in this example is an aggressive attempt to have the recipient believe in its legitimacy. The sender points out previous organizations' names used to commit these types of scams and goes as far as using the sitting president and first lady as participants in compensating recipients of the unsolicited e-mail. Recipients are requested to provide a large amount of personal information that can be used for identity theft. Requests will also be made by the sender to have the recipient provide up-front fees.

From: Mr. Gabriel Jones <grimesndg@hotmail.com>
To:
Subject: ARE YOU STILL ALIVE?.

USA FUND RECOVERY COMMITTEE.
Washington DC, U.S.A.
Tel: +1(650) 308-9573
ATTENTION:

We are the United States fund recovery committee recently commissioned by First Lady Michelle Obama last year 2013. Our responsibilities are to recover: stolen funds, properties, Compensation payments, lottery winnings,Fund Inheritance, Contract Funds, e.t.c. You are receiving this email because you are listed as a potential beneficiary of fund yet to be paid to you.

In your own case we have discovered that you are being owed the sum of $200.000 (Two Hundred Thousand United States Dollar) in Our recent mass investigation carried out in some countries including Nigeria with the help of the REAL FBI, and INTERPOL, we were able to arrest 12 men and 6 women.

These arrested men and women have all confessed to be impostors and fraudster who have been scamming people for many years now, they also stated they are many people out there who are in the same fraud business with them.We found out that there are many impostors who are using the following offices for scam activities: FBI, CIA,HOMELAND SECURITY, INTERPOL, SECRETARY OF STATES (USA), IMF, BANK OF AMERICA, WORLD BANK, CENTRAL BANK OF NIGERIA, SENATE PRESIDENT OF NIGERIA, EFCC NIGERIA,ANTI TERRORIST OFFICE, MONEY LAUNDERING OFFICE.

The President of the United States and his wife instructed that you stop communicating with the above fake offices to avoid being scammed again.

We were able to retrieve your email address from the arrested fraudsters, therefore, you are needed to submit the below details as outlined for immediate processing and payment of your fund and I will respond to you as soon as we receive your full details: here outlined is our office telephone number (+1(650) 308-9573) you can call immediately you receive this mail for more verification and confirmation as to the calming of your fund.

1, Your Names:
2, Your Home Address:
3, Your Country:
4, Your City:
5, Sex/Age :
6, phone number:
7, Your Private/secure email address:
8. Your Present Occupation:
9. your copy of your ID

Your quick response to this email notice with the above information is highly appreciated.

Yours Sincerely,
Mr. Gabriel Jones
Head of Committee

EXAMPLE B.14

The letter for Example B.14 is an example of an attempt at revictimization or continuation of an advance fee fraud. Many recipients of this letter who have not participated in the scam will simply delete the unsolicited e-mail. Individuals who have participated in the scam and are beginning to believe they might be a fraud victim will view this letter in a positive light. They might have fallen victim to an advance fee fraud, but Interpol and the FBI are on the case to retrieve their money. Unfortunately for those believing the letter provides an offer of assistance, they will become more involved in the fraud and provide additional advance fees.

> **From:** INTERNET FRAUD UNIT <info@interpol.org>
> **To:** undisclosed-recipients:;
> **Subject:** Urgent

Good Day

This is the internet fraud unit of the Interpol police; we are mandated by the British High Commission and the FBI to combat internet fraud. Our monitoring device picked up several signal transaction on your server and since then we have been monitoring all your internet transaction and we have just discovered that you have been into series of transaction.

From our investigation you have been into a transaction worth of millions of dollars which you have spent money on, and you have been dealing with the wrong people. A compensation of six hundred and fifty thousand united state dollars ($650,000.00) has been allocated to Americans, Arabians, Europeans, Canadians and Asian citizen who have been scammed and harassed on the internet. We are supported by the UNITED NATIONS and have been investigating emails directed to selected individuals.

We want to clear your doubts; you are to continue your transaction with Robert Nicholas of the compensation payment department immediately. Please you are to notify us when you receive this email.

You are not to disclose this information to a third party as we are on the trail to get all perpetrators of cyber crime.

Thank you for your understanding

Faithfully
Bryan Anderson
Head Internet Fraud Unit

Appendix C: Work-at-Home, Mystery Shopping, Inheritance, and Lottery Schemes

Appendix C consists of actual unsolicited e-mails sent in an attempt to generate work-at-home, mystery shopping, inheritance, lottery schemes, and phishing e-mail scams. No changes were made to the e-mails as far as the From, To, and Subject lines. These lines are posted exactly as received. No changes were made to the actual e-mails regarding the written wording. Poor spelling and grammar issues are common in many advance fee fraud letters and are a warning sign of potential fraud. All of the examples provided were received in 2014.

EXAMPLE C.1

This example is an actual unsolicited e-mail received from a person claiming to represent a legitimate mystery shopping company. The actual mystery shopping company name and business address used in the e-mail are legitimate, but the contact name provided in the e-mail is not a legitimate employee of the organization. Individuals committing mystery shopping frauds will hijack the trade name of a legitimate mystery shopping company to add credibility to their work-at-home offer.

SUBJECT: Become a Mystery Shopper Today

We have a mystery shopping assignment in your area and we would like you to participate.

Mystery Shopper is accepting applications for qualified individuals to become mystery shoppers. It's fun and rewarding, and you choose when and where you want to shop.

You are never obligated to accept an assignment. There is no charge to become a shopper and you do not need previous experience.

Mystery Shopper NEVER charge fees to become a shopper, mystery shoppers are paid a prearranged fee for a particular shop, We have available for immediate assignment an inspection of the customer service of any Western Union in your area. This fee will be paid upfront. During this shop you will visit the location and make several observations as regards the customer service. You will be required to interact with the shop clerk. You may conduct the shop alone or as a couple.

The assignment will pay $170.00/assignment.

Kindly Fill Out the application form below and we will get back to you shortly with the assignment.

You can also send the below required information as plain text email.

PERSONAL INFORMATION:
First Name..
Middle Name..
Last Name..
Street Address(Not PO Box)..
City, State, Zip Code..
Cell Phone Number..
Home Phone Number..
Age..
Current Occupation..
Alternate Email Address..
AVAILABILITY: Days/Hours Available

Monday.
Tuesday.
Wednesday.
Thursday.
Friday.
Saturday.
Sunday.
Hours Available:

We await your urgent response.

Thank you for your help. We look forward to working with you.

Sincerely,

Timothy White.
####### ########, Inc.
PO Box ##### Knoxville, TN 37950

EXAMPLE C.2

Example C.2 is an unsolicited notification that offers mystery shopping employment opportunities. The individuals involved in this scam took the name of an actual mystery shopping organization in an attempt to add legitimacy to the offer. Recipients should be alerted to the * added on the From line and the e-mail address of the sender. A legitimate US organization would not have an .edu domain name. The .edu domain is intended for educational organizations.

> **From:** Mystery Shopper Inc® <svasikarla@csun.edu>
> **To:** Undisclosed recipients:;
> **Subject:** Employment Opportunity

Dear Shopper,

Please click here to read about job description

www.Secretshopper.com

Regards,
© Secret Shopper Inc

EXAMPLE C.3
The unsolicited e-mail shown in Figure C.1 provides the recipient with a success story of a single mother who has made large amounts of money in a work-at-home job. The sender uses flashy pictures and the names of some prominent news organizations in an attempt to add validity to the offer. The main focus of this work-at-home offer is to have the job seekers pay to go through a work-at-home certification program that will authorize them to be a certified online worker.

Figure C.1   Unsolicited e-mail promises high paying work-at-home jobs.

From: Sandra Miller <XeGPkYz@p9Vp3BS.srixamy.com>
To:
Subject: **Needed: 23 Positions available working from home - $379/day** 8712

If you'd prefer not to receive future emqails, Unsubscribe Here.

8984 /Cottage Canyon Dr - Cedar Hills, Utah 84062

EXAMPLE C.4

The work-at-home job opportunity discussed in this example is for a domestic logistics manager position for a company operating out of Denmark. Individuals hired for this position will be tasked to receive through the US mail items purchased through fraudulent means. The items are to be repackaged and mailed to an international address. Individuals targeted for this work-at-home scam are typically paid via a cashier's check. The amount of the check received is to cover the employee's salary and shipping expenses. As with most of these scams, the cashier's check is for an amount larger than the expenses and the recipient is tasked with depositing the check and wire transferring the balance to a third party.

The rationale provided for the suspicious payment methods is that the international company has yet to establish banking accounts in the United States. The individuals targeted in this scam are advised future payments will come from checks drawn on a US financial institution.

Unfortunately, the initial cashier's check is counterfeit and will eventually be returned against the bank account of the targeted individual.

From: Jyoungblood <comamasksid@asia.com>
To: Postmaster <jyoungblood5@cox.net>
Cc: Administrator <merideth3@cox.net>
Subject: US Logistics Manager Position Open

Mountship is an international shipping company established in Denmark.

We are seeking top 7 candidates to increase the number of our employees on the US territory.

This position position is home based, and entails receiving, inspecting, splitting/combining and preparing parcels to be shipped out to various company's customers outside the US. The job will also entail using a company's control panel to document/print packing and shipping activities.

These are day shift openings.

Company offers a salary of $1800+ per month ($50 per package processed).

To perform the job successfully, employee must be able to perform each and every essential task satisfactorily and independently. The requirements stated below represent knowledge, skill, and/or ability required.

Must be well organized and execute the tasks in timely manner.

Must be able to perform the job from home independently, at home.

Must be proficient in - Microsoft Word, Excel, PDF documents, etc. Must have a PC with stable internet connection, printer.

Must be able to process incoming packages and prepare these for outgoing shipments.

If you want to apply for this job, please submit your up-to-date resume for immediate consideration.

SheaJukesogy@yahoo.com

EXAMPLE C.5
Example C.5 is an unsolicited e-mail attempt that hopes to gain the attention of the recipient by informing them they could be entitled to a monetary payout from an unknown deceased relative. The recipient is asked to provide personal information that can be used to commit identity theft. Individuals responding to this type of notification will be informed they actually had an unknown deceased relative and are entitled to a large monetary payout. Prior to receiving their long-overdue payout, they will need to provide some type of up-front fee to cover taxes or administrative or processing fees.

> **From:** Admin Staff <dmintafoff@administaff.com>
> **To:** undisclosed-recipients:;
> **Subject:** Re: Heir Hunters
> Re: Heir Hunters
> Attn: Please,
>
> I am writing you from the Heir Hunters Company in the United Kingdom, we are Heir Hunters detectives looking for distant relatives of people who have died without making a will.
> United Kingdom government last year made over GBP80M from unclaimed estates.
> When people die intestate (without valid WILL) and with no known relatives, list of these unclaimed estates are published by the Treasury.
> The race is now on for heir locators to track down the often distant relatives in line for a windfall. Often heir hunters pick more unusual names first, as they are easier to trace.
> We came across your profile and email while searching through genealogy database, we will be glad if you can get back to us with your full names and address to see if it corresponds with the information we have in the genealogy database in order to carry out the necessary verification processes and to get your claim across to you without any delay.
> Heir Hunters have handed over millions of funds to heirs who have no idea of their fortune. We will gladly answer any of your questions.
>
> Very Truly Yours
> Admin Staff.

EXAMPLE C.6
The recipient of this unsolicited e-mail is informed they are the winner of a $1 million prize. Attempting to add legitimacy to the notification, the name of the news organization CNN is used. In a further attempt at legitimacy, a confidentiality notice is provided in the notification.

From: David Torres <datorres@delmar.edu>
To:
Subject: CNN 2014 Draw.

YOU WON £1,000,000.00GBP IN 2014 CNN AWARD. Contact E-mail:
cnn5000@rogers.com

Confidentiality Notice: The information contained in this email, including attachments, may be privileged, proprietary, and/or confidential as provided by law. The information in this email is intended only for the use of the individual or entity to whom it is addressed. If you have received this communication in error, please notify the sender by replying to the email message and immediately return the email, attachments, and any and all copies to the sender. If you are not the intended recipient of this email and received it in error, please be advised that you may be subject to civil liability for any use of privileged, proprietary, and/or confidential information contained herein.

EXAMPLE C.7
The recipient of this unsolicited e-mail is informed that they have won a $1.4 million prize. In an attempt to add legitimacy to the notification, the name of Blackberry is used.

The goal of the sender is to collect personal information from the recipient to conduct identity theft fraud.

From: Black berry Promo <blackberryasiawin@kimo.com>
To: jyoungblood5@cox.net
Subject: Congrat ulations

Your email as w on US 1 400 000.00 in the ongoing Black Berry Asia online promo 2014, For claims send your names & mobile number.

EXAMPLE C.8
The recipient of this unsolicited e-mail is informed they have received an inheritance. The goal of the sender is to have the recipient open the attachment. Once the recipient clicks on the link provided, dangerous malware/spyware can be loaded onto their computer.

From: INHERITANCE CLAIMS DEPT <inheritanceclaimsdept@gmail.com>
To: undisclosed recipients: ;
Subject: VIEW ATTACHED FILE FOR MORE INFO:
Attachments: Inheritance Funds Letter Attached.pdf (235.1 KB)

Open Attachment Inheritance Funds Letter Attached.pdf

EXAMPLE C.9
The letter in Example C.9 was delivered through an unsolicited e-mail informing the recipient of a large monetary grant award. For whatever reason, the sender is using the Olympics as the entity generating the award, which is to be delivered in British pounds. Along the lines of many other advance fee letters,

the sender is requesting the recipient provide basic personal information. Once the personal information is received, a request for an advance fee to be paid will follow.

From: info@www.net
To: Recipients <info@www.net>
Subject: YOUR GRANT AWARD

LONDON OLYMPIC GRANT AWARD has AWARDED £1,000,000.00 pounds to you as a grant award. Meanwhile your urgent respond is highly needed with the re-onfirmation of your details such as: Your Name: Country: Telephone Number: Age: Sex: Occupation: send the following details to our delivery officer below, to enable him deliver your grant award document and certify check of £1,000,000.00 pounds to you in person immediately. this document well facilitate the clearance of your grant award funds in your bank. Please endeavor to quote your REF Number: BDA/01/034/561/56D BATCH No: 34/0065/KJY, Qualification numbers (N-222-6647, E-910-56).

Regards.
Delivery Officer.
Mr Owens. Jackson
Tell: +447024021326
Email: owensjackson@kimo.com

Several of the scam letters posted in Appendix C provide PDF file attachments. The hope of the sender is that the recipient will open the PDF file to obtain further information and details of the award. Because many of these attachments contain links that download unauthorized software onto the recipient's computer, none were opened. From a computer safety perspective, whatever information is present on these provided attachments was not accessed or provided.

EXAMPLE C.10
With this unsolicited e-mail notification, the recipient is informed that their e-mail address was randomly picked to receive a $500,000 cash payment. In an attempt to add legitimacy to the alert, the sender uses the name of the Microsoft Management Team.

From: Mr.Neil Trotter <kjju6787@oct-net.ne.jp>
To: undisclosed-recipients:;
Subject: Re:Euro Millions Lottery Winner

Dear Friend,

Greetings to you and your family, I hope this communication finds you well. You will be curious as to why I have selected you to receive the cash sum of ($500,000.00USD, Please see our interview by visiting the web page below: I am a car mechanic who is also a racing driver; I am winner of Euro Millions Jackpot on March 14, 2014 http://www.huffingtonpost.co.uk/2014/03/18/neil-trotter-euromillions-winner_n_4984234.html

I grew up knowing I will be a millionaire one day, I thank God for this bountiful blessing which am not going to benefit alone, I have decided to help my families, friends and well wishers. I saw your profile on a list of registered email addresses provided to me by Microsoft Management Team when I disclosed my intentions to donate; your email was picked after the round table donation draw. I will like to assure you of the authenticity of my good will, this donation is not involve in any illegal acts/activities rather is my burning desire to help others to partake from my lucky winning, we have much to give away, I believe this is my chance to help and alleviate people. I will advise you to be calm not to throw this great opportunity away because of bad feelings or ignorance, millions of people would die for this great moment because they have never been so lucky before. Reply to me if you are interested but decline if you are not; provide the following details to enable me provide additional i

Full Name:
Telephone number:
Age:
Occupation:

Keep this message as a surprise package for your love once but please don't be stingy with this gift because I myself gave out freely without sentiments, this donation have been clarified by the global financial board so is free from money laundry and terrorism. I am too busy with charity projects, no time talk to you on phone but can direct you to the approved paying bank for donation release proceedings. The donation has legal personality; please disregard any person or group of people impersonating my name without providing this security reference confirmation code authorized by me (NEIL/TRTT/EURO/XXAS3), my email (mrneiltrotter2014@gmail.com)
God bless you and happy Celebrations in Advance.

Regards,
Mr.Neil Trotter
Euro Millions Lottery Winner

EXAMPLE C.11

The goal of this unsolicited e-mail is to attract the attention of the recipient by notifying the recipient that they have won a sweepstakes bonanza. Senders hope the recipients click on the PDF link provided to obtain additional information on their prize. By clicking on the link, individuals are opening their computer up to the unauthorized downloading of malware/spyware.

From: Lardenoije, Celine <c.lardenoije@orbisconcern.nl>
To: win@winer.be
Subject: Email Ticket NO: 8-24-48-12-6-3
Attachments: BONANZA.pdf (275.7 KB)

Email Ticket NO: 8-24-48-12-6-3
Reply to Email:freef10@aol.com

PLEASE VIEW THE ATTACHMENT FOR THE FULL WINNING DETAILS, YOU HAVE WON FREE LOTTO STYLE EMAIL SWEEPSTAKES BONAZA THAT BRUSSELSBELGIUM.CONTACT: MR.Frank Mathis
BELGIUM.TEL:0032-466-045-509 OR +1132-466-045-509

EXAMPLE C.12

Example C.12 informs the recipient that they are part of a random e-mail-based selection process. Recipients of this e-mail are enticed by the notification that they were selected from a pool of 450,000 potential winners. To further increase the excitement of the recipient, they are informed of winning an additional prize of a BMW along with the promised cash payout.

As with other random prize-winning unsolicited e-mail notifications, the recipient is asked to provide up-front personal information that can later be used for identity theft. Prior to the identity theft taking place, the recipient is asked to provide some type of up-front fee to cover taxes, processing fees, administration fees, and so on.

From: MRS.SUSANNE KLATTEN <flipscomb@troyllcwv.com>
To:
Subject: YOUR $5 MILLION USD CONTACT HIM NOW

Dear Winner,

This is to inform you that you have been selected for a prize of a brand new 2013 Model BMW 7 Series Car and a Check of $5,000,000 million USD from the international balloting programs held in the UNITED KINGDOM.

The selection process was carried out through random selection in our computerized email selection system (ESS) from a database of over 450,000 email addresses drawn from all the continents of the world which you were selected.

CONTACT YOUR AGENT : Mr. Maxwell Steven

Name: Mr. Maxwell Steven
Email: mallstevenchambers@yahoo.co.uk
Phone number: 785-285-6422

You are also advised to provide him with the under listed information as soon as possible:

1. Name In Full :
2. Residential Address :
3. Age/Sex :
4. Phone :
5. Occupation:
7. Present Country :

Mrs. Susanne Klatten.
Holdings in Altana and BMW.
(BELOW IS MY PROFILE)
http://en.wikipedia.org/wiki/Susanne_Klatten

EXAMPLE C.13

Example C.13 is an introduction letter informing the recipient that they are due an inheritance being processed through the Bank of Nigeria. As you can see after looking over the sample advance fee letters in this appendix and in Appendix B, the authors of these letters are working to write in a more professional manner. In an attempt to add credability to the letter, the writer has included a statement of confidentiality. The letter also discusses how other letters of this nature have requested the recipients pay various types of advance fees. In this letter, the recipient is informed there is no up-front fee required to have paperwork processed.

No matter the language contained in this or other types of letters, there will eventually be a request for some type of up-front payment or a request for detailed personal information. The personal information will eventually be used for identity theft fraud.

Form: CBN CONSULTANT <postmaster@393939.com>
To: undisclosed-recipients:;
Subject: RE;YOUR OVER DUE PAYMENT

Dear Beneficiary,

I hope that this correspondence is received with the urgency and the expediency required. It has come to the notice of the Board of Trustees at the CBN that your present inheritance claims application being handled by the Remitting Bank in Nigeria is experiencing some man made irregularities.To this effect,it has become necessary for the Board of Trustees to invite trained Fund Transfer/Assets transfer Specialists from the United States to resolve and regularize your fund release with immediate effect and stop all further fund discrepancies.

We at Howard & Associates have been duly consulted by the CBN Board of Trustees and have been fully informed about how the staff of the remitting bank have been taking advantage of you by telling you to pay unnecessary exorbitant charges which will only make your fund payment a long drawn out process. Due to this we have decided to step into the process of your fund transfer to enable your funds to be transferred within the soonest possible time without needing to pay all the huge sums of monies that are being demanded from you by the remitting bank, you are to get back to us immediately.

All processes to have your funds paid to you immediately through the Federal Reserve Bank in New York have been initiated to cut out unnecessary costs.You are advised to keep this communication highly confidential as the CBN Board of Trustees have asked us to resolve this fund payment independent of the office of the CBN Governor to identify the the principal participants in this unethical payment procedure.Furthermore,you are hereby advised to pay no further fees or charges to the Remitting Bank in Nigeria as well as any person or persons, Real or Fictitious, prostates and institutions as they shall no longer be handling your payment process.

We shall await your immediate correspondence with your direct telephone numbers so that we may conclude your payment immediately contact the claim officier through this emailaddress : william.associates@barid.com

Yours Faithfully,
Mrs,Presa Bill.
Howard & Associates c/o CBN.

Statement of confidentiality: "the information in this email and in any attachments contains confidential information and is intended solely for the attention and use of the named addressee(s). It may not be disclosed to any person without authorization. If you are not the intended recipient, or a person responsible for delivering it to the intended recipient you are not authorized to and must not disclose, copy, distribute or retain this message or any part of it."

EXAMPLE C.14

The sender of this unsolicited e-mail hopes to get the attention of the recipient by using the name of the US Postal Service. A check of the From line should alert the recipient that the e-mail was not generated by USPS. The intent of this unsolicited e-mail is to have the recipient click on the Print Shipping Label tab. By clicking on this tab, the recipient is subjecting their computer to the downloading of dangerous software, mainly malware and spyware.

From: USPS <support@myrtletracesc.org>
To: jyoungblood5@cox.net
Subject: Postal Notification Service

USPS.COM

Notification

Our companys courier could not make the delivery of parcel to you address at 10th September.

Print your label and show it in the nearest post office to get a parcel.

Print Shipping Label

EXAMPLE C.15

The goal of this unsolicited e-mail is to attract the attention of the recipient with an offer of money from the International Monetary Fund (IMF). The IMF has identified the names used in previous advance fee letters as fraudulent and that this correspondence is legitimate.

From: Fatima Perez <perez@internationalmoney.com>
To:
Subject: Contact Mrs.Fatimam Pereza For Your Funds

INTERNATIONAL MONETARY FUND (IMF)
HEAD OFFICE NO: 23 ADEBOYE ST,
APAPA Benin-Cotonou.
CALL: +22961173066

Attn: Beneficiary,

This is to intimate you of a very important information which will be of a great help to redeem you from all the difficulties you have been experiencing in getting your long over due payment due to excessive demand for money from you by both corrupt Bank officials and Courier Companies after which your fund remain unpaid to you.

I am Mrs Fatimam Pereza highly placed official of the International Monetary Fund (IMF).It may interest you to know that reports have reached our office by so many correspondences on the uneasy way which people like you are treated by Various Banks and Courier Companies Diplomat(s) across Europe to Africa and Asia London UK, and we have decided to put a STOP to that and that is why I was appointed to handle your transaction here.

Listed below are the name of mafias and banks behind the non release of your funds that I managed to sneak out for your kind perusal.

1) Prof. Charles soludo
2) Senator David Mark
2) Micheal Edward
3) Chief Joseph Sanusi
3) Sanusi Lamido
4) Dr. R. Rasheed
5) Mr. David Koffi
6) Barrister Awele Ugorji
7) Mr. Roland Ngwa
8) Barrister Ucheuzo Williams
9) Mr. Ernest Chukwudi Obi
10) Dr. Patrick Aziza Deputy Governor - Policy/Board Member
11) Mr. Tunde Lemo Deputy Governor - Financial Sector

All Governmental and Non-Governmental prostates, NGO's, Finance Companies, Banks, Security Companies and Diplomat(s) which have been in contact with you of late have been instructed to back up from your transaction and you have been advised NOT to respond to them anymore since the IMF is now directly in charge of your payment. Your fund will be transferred to you directly from our source with immediate effect and we shall give you further details on how your fund will be released. You can as well call me as soon as you send the E-mail so that you will be given an immediate response

I hope this is clear. Any action contrary to this instruction is at your own risk. Respond to this E-mail on (fatimamperez8@gmail.com).

Regards,
Fatima Perez
+22961173066

EXAMPLE C.16
Numerous individuals who want to commit advance fee fraud are using the name Neil Trotter, who was an actual past Euro Lottery winner. The sender informs the recipient this actual notification is legitimate and all others are bogus. Recipients are asked to provide personal information that is most likely used for identity theft fraud.

From: European National Welfare Neil Trotter Donation <msantama@ipn.mx>
To: Recipients <msantama@ipn.mx>
Subject: SOSPECHOSO: Re: End of July Donation Newsletter. Registered £2,500,000.00 GBP In Your Name.

Be informed on your cash donation of £2,500,000.00 GBP the European National Welfare Donation Committee has sanctioned your details to be approved for the ongoing donation organized by few honorable winners of the past Euro Millions Games. Due to recent illegal activities of impostor posing as the actual Euro Million winners, it has been banned by the Lord Mayor of London Mayor Boris Johnson that from hence forth lottery winners of great social firms are not permitted by law to make direct contact or distribute charity donations personally to other selected winners because this means has been abused by spammers to cheat numerous number of legal retired citizens. <?xml:namespace prefix = "o" ns = "urn:schemas-microsoft-com:office:office"/>

Due to these above reasons we the European National Welfare Scheme Committee are mandated under the UK law Act 263, of Welfare to communicate your winning amount of £2,500,000.00 to you, which was donated to you by past honorable Euro Millions Winners with major donation from Mr. Neil Trotter.

Furthermore as a lucky winner you are entitled to enroll one member of your family or friend into the Auto Mechanic Game play solely organized by Neil Trotter Auto Mechanic, Race Driver and current Euro Million Winner of £107,932,603.20. Please confirm the identity of your major donor on the BBC news/interview:

http://www.bbc.com/news/uk-england-london-26627075

Please activate your winnings by reconfirming these details: Full Name - Sex-Address – Phone - Family Member Name.

Area Co-coordinator
Charity Donation Program
International Alert & Information's Dept.
© 2014 UK European National Welfare Scheme.

Index

Note: Page numbers ending in "f" refer to figures. Page numbers ending in "t" refer to tables.

For Product Safety Concerns and Information please contact our EU
representative GPSR@taylorandfrancis.com
Taylor & Francis Verlag GmbH, Kaufingerstraße 24, 80331 München, Germany

www.ingramcontent.com/pod-product-compliance
Ingram Content Group UK Ltd.
Pitfield, Milton Keynes, MK11 3LW, UK
UKHW021018180425
457613UK00020B/977